ENVIRONMENTAL LAW HANDBOOK

Fourth edition

TREVOR HELLAWELL

Legal Training Consultant

law society publishing

ISBN 1–85328–721–0

Fourth edition published in 2001 by Law Society Publishing
113 Chancery Lane, London WC2A 1PL

Typeset by Columns Design Ltd, Reading
Printed by Antony Rowe Ltd, Chippenham, Wilts

Contents

Preface to the Fourth Edition

After a gestation period akin to that of a bull elephant – and almost as difficult to describe – the contaminated land regime finally saw the light of day on 1 April 2000. Whether this was an auspicious date to pick remains to be seen, but at last practitioners can advise with some greater certainty as to its implications. The final version differs little in scope from the earlier drafts but there were some last-minute subtleties introduced which make it worth revisiting.

As the new regime was being introduced, the UK became enmeshed in the introduction of the Pollution Prevention and Control Directive (involving a new regime to be known in the UK as IPPC), a much more far-reaching version of our own integrated pollution control (IPC) system, now a decade old and bedevilled by its own enforcement difficulties. The ramifications of the Pollution Prevention and Control Act 1999, and its associated Regulations, will take the whole of the roll-out period of seven years, and more, to become fully understood and workable, but new operations are to be subject to the new regime forthwith.

These innovations, and several topical cases, the Milford Haven appeal in particular make this a good time to review this book and refresh the parts that have not been reached for some time.

I have taken the opportunity to revise and update all the chapters, but especially those on liabilities (to encompass IPPC), contaminated land (to reflect the final version of the legislation) and property transactions (to include a new precedent on apportionment of liabilities). There is also a new contacts section, and a completely new chapter on European law.

I would like once more to take this opportunity to thank all my colleagues on the Law Society's Planning and Environmental Law Committee for their continued support, the Secretary to that Committee, Steven Durno, for his generous help with Chapter 8, and the editorial and administrative staff at Law Society Publications for their sterling efforts in compiling the Contacts list, and getting this edition to print on time, despite my baby daughter's efforts to delay my contribution.

The law is stated as at 1 October 2000.

Trevor Hellawell

Warwick
October 2000

Table of cases

Table of statutes

Table of statutory instruments

Note: Please see Chapter 8 for European legislation.

Abbreviations

BAT	best available techniques
BATNEEC	best available techniques not entailing excessive cost
CEPS	corporate environmental policy statement
DETR	Department of Environment, Transport and the Regions
DoE	Department of the Environment
EA	Environment Act [1995]
EDA	Environmental Data Association
EIL	environmental impairment liability
EMAS	EC Eco-Management and Audit Scheme
ENDS	Environmental Data Systems Ltd
EPA	Environmental Protection Act [1990]
ERI	environmental remediation insurance
ES	environmental statement
FPL	first-party liability
FRI	full repairing and insuring
GPDO	General Permitted Development Order
HSE	Health and Safety Executive
IA	Insolvency Act [1986]
IEA	Institute of Environmental Assessment
IPC	Integrated Pollution Control
IPPC	Integrated Pollution Prevention and Control
LAAPC	Local Authority Air Pollution Control
LIP	licensed insolvency practitioner

LPA	local planning authority
MAFF	Ministry of Agriculture, Fisheries and Food
PCB	polychlorinated biphenyl
PPC	Pollution Prevention and Control
PLL	pollution legal liability
RICS	Royal Institution of Chartered Surveyors
SAC	special area of conservation
SPA	special protection areas
SPZ	special planning zone
SSE	Secretary of State for the Environment
TCPA	Town and Country Planning Act
UST	underground storage tanks
WIA	Water Industry Act [1991]
WRA	Water Resources Act [1991]

CHAPTER 1

Environmental liabilities

1.1   INTRODUCTION

All environmental considerations – in whatever type of transaction – are, ultimately, liability-driven. What liabilities may a buyer of land or a company, a developer, a banker, an insolvency practitioner or a professional adviser be facing?

Much has been said and written about the extent, and potential cost, of environmental liabilities over recent years. Much of the rhetoric could be said to have caused some over-reaction in the financial and business community.

True, such liabilities can be expensive, and one may have to take a decision to back out of a deal or walk away from a purchase if the risks are too great, but equally, there may be many instances where the perception of the risk is much worse than the reality.

What is needed is full information – about the legal position, the practical stance taken by the regulatory bodies, and the actual state of contamination in the ground. With such knowledge, one can take informed decisions about a transaction, and take all the necessary steps and precautions to secure the appropriate protections.

This chapter is intended to set out the basic legal position. Later chapters will deal with the practical considerations involved in specific types of transaction, and will discuss who to use to assess the state of an actual contamination or pollution incident.

1.2   CRIMINAL LIABILITIES

1.2.1   The liabilities

Environmental Protection Act 1990 (EPA 1990)

PART I – IPC/LAAPC OFFENCES

Part I of the EPA 1990 governs the system of Integrated Pollution Control, or IPC, and the related system of Local Authority Air Pollution Control, or LAAPC.

These systems require the more polluting industries (defined in the Prescribed Processes and Substances Regulations 1991, SI 1991/472 as amended) to be licensed by the Environment Agency (if a so-called 'Part A' process), or the relevant local authority (if a so-called 'Part B' process), before being carried on.

Under s.23 generally it is an offence for a person:

- to carry on a prescribed process except under a licence (an 'authorisation', occasionally referred to as a 'consent') and in accordance with its conditions;

- to fail to comply with enforcement or prohibition notices served by the regulatory body;

- to obstruct an inspector in the exercise of his powers; or

- to commit deception, forgery and the like in any application or other documentation.

One condition of the authorisation will always be to use 'best available techniques not entailing excessive cost' (BATNEEC) to minimise polluting discharges. Other conditions will include specific limits on emissions to air, land and water together with further 'house-keeping' conditions as to monitoring, record-keeping and reporting.

Part I of the EPA 1990 is in the process of being superseded by Integrated Pollution Prevention and Control (IPPC), in accordance with the UK's obligations under the Integrated Pollution Prevention and Control Directive (96/61).

INTEGRATED POLLUTION PREVENTION AND CONTROL

The UK has passed the **Pollution Prevention and Control Act 1999** (Royal Assent, 27 July 1999) and published the relevant Regulations (Pollution Prevention and Control (England and Wales) Regulations 2000, SI 2000/1973 (together with the Scottish version)) which will roll-out the new system in full by 2007.

The main changes under the new regime, compared with the old, are:

- more processes will be regulated than was formerly the case (new industry sectors covering intensive farming and the food and drink processing industries are to be regulated for the first time);

- a new, three-tier system is to be introduced, comprising Part A1 processes, Part A2 processes and Part B processes, the first regulated by the Environment Agency, the latter two by local authorities;

- many existing processes will be redesignated (essentially, the division becomes: Part A1 (old Part A), Part A2 (new industry sectors and some old Part B processes), Part B (remainder of old Part B));

- 'installations' are to be given 'permits' (this may seem like an exercise in semantics, but amounts to more than that when one investigates the definition of an 'installation'; it is a series of technically interlinked processes, which in turn suggests that the new licensing regime is going to take a more holistic view of site management issues than the old (one site with three linked processes being governed by one permit, rather than three, as now);

- inputs to, as well as outputs from, regulated installations are to be monitored;

- land quality assessments are to be required at the start and end of any regulated activity (so as to be able to identify any land contamination attributable to the regulated activity, for which the operator can be made to pay);

- BATNEEC becomes BAT ('best available techniques'), though this is more an apparent change than a real one, the technological benchmarks still being set by reference to industry-wide standards agreed centrally.

Practical problems with the new regime include:

- difficulties of definition in marginal cases (when is a process 'inter-linked' with another);

- disparity in the methodology of the land quality assessments at the start and end of the activity resulting in inaccurate assessment of the state of land contamination on the site;

- the lack of any discretion to decline to require small operators to get a permit;

- local authority control of Part A2 processes (which require regulation of emissions to all three media – air, land and water – not something the local authorities are historically familiar with);

- the long roll-out period (1999–2007);

- new, and as yet unfinalised, fee structures;

- whether an environmental management system is going to be necessary in order to achieve compliance with all the new requirements of the permit (in fact, if not in theory).

PART II – WASTE RELATED OFFENCES

Part II of the EPA 1990 governs the system for the regulation of waste. A licence from the Environment Agency is required by anyone who is in the business of dealing with, treating or disposing of 'waste', as defined in Regulations.

The waste management licensing regime was introduced on 1 May 1994 by the Waste Management Licensing Regulations 1994, SI 1994/1056 (WMLR 1994), and the detailed provisions are to be found in these Regulations. A number of Guidance Notes were published at the same time (and have been updated subsequently), and a solicitor needing to undertake further research in this area should have regard to them.

Those who merely produce waste as a natural concomitant of a process or activity need to comply with the statutory duty of care contained in s.34 in relation to that material.

This involves those generating and holding waste temporarily, pending its ultimate removal elsewhere, to:

- identify accurately the different types of waste generated and, ideally, segregate them (the key differentiation to be made being that between ordinary waste and 'special' waste within the meaning of the Special

4

Waste Regulations 1996, SI 1996/972 (oily, toxic, flammable or dangerous wastes);

- store it securely (against leakage and interference);

- label it accurately;

- complete transfer notes (if ordinary) or consignment notes (if special) for it;

- hand it over to a licensed carrier for removal, with the transfer or consignment note;

- take reasonable steps to ensure that no offence is committed by anyone dealing with the waste at any time (a potentially onerous element requiring supervision of other people's actions and activities).

Under s.33 (as amended by Regulations) it is an offence for a person:

- to deposit, abandon or dump or knowingly cause or permit to be deposited, abandoned or dumped 'controlled waste' (now occasionally known as 'Directive waste') without or in breach of a licence;

- to dispose of or recover (or knowingly cause or permit the disposal or recovery of) 'Directive waste' without or in breach of a licence;

- to treat, keep, dispose of or recover 'Directive waste' in a manner likely to cause pollution or harm to health;

- to breach any condition of a waste management licence; or

- to breach the duty of care contained in s.34.

'Directive waste' is anything which is 'discarded', i.e. abandoned, dumped, disposed of or put in its final resting place, or subjected to a recovery operation without which it is useless.

If one person discards material because he has finished with it, but can find a buyer for the material who can and will use it in its unchanged form, the material is not yet waste, as it has not yet 'fallen out of the commercial chain of utility'.

The offences of 'depositing' or 'causing' (as redefined) will require proof of some positive act on the part of the defendant; 'permitting' is the act of allowing something to occur, once it is known that it is likely to occur, though there is no need to show knowledge of the illegality of the deposit.

Matter cannot be 'waste' and regulated under Part II if and to the extent that it is already regulated under the IPC regime in Part I of the Act, or the IPPC regime which supersedes it.

It is also worthy of note that many waste related activities, particularly landfill, are now to be regulated under IPPC, rather than Part II of the EPA 1990, as a result of the implementation of the PPC Directive.

PART IIA – CONTAMINATED LAND

The new Part IIA of the EPA 1990, discussed fully in Chapter 2, contains the contaminated land provisions (ss.78A–78YC).

These sections provide that it is an offence for the person served with a remediation notice by a local authority in respect of contaminated land, to fail, without reasonable excuse, to comply with any of the requirements of the notice.

The 'person served' is the appropriate person as defined in Part IIA and Guidance Notes, i.e. the original polluter, or the owner or occupier if the original polluter cannot be found, subject to complex exclusionary tests in the Guidance Notes.

Matter cannot be 'contaminated land' to the extent that it is already regulated under Part I or II of the Act, or the new IPPC regime.

These provisions are now in force, having been brought in on 1 April 2000 – see the Contaminated Land (England) Regulations 2000, SI 2000/227, and Chapter 2.

The full effect of the regime should make itself felt in or around July 2001, when the 15-month strategic phase-in period expires.

PART III – STATUTORY NUISANCES

Part III of the EPA 1990 codifies the existing law on statutory nuisances – smoke, dust, smell or premises or accumulations, etc. which are a health or pollution risk.

Under ss.79–80 it is an offence for the person served with an abatement notice by a local authority in respect of a statutory nuisance, to fail to comply with the notice. The 'person served' is the person responsible for the nuisance or, if they cannot be found, the owner or occupier of the premises.

Proceedings under this Part of the Act cannot be brought, other than in very limited circumstances, once a licence has been issued to a process operator under Part I or II of the Act, or the new IPPC regime, as it is these regimes that are designed to control all aspects of regulated emissions, including nuisance aspects.

Moreover, once land is in a 'contaminated state' within the meaning of para. 89 of Schedule 22 to the Environment Act 1995, it cannot, to that extent, be regarded also as a statutory nuisance.

The definition of 'contaminated state' catches land which is in such a state by reason of substances in, on or under it that there is a possibility of harm.

This is not the same as 'contaminated' for the purposes of Part IIA (where the risk of harm must be 'significant') and one is therefore left in the position where polluted land that is not serious enough to be designated as contaminated, is not able to be called a statutory nuisance either.

A local authority is therefore left powerless to deal with it. Arguably, this is a defensible position given that if land is not so dangerous as to be officially 'contaminated' it is, by definition, not going to cause any harm and can therefore be ignored.

Water Resources Act 1991 (WRA 1991)

POLLUTION OFFENCES

The WRA 1991 is the Act that determines the powers and duties of the Environment Agency and it creates a series of water pollution offences which the Environment Agency, and others, can use to prosecute polluters. Under ss.85–89 it is an offence for a person:

- to cause or knowingly permit poisonous, noxious or polluting matter or any solid waste matter to enter any 'controlled waters';

- to breach any prohibition or condition imposed under s.86 relating to discharges from a drain or sewer;

- to cause or knowingly permit trade or sewage effluent to be discharged into controlled waters or by pipe into the sea;

- to cause or knowingly permit trade or sewage effluent to be discharged, in breach of any prohibition or condition imposed under s.86, from buildings or plant onto land or into lakes or ponds which are not inland freshwaters;

- to cause or knowingly permit any matter to enter inland freshwaters so as to tend to impede the proper flow of the waters in a manner leading or likely to lead to a substantial aggravation of pollution or its consequences; or

- to contravene a prohibition under s.86.

Although these provisions seem absolute in their terms, the Environment Agency has power to issue discharge consents, and, provided their terms are complied with, no offence is committed.

The offence of 'causing' a pollution offence will require proof of a positive act or omission on the part of the defendant – dumping, leaking, over-filling, operating inefficiently, breaching bund walls, hosing excess chemicals down broken drains and the like. Simply carrying on the activity that caused the pollution is enough. It is not necessary to prove knowledge, negligence or fault. As long as the activity was itself intentional, all that is needed is a causal link between the activity and the pollution. Being part of the cause is also sufficient.

Note also the case of *Empress Car Co. (Abertillery) Ltd* v. *National Rivers Authority* [1998] 2 WLR 350, HL where a site owner was found guilty of a water pollution offence notwithstanding intervention by vandals who broke into the premises and opened the taps on an oil storage tank.

'Permitting' the pollution can consist in merely allowing pollution to remain, i.e. not removing it, if it was possible to do so.

The 'offence' is that of 'knowingly' permitting. What degree of knowledge is required?

There is some authority (*Schulmans Incorporated Ltd* v. *National Rivers Authority* [1993] Env. LR D1) for the view that, in addition to actual knowledge of the circumstances, turning a blind eye to the obvious or deliberately refraining from enquiry for fear of the truth, may attract liability.

This ambiguity over the definition of 'knowingly permitting' means that a purchaser or current owner may be liable for ongoing water pollution caused originally by someone else.

Clients must not imagine that deliberately contrived ignorance of the fact and extent of pollution will get them off the hook. A defence of 'I didn't want to know, so I didn't bother looking' will not work.

If they could have found out about the pollution (for example, by survey or investigation), could have done something to correct it and failed to take those steps, they may be said to have 'knowingly permitted' it.

Solicitors should note the recent cases involving the run-off of fire-fighting water into controlled waters. The courts have decided that this is still the offence of 'causing' water pollution committed by the site owner, not the Fire Service.

There is the additional offence of 'failing to comply with consent conditions'. This offence can be committed by any person who is subject to the benefit and burden of the consent itself, whether or not they own any land or carry on any industrial activity themselves. This was established by the case of *Taylor Woodrow Property Management Ltd* v. *National Rivers Authority* [1994] Env. LR 20, where the consent was issued to Company A, but associated Company B was responsible for policing the outfall to the river. Despite not owning the land, and not carrying on any activities, Company B was successfully prosecuted for allowing polluting matter to enter waters in breach of the consent.

Ignorance of the law has never been a defence; it now seems that ignorance of the facts is no defence either. Failure to make all reasonable enquiries, and then take steps to stop any pollution from occurring, may therefore be a criminal offence.

Under these WRA 1991 provisions, private prosecutions can also be brought – the Environment Agency is not the only body with power to bring such prosecutions.

Since the last edition of this book, the Crown Court and the Court of Appeal have had the opportunity to consider water pollution issues afresh, and in particular, reconsider the appropriate levels of penalty, in the *Milford Haven Port Authority* appeal.

Originally convicted in the Cardiff Crown Court of a s.85 water pollution offence arising out of the Sea Empress oil spillage disaster, Milford Haven Port Authority was fined £4 million (four times the previous highest fine). It appealed against sentence, and in March 2000 the Court of Appeal agreed that the original fine was 'manifestly excessive', and reduced it to £750,000.

It took the opportunity to set out the factors relevant to penalty, and echoed its original advice given in the case of *R* v. *F Howe & Sons (Engineers) Ltd* [1999] 2 All ER 249, CA, a Health and Safety case.

The factors amongst others are:

- the degree of deliberacy or intention involved;

- the presence or absence of a profit motive;

- whether harm to persons was caused and its degree;

- whether an immediate plea of guilty was entered;

- the adequacy of relevant management systems.

The Milford Haven reduction was justified on the grounds that, though serious, it was unintentional and no loss of human life resulted.

At around the same time, the Home Office Sentencing Advisory Panel also reported. It expressed the view that environmental penalties were inconsistent, and generally, too low. However, the Court of Appeal declined to follow its recommendations on the approach to sentencing in such cases, preferring to follow its earlier views as expressed in *Howe*.

PROCEDURAL OFFENCES

Under new ss.161A–161D inserted by the Environment Act 1995, it is an offence for a person served with a works notice by the Environment Agency to fail to comply with any of the requirements of the notice.

The 'person served' is the person who caused or knowingly permitted the polluting matter to be present.

This provision was expected at the same time as EPA 1990, Part IIA (April 2000), but was in fact introduced nearly a year earlier, on 26 April 1999 (see the Anti-Pollution Works Regulations 1999, SI 1999/1006).

Pressure has been brought to bear for this procedure to be applied by the Environment Agency in accordance with similar principles to those imposed on local authorities by Guidance Notes in respect of contaminated land and this is to be achieved by a memorandum of understanding with the Environment Agency.

However, the overlaps between the two regimes are at best undesirable, and at worst, unworkable, and the primary legislation is to be altered to eradicate unnecessary overlaps.

In the author's view, the works notice is a much more appropriate tool to use in respect of water pollution risks than the remediation notice relating to contaminated land as the risks to water are easier to discern, and need not be so serious in order to warrant official designation.

The question still remains – who deals with contaminated land which is polluting water – the local authority under EPA 1990, Part IIA or the Environment Agency under WRA 1991, ss.161A–161D? Logic would dictate that it should be the latter (emergency, need to act quickly, statutory obligation to maintain water quality, more resources) but the Regulations suggest that it is the former body – the local authority – which has jurisdiction.

Currently there is nothing in the new provisions requiring the Environment Agency to take specific account of Guidance but the Secretary of State has made Regulations governing form, content and procedure.

Water Industry Act 1991 (WIA 1991)

DISCHARGE OFFENCES RELATING TO TRADE EFFLUENT

The WIA 1991 sets out the powers and duties of the privatised water companies.

Under s.118 it is an offence for an occupier of trade premises to discharge trade effluent into public sewers without or in breach of sewerage undertaker's consent as to the nature and composition, the quantity and rate of the discharge and identification of the sewers into which the discharge can be made.

Defences

Some of these offences have statutory defences.

In particular, EPA 1990, s.33(7) (waste offences) contains defences if the defendant can show that, in the process of depositing waste illegally:

- all reasonable precautions were taken; or

- he was acting under instruction from an employer; or

- the activities were undertaken in an emergency to avoid harm to the public.

Under EPA 1990, new s.78M(2) it is a defence to a prosecution for failure to comply with a remediation notice to show that the reason it was not complied with was because a joint polluter could not or would not pay their allocated share of the cost of compliance.

Under EPA 1990, s.80(7) it is a defence to a prosecution in respect of a statutory nuisance on industrial, trade or business premises to show that the best practicable means were used to counteract the effects of the nuisance.

Under WRA 1991, s.87(2) a sewerage undertaker shall not be guilty of an offence under s.85 of 'polluting controlled waters' by reason only of the fact that a discharge from a sewer or works vested in the undertaker contravenes conditions of consent relating to the discharge if:

- the contravention is attributable to a discharge which another person caused or permitted to be made into the sewer or works;

- the undertaker either was bound to receive the discharge into the sewer or works or was bound to receive it there subject to conditions which were not observed; and

- the undertaker could not reasonably have been expected to prevent the discharge into the sewer or works.

National Rivers Authority v. *Yorkshire Water Services* [1995] 1 AC 444, HL

Sections 88–89 (water pollution offences) of WRA 1991 contain defences if the defendant can show, in relation to authorised discharges, that:

- a polluting discharge took place in accordance with licence conditions;

and in relation to unauthorised discharges that:

- the discharge took place in an emergency to avoid danger to life or health;
- all reasonable steps were taken to minimise the harm; and
- particulars were furnished to the authorities as soon as possible.

Penalties

Depending on the offence, and the identity of the defendant, the potential maximum penalties are:

- six months' imprisonment, or a £20,000 fine in the magistrates' court;
- two to five years' imprisonment, or unlimited fines in the Crown Court.

Under the new contaminated land provisions, daily default fines are imposed for non-compliance with a remediation notice.

An average fine for a first offence, with good mitigation, is around £2,000–£5,000, with costs, but see the earlier comments regarding sentencing policy and guidelines.

1.2.2   How do I protect my client?

Against criminal liabilities the first piece of advice has to be 'forget insurance'. One cannot insure against this type of risk. If a client is prosecuted for any of the offences listed above, the main 'protections' are those familiar to criminal practitioners everywhere – avoidance and mitigation.

Avoidance and mitigation

1   AVOIDANCE

If one accepts, as seems to be the case, that the offences are offences of strict liability, is there anything that one can do to avoid prosecution and conviction? It would be wrong to assume that there is no way out of a conviction, and there follows a list of matters to consider.

i. Identity of the defendant. It is conceivable, especially within complex corporate groups, that the prosecutor has inaccurately identified the defendant company which actually carries on the process that has caused the discharge. Section 127 of the Magistrates' Courts Act 1980 provides that mere typographical errors will not invalidate the proceedings, but clearly, if a wholly different legal person has been prosecuted from the one that ought to have been prosecuted, then the proceedings will have to be withdrawn and recommenced.

ii. Statutory defences. Some of the offences carry with them statutory defences, and of course it is essential to check the statute to see whether the client could benefit from any of these defences, which mainly involve circumstances of emergency.

iii. Common law defences. There may be some common law defences. These are limited in scope, but if one can show that some natural event was the initial cause of the discharge then a defence may be made out if one can prove that the natural event was so extraordinary and exceptional as to be unforeseeable.

iv. Duplicity of informations. The prosecutor may need to take care in the drafting of the informations to ensure that they are not duplicitous. This is particularly so when the discharge complained of has been an intermittent one. If an information charges a defendant with numerous discharges occurring between certain dates it is at least arguable that the information contains allegations of more than one offence and is therefore invalid.

v. Evidential gaps. As the offences are triable either way, advance information is available under the Magistrates' Courts (Advance Information) Rules 1985, SI 1985/601. All the defendant need do is request copies of the prosecution evidence in advance, and it will be provided. It is always worth checking to see whether the prosecution evidence actually sustains the allegation made in the proceedings.

There have been difficulties in the past of proving the entry of noxious or polluting matters into 'controlled waters', as the testing of the discharge was performed at an inappropriate point (e.g. in a sewer). There have also been difficulties in proving the initial source of a particular contamination. Clearly if the prosecution evidence is deficient, it is not entitled to a conviction.

vi. Failure to comply with proper procedures. The water pollution legislation formerly provided proper procedures for, among other things, sampling. Any sample taken by inspectors had to be divided into three parts, and one of three parts sealed and handed to the defendant for their own analysis. If this procedure had not been properly followed, the evidence of the sample was inadmissible. There was once much interest in this area, culminating in the Court of Appeal ruling in Attorney-General's Reference (No. 2 of 1994), *R.* v. *Thames Water Utilities Ltd* [1994] 1 WLR 1202. The tri-partite sampling process was abolished by provisions in the Environment Act 1995 but it may still be thought of as good practice.

vii. Relationship with regulatory bodies. It may be worth negotiating with the prosecuting body on the basis that the defendant has always in the past had a constructive and responsible approach to the environment, taking advice and measures to prevent discharges of the type complained of. It may persuade the prosecuting authority not to proceed if one can point out that this good relationship is in danger of suffering, and the client's responsible attitude with it.

The aim of discussing these possibilities is of course to persuade the prosecutor to withdraw the proceedings altogether, but another alternative to consider is agreeing with the prosecution to the imposition of a formal caution rather than going through the full litigation and conviction process. Some of the regulatory bodies have been keen to proceed along this line.

2   THE TRIAL

If one cannot avoid a prosecution, the next question is how should the client plead at the trial itself? The short answer is that the client should plead not guilty if there are evidential gaps or procedural problems which would deny the prosecution a conviction. There is no ethical problem in pleading not guilty, as that merely puts the onus on the prosecution to prove its case. If the prosecution is unable to discharge the burden of proof, then the client is entitled to an acquittal.

If the evidence looks watertight, then the standard advice is probably to plead guilty and to mitigate, putting forward the best explanation of the event that one can.

Bear in mind also the Court of Appeal's comments on the discount to be received by a plea of guilty (standard advice in most cases) in the *Milford Haven* case.

3 MITIGATION

The standard approach to mitigation adopted by criminal practitioners is fairly easily adapted for use in environmental cases. Broadly, the age and history of the defendant, the circumstances surrounding the offence, the behaviour since the offence and the indirect effect of conviction or sentence are all matters on which the magistrates can be addressed.

i. Age and history of the defendant. The magistrates should be informed about the history of the company and its activities, how long it has occupied its site and its record in relation to previous incidents and accidents. In addition, one can concentrate on the client's commercial attitude to the environment, its past record of taking advice and preventative measures to avoid damaging discharges and its past relations with the regulatory bodies, in an attempt to persuade the court that the client is a responsible citizen, not an 'amoral calculator' which is prepared to discharge into the environment if that is the best commercial decision at the time.

ii. Circumstances surrounding the offence. It is always worth pointing out that, since the offences require no fault on the part of the defendant, in fact there was no fault present on the part of the defendant. It is also worthwhile pointing out the facts and the effects of the incident in context. In this regard, a keen appreciation of the chemical effects of the polluting discharge is helpful. For example, how much oxygen does the chemical strip from a watercourse at a given temperature and flow rate, and how much oxygen do trout, plants, etc. need to survive? How much damage was in fact done? In appropriate cases it is worthwhile pointing out that the company derived no financial benefit from the fact of the discharge and there was no cover up of the incident either.

This begs a question as to whether the client should report an incident as soon as it occurs, notwithstanding the privilege against self-incrimination. The author's, perhaps rather purist, view is that if the company is a responsible environmental citizen, then it should, as a matter of policy, report incidents so that the damaging effects can be minimised as soon as possible, and then use this fact in mitigation at a later date.

iii. Behaviour since the offence. Credit will be given for the plea of guilty (if that has indeed been the plea), and it will be given also for immediate voluntary clean-up and restocking of fish and plants, etc. voluntary payment of costs and expenses, and the taking of further advice and remedial and preventative measures to ensure non-recurrence. It would help also if the company can demonstrate that it has reviewed comprehensively its internal operating procedures, made any necessary investments in new plant and machinery and even that it has supported local initiatives which may not be directly connected with this specific incident.

iv. Indirect effect of conviction or sentence. In appropriate cases, mention the potential damage to relations with the regulatory bodies, the financial and cash flow effects of a harsh penalty and the knock-on employment implications in the locality if a company is forced out of business as a result of harsh fines.

See also the Court of Appeal's comments in the *Milford Haven* case.

4   OTHER STEPS

It would be foolish for a client, or a solicitor, to underestimate the PR impact of a conviction. It is therefore essential that the client be prepared for the barrage of questions that may follow from a conviction on a guilty plea. Press and other media releases should be prepared in advance and clients should be counselled in how to deal with press questions which may be put to them on the steps of the court.

As a follow-up, solicitors should give any necessary advice to their clients about environmental compliance and of course the clients should take any remedial steps which may have been promised in the plea in mitigation in order to prevent recurrence of the incident.

1.3   NON-CRIMINAL LIABILITIES

1.3.1   Civil liability

Nuisance

After the landmark decision of the House of Lords in *Cambridge Water Company* v. *Eastern Counties Leather plc* [1994] 2 AC 264, HL a person may be liable in damages for current or future contamination if he commits the tort of nuisance. The House recast this tort, and someone commits it if he owns or occupies land and/or acts on it in a way which causes injury, loss or damage by creating a nuisance, whether by continuing activities which cause gradual pollution, or by a one-off escape of harmful material.

For such incidents there is strict liability, i.e. there is no need to prove fault or negligence on the part of the defendant. It does not matter, therefore, what steps were taken to prevent the escape. If it occurs at all, liability may follow.

The only prerequisites to liability are:

- a non-natural/non-reasonable (i.e. industrial or commercial) use of the land;

- that harm of the relevant type must have been reasonably foreseeable at the time of creation of the nuisance, or the collection of the harmful material.

This latter point was widely hailed as meaning that one cannot be liable for historic pollution, but this analysis misunderstands the judgment. One can be liable for the effects of historic pollution if, at the time one caused it, one could have foreseen the damaging results of it. The damaging consequences of certain types of pollution have been foreseeable on this test for many years, or even decades.

Undoubtedly, things have been done in the recent past, and are being done today which can be said to have very foreseeable consequences. If problems are caused in the future, businesses will be held liable – the only real obstacle being the burden of proof which a claimant would have to discharge to win his case. One can, however, predict decades of litigation ahead.

The position of the defendant – who could be the owner of the land, the occupier, the controller of the source of the nuisance or the creator of the nuisance itself – is made more precarious by the fact that liability under the rule is strict. It will not matter what steps were taken to prevent the harm: if an escape occurs and causes foreseeable damage, the defendant will be liable for all the ensuing consequences.

The main elements of *Cambridge Water* have been confirmed in the case of *Graham and Graham* v. *ReChem International Ltd* [1996] Env. LR 158. This case confirmed the strict liability principle and confirmed that the defendants knew in 1977 of the potential harm caused by their emissions and would have been liable for all the consequent damage from then on, but went against the plaintiffs because they could not establish on the evidence that the emissions had actually caused the loss complained of. It did also establish, however, that a defendant can be civilly liable if his acts were only part of the cause.

Moreover, in the judgment, the House went on to imply that whilst a landowner/occupier will not generally be liable for unforeseeable historic contamination, he nonetheless could be liable for the consequences of it if, since the time the damage became foreseeable, it has been possible to stop the nuisance, and no such steps have been taken.

It seems therefore, that even if you are not liable for starting a nuisance, you can be liable for not stopping it.

To this extent, the *Cambridge Water* case merely equates the position of existing landowners with the position of buyers, which has been settled law for some time. Buyers of contaminating land, and those enforcing security over it, will only be liable for continuing nuisances created by predecessors in title if they knew or ought to have known of the nuisance, could reasonably foresee it causing harm and could have taken reasonable steps to prevent or abate it, but failed to do so (*Sedleigh-Denfield* v. *O'Callaghan* [1940] AC 880, HL; *Goldman* v. *Hargrave* [1967] 1 AC 645, HC (Aus); *Leakey* v. *National Trust* [1980] QB 485, CA).

Moreover, compliance with an authorisation or lawful planning permission does not provide a defence against a civil action for nuisance (*Wheeler* v. *Saunders* [1995] 3 WLR 466, CA, confirmed (amongst other interesting points) by *Hunter* v. *Canary Wharf Ltd* [1997] AC 655, HL).

Solicitors should note the added difficulty surrounding limitation. A claimant would have six years (three if personal injury is claimed) from the date on which the damage was caused to him in which to sue. This date may be long after the creation of the original nuisance, or the original incident.

Note also the two recent cases of *Blue Circle Industries plc* v. *Ministry of Defence* [1998] 3 All ER 385, CA (a judgment in excess of £6 million), and *English Partnerships* v. *Mott MacDonald* (reported in ENDS Report, April 1999, a judgment in excess of £18 million), both of which turned on the question of the quantification of damages, and both of which agreed that the market value of the property (volatile though that may be), rather than the cost of clean-up, is the starting point for determining damages in civil cases involving land contamination.

Statutory tort

A person may also be liable in damages if he commits a statutory tort under EPA 1990, s.73(6). This section provides that, where any damage is caused by waste deposited in or on land in such a manner as to constitute an offence, the person who deposited it, or who knowingly caused or permitted it to be deposited, is liable for the damage.

Negligence

To sue in negligence the claimant must show a duty of care owed to him by the defendant and breach of that duty which resulted in foreseeable harm to the claimant or his property.

This duty is hard to establish in most situations of environmental incident, and there is the additional problem that any latent damage caused by a negligent act is statute-barred after 15 years from the date of the original incident by the Latent Damage Act 1986.

Trespass

The claimant must show direct entry on to, and damage to, his land by the emissions of the defendant. This has usually proved difficult to show.

Breach of statutory duty

One should also note the possibility of a claim based on statutory duty, e.g. under the Occupiers' Liability Act 1957 or the Defective Premises Act 1972.

The *Blue Circle Industries* case was based on statutory duties in the Nuclear Installations Act 1965, and resulted in an award of over £6 million against the Ministry of Defence.

How can I protect my client against civil liability?

One possibility is insurance – this subject is discussed more fully in Chapter 6.

The main protection for the client, apart from the obvious logistical difficulties for a claimant in proving causation, will be in the form of expert evidence. An environmental investigation should be carried out to ascertain the exact state of land or operations at a given point in time, e.g. on a purchase.

This will inform the client:

- of the current state of contamination;

- whether there are any obvious remediable problems which need attention;

- to what extent any such contamination is now beyond remediation by the client.

The client will be liable in the future for the consequences of any contamination which he could have discovered and corrected. An expert's report which states that at a certain date certain contamination was not present, or was present but could not be corrected, should exonerate a client in future litigation over the effects of that historic contamination.

Chapter 7 deals with the considerations to be borne in mind when engaging consultants.

1.3.2   Clean-up costs

A wholly novel type of liability arises in the environmental context – clean-up costs. Any discussion of this liability is fraught with difficulties, marred by the experience of the United States in the clean-up activities of the Environmental Protection Agency under the so-called Superfund legislation, which has so far been perceived to have cost billions of dollars to little real effect.

The clean-up powers of the regulatory agencies are as set out below:

Environmental Protection Act 1990

PART I – IPC MATTERS

Under s.27 where the commission of an offence under s.23 causes any harm which it is possible to remedy, the chief inspector may remedy the harm and recover the cost from the person convicted of the offence. It follows that this can only be claimed after a successful prosecution.

Similar powers, but not requiring a prior conviction, are to be found in the new IPPC regime (see Regs. 22 and 33 of the Pollution Prevention and Control (England and Wales) Regulations 2000).

PART II – WASTE MATTERS

Under s.59, if any controlled waste is deposited in or on any land so as to constitute an offence, the Environment Agency may by notice require the occupier to remove the waste, and if he does not, can do the required work and recover the cost from the occupier, or in some circumstances, from the person who deposited the waste or who knowingly caused or permitted it to be deposited.

ENVIRONMENTAL LIABILITIES

PART IIA – CONTAMINATED LAND

Under EPA 1990, s.78N a local authority, having identified contaminated land in its area, may do such works as are appropriate by way of remediation to the relevant land in such circumstances as the section permits, mainly non-compliance with a remediation notice, or emergency.

If works are carried out, the authority can recover reasonable costs from the appropriate person, subject to Guidance and any hardship caused.

Costs may include interest if the appropriate person is both the original polluter and the current owner of the contaminated land.

See Chapter 2 for a fuller discussion of these powers.

PART III – STATUTORY NUISANCES

Under s.81, where an abatement notice has not been complied with, the local authority may abate the nuisance, and recover the cost from the person by whose act or default the nuisance was caused, or from the owner for the time being of the land.

Water Resources Act 1991

ANTI-POLLUTION WORKS

Under the recently modified ss.161, 161A–161D of WRA 1991 where it appears to the Environment Agency that any poisonous, noxious or polluting matter or any solid waste matter is likely to enter, or to be or to have been present in any controlled waters, the Environment Agency may carry out works to prevent its entry, remove it and remedy any damage.

Such powers may now only be exercised if:

- the Environment Agency considers immediate works to be necessary; or
- nobody can be found on whom the Environment Agency could serve a 'works notice' requiring remediation of the problem; or
- a works notice is served but is not complied with.

The Environment Agency can recover any costs reasonably incurred from the person served with the notice.

See Chapter 2 for a fuller discussion of these powers.

1.4   INDIRECT COSTS

Environmental liabilities comprise not just the risks mentioned above, but other factors such as:

- legal costs;
- adverse press coverage, which can affect consumers and affect purchasing decisions;
- reduced profitability;
- downward pressure on a company's share price;
- effect on the company's cash flow and thus its ability to service its debt burden;
- insolvency and potential closure.

1.5   PERSONAL LIABILITY OF DIRECTORS AND OTHERS

Directors and others may be made directly liable for the various criminal liabilities mentioned above if they can be said to fall within the statutory wording creating the offence (e.g. by causing or knowingly permitting a water pollution offence).

Directors and other company officers may in addition be made indirectly liable for many of the criminal offences of their companies by virtue of EPA 1990, s.157, which provides that:

> 'where an offence under any provision of this Act committed by a body corporate is proved to have been committed with the consent or connivance of, or to have been attributable to any neglect on the part of, any director, manager, secretary or other similar officer of the body corporate or a person who was purporting to act in any such capacity, he as well as the body corporate shall be guilty of that offence and shall be liable to be proceeded against and punished accordingly.'

Similar provisions are to be found in WRA 1991, s.217(1) and WIA 1991, s.210.

It follows from this provision, that whether or not the company is prosecuted for an offence, its directors can be, and they can be imprisoned for up to five years, depending on the offence.

Any other person – employees, contractors, parent companies, lenders – may also be made liable by virtue of EPA 1990, s.158 if they are involved in the activities of the company. It provides:

> 'where the commission by any person of an offence under Parts I, II, IV or VI or section 140, 141 or 142 above is due to the act or default of some other person, that other person may be charged with and convicted of the offence by virtue of this section whether or not proceedings for the offence are taken against the first-mentioned person.'

This does not include statutory nuisances.

Similar provisions are to be found in WRA 1991, s.217(3) but there are no similar provisions in the WIA 1991.

A director, or other employee, a contractor, or even a parent company, may be caught by this provision if he or it commits some act or default which results in an offence being committed.

1.6   LIABILITY OF LENDERS, RECEIVERS AND OTHER TYPES OF INSOLVENCY PRACTITIONER

1.6.1   Administrative receivers

General

A receiver appointed by a bank or other lender under the terms of a normal floating charge debenture taken over the whole or substantially the whole of a company's assets will be an 'administrative receiver' by virtue of the Insolvency Act 1986 (IA 1986), s.29.

The main implications and effects of this are that:

- the IA 1986 provides that such an individual will be the agent of the company (s.44);

- the appointee is given very wide powers to deal with the assets of the company, together with wide powers of management.

The breadth of the powers of the administrative receiver are, to some extent, a cause for concern in that, very often, the receiver becomes very closely allied to the activities of the company over which he is appointed.

This can link him with its environmental liabilities. However, he enjoys statutory exemption for liability for contaminated land so long as he acts normally in the execution of his functions.

Criminal liability

DIRECT LIABILITY

Notwithstanding the statutory exemption in respect of contaminated land, receivers may still be made criminally liable directly under EPA 1990 if:

- they carry on a business in breach of an IPC licence or an IPPC permit;

- they cause or permit the deposit of waste, or breach the duty of care;

- they are responsible for a statutory nuisance and fail to comply with an abatement notice;

under the WRA 1991 if:

- they cause or knowingly permit a pollution offence;

and under the WIA 1991 if:

- they occupy trade premises and discharge trade effluent in breach of sewerage undertaker's consents.

Whether this is possible depends on the ability of the prosecuting authority to prove the receiver's causal involvement in the incident, and this will in turn depend on the extent of the receiver's actual involvement in the management of the business.

A typical receiver will normally be wishing to sell the business as a going concern, and will therefore be thinking in terms of keeping the operation going until a buyer is found. He will therefore be continuing the activities of the company under his powers of management, and if offences are committed in this period, the receiver may be exposed to the risk of prosecution, as it is his activities which have 'caused' the offence.

At the very least, he will be expected to understand the nature of the business over which he is appointed, and so must be said to be 'knowingly permitting' any offences which occur. A receiver must therefore investigate the potential environmental liabilities and risks fully before appointment.

Most of the offences are of strict liability, and a receiver is therefore likely to be liable personally unless he can take advantage of some statutory defence, e.g. under EPA 1990, s.33(7) or WRA 1991, ss.88–89.

A receiver's agency will not protect him from prosecution for a criminal offence.

INDIRECT LIABILITY

Receivers may be made indirectly liable by virtue of EPA 1990, s.157 (or the sister provisions, WRA 1991, s.217 and WIA 1991, s.210), if it can be said that a receiver is 'a person who was purporting to act' in the capacity of a company officer.

A receiver is an 'office-holder' within the meaning of the IA 1986. Whether a receiver is an 'officer' of the company, however, is debatable, but he may be 'someone purporting to act in that capacity', in that the receiver has *de facto* power of control over company operations once appointed.

There may, in addition, be liability under EPA 1990, s.158 (or its sister provisions in WRA 1991 and WIA 1991) if he commits some 'act or default' which results in an offence being committed. It is submitted that this may include merely continuing with existing business operations.

Non-criminal liability

NUISANCE

A receiver may be liable in nuisance if he is appointed over the assets of a company, one of which is land giving rise to a nuisance, for example, due to contamination.

The receiver could arguably be said to be an 'occupier' of the land or, depending on the circumstances, the creator of the nuisance, and as such could be sued in tort.

After *Cambridge Water*, it seems clear that if it is now beyond the power of the receiver to rectify a contaminating situation, he will not be liable in nuisance.

However, if it is within the receiver's power to rectify a situation, it matters not that the nuisance had begun before the receiver was appointed; failing to abate or prevent it from continuing after that date may be sufficient to attach liability for all the foreseeable consequences of the activity.

Of course, the receiver will be strictly liable in civil law for the foreseeable consequences of any operations carried on by him while in office.

It is perhaps unlikely that, given the short time of his occupation, a plaintiff would be able to show all the necessary elements of the claim as against the receiver, so the risk of civil suits should not be overstated.

CLEAN-UP COSTS

Environmental Protection Act 1990

Part I – IPC matters

Receivers will be liable for the cost of remedying damage caused by IPC offences only if they are convicted of the appropriate IPC offence (but note the different wording of Regulations 22 and 33 of the Pollution Prevention and Control (England and Wales) Regulations 2000 regarding IPPC).

Part II – Waste matters

Receivers can be liable under s.59 (cost of removal of waste) if they are the 'occupier' of the land in question. Is a receiver an 'occupier'? The term is not defined in the Act, but case law would have it that the person in possession of the property is its occupier. A receiver will be so regarded as he is generally given full power to possess and control the property.

Section 59 requires the deposit to constitute an offence under s.33 before the power to recover costs exists, so a receiver could raise the statutory defences in s.33 as a defence to a claim for clean-up costs. Section 59 also has its own 'innocent occupier' defence.

Part III – Statutory nuisances

A receiver can be liable for the cost of abating a statutory nuisance if his act or default caused the nuisance.

It is debatable, therefore, whether the cost of abating a nuisance which arose before the receiver's appointment, but continues after, would be recoverable from him. It probably is not, though it is possible to argue that continued inactivity by a receiver with regard to known problems could amount to 'default'.

Water Resources Act 1991

A receiver could be liable for the costs of preventing or remedying a water pollution incident if he can be said to have either caused or knowingly permitted it.

It is submitted that the test of causation or permission will be the same as in criminal law, i.e. strict liability for matters which the receiver should or could have known about. Receivers can therefore expect to be made personally liable for these costs, though the receiver's agency, as long as it subsists, should protect him from clean-up costs.

Clean-up costs enjoy no preference in an insolvency.

1.6.2 Administrators

Administrators appointed by the court under the IA 1986 have the function of taking control of the activities of a company, in the shoes of the directors, in order to achieve one or more of the purposes specified in the Act – broadly, the financial regeneration of the company, or a better realisation of its assets.

An administrator enjoys very wide powers of management over the company, and therefore faces potentially the same sort of exposure to environmental liability as a receiver, and for the same reasons. Likewise, he may well be regarded as an occupier of land owned by the company, but probably not its owner.

However, there are certain differences in the nature of the two appointments, and the legislation surrounding them, that put an administrator in a stronger position.

First, an administrator is an appointee of the court, not merely of some party in contract with the company.

Second, he benefits from a statutory stay on all proceedings or actions while in office. No proceedings may be brought without the leave of the court, and such leave will only be granted if it is in the interests of the creditors as a whole to do so. It is possible to envisage circumstances where a court may take the view that it is in the interests of the creditors to allow clean-up actions to be brought, but those circumstances would be rare indeed.

Moreover, the IA 1986 provides that the administrator's discharge, at the end of his period in office, releases him from 'all liabilities'.

It is suggested that this combination of provisions effectively means that he cannot be prosecuted for his activities while in office, and is exonerated on his departure.

1.6.3 Liquidators

The function of a liquidator, by contrast, is to wind up the company. In the process, liquidators are also given very wide powers to deal with the assets

27

of the company, and manage its business. Notably, though, and unlike the situation in a bankruptcy, the assets do not actually vest in the liquidator. He is merely given powers to deal with them. He would probably be regarded as the occupier of any land, but not its owner.

Potentially, then, a liquidator faces similar potential exposure to environmental liabilities as receivers. However, it is not the possession of powers which is fatal to the office-holder, but the exercise of them.

Can the office-holder be said to have 'caused' an offence, by the actions which he took? This requires activity, and whereas a receiver is usually carrying on the business activities pending sale, a liquidator will usually be running them down. If, in that process, a liquidator takes steps or performs activities which have a polluting impact, then he would be exposed to liability on the same principles as set out above, but in the absence of such direct involvement, liquidators should be safe.

1.6.4 Supervisors of voluntary arrangements

The function of supervisors is, as the name suggests, to implement an agreed scheme between the company and its creditors for the payment of its debts. There are no powers beyond this. As such, it is difficult to see how such office-holders could be made liable for any of the risks that are set out above.

To the extent that the regulatory agencies and potential civil plaintiffs can be said to be creditors of the company, they may be affected by the rules relating to advertisement of creditors' meetings, and the voting rules at such meetings where arrangements for the payment of liabilities, including environmental liabilities, are discussed and approved. Once approved by the requisite majority attending the meeting, the scheme is binding on all creditors who could have attended the meeting – whether or not they did so.

1.6.5 LPA receivers

Rather like supervisors, 'LPA receivers' usually have no powers to run the company or deal with its assets. They are usually appointed merely to collect rent from property, and as such it is difficult to see how they could be saddled with any of the liabilities mentioned above.

However, such powers can be given by contract between the company and the appointor of the receiver, and if such powers of management are given, and in fact used by the receiver, then liability may follow, depending on the circumstances and the extent of the receiver's involvement in the polluting event.

It is generally thought unlikely, however, that such receivers would be treated as occupiers or owners of any property owned by the company.

1.6.6 Lenders

Criminal liability

DIRECT LIABILITY

In much the same way as administrative receivers (see para. 1.6.1), lenders may be made criminally liable directly under EPA 1990 if:

- they carry on a business in breach of an IPC licence or IPPC permit;

- they cause or permit the deposit of waste or breach the duty of care;

- they are responsible for a statutory nuisance and fail to comply with an abatement notice;

under the WRA 1991 if:

- they cause or knowingly permit a pollution offence;

and under the WIA 1991 if:

- they occupy trade premises and discharge trade effluent in breach of sewerage undertaker's consents.

Whether this is possible depends on the ability of the prosecuting authority to prove the lender's causal involvement in the incident, and this will in turn depend on the extent of the lender's actual involvement in the management of the business.

The lender is only likely to be involved in the management of the business if it goes into occupation of the business as a mortgagee in possession, or issues instructions to the directors or receiver which are acted upon. Most of the offences are of strict liability, and a lender which is a mortgagee in possession or which is issuing instructions is therefore likely to be liable personally unless it can take advantage of some statutory defence, e.g. under EPA 1990, s.33(7) or WRA 1991, ss.88–89.

INDIRECT LIABILITY

Lenders could potentially be indirectly liable under EPA 1990, ss.157 and 158 or WRA 1991, s.217 (see para. 1.5) if they became so involved in the running of the business, for example, by issuing instructions to the management team, that they could, in effect, be said to be acting in the capacity of an officer of the company, or someone whose act or default caused the offence.

A lender would not be liable indirectly under any indemnity given to a receiver, as this would not cover criminal liabilities.

Non-criminal liability

CIVIL LIABILITY

Again, like receivers, lenders may be directly liable, if they can be said to be owners or occupiers, or creators of a nuisance, or if they can be said to be persons who caused or permitted an unlawful waste deposit. This is likely only if the lender is a mortgagee in possession, or is otherwise actively involved in the management of the company's operations, but as such lenders may be in possession longer, and have more assets than a receiver, the temptation for a plaintiff to sue may be rather greater.

The principles of *Cambridge Water* will apply to lenders, so they will not be liable for starting a nuisance if they failed to foresee the risk of damage, but they may be liable for not stopping it if they could have done so.

Lenders may be made indirectly liable for such damages through the indemnity given to the receiver, depending on the wording and extent of that indemnity.

CLEAN-UP COSTS

Lenders may be liable directly for clean-up costs if they are convicted of an IPC offence (or the differently worded IPPC equivalent provision), if they can be said to be occupiers (EPA 1990, s.59), or they cause a statutory nuisance or they cause or knowingly permit water pollution. These possibilities are likely only if the lender is a mortgagee in possession, or is otherwise actively involved in the management of the company's operations.

Lenders may be made indirectly liable for such costs through the indemnity given to the receiver, depending on the wording and extent of that indemnity.

1.6.7 Liability of lenders for contaminated land

The financial sector's primary concern was always that there should not be a 'deep pocket' regime in which lenders could be pursued, regardless of their responsibility for any contamination, if no directly liable party could be found. Such cases now appear less likely, but it is still possible that a mortgagee in possession of a site may be looked upon as the person who 'caused or knowingly permitted' contamination to be present (the 'Class A' person), or the owner or occupier of the land, thus making them the appropriate person on whom to serve a remediation notice.

The term 'owner' is now defined as 'a person (other than a mortgagee not in possession) who ... is entitled to receive the rack rent' (i.e. the yearly amount of rent that a tenant could reasonably expect to pay on the open market). A mortgagee in possession who is entitled to receive the rack rent will therefore be treated as the owner and, accordingly, as liable to be served with a remediation notice if an original polluter cannot be found.

1.6.8 Liability of insolvency practitioners for contaminated land

The Environment Act 1995 provides that:

> a person acting as an insolvency practitioner shall be personally liable under this Part [i.e. for contaminated land] only to the extent that –
>
> (a) harm,
>
> (b) pollution of controlled waters, or
>
> (c) the condition of any land by reason of substances in, on or under the land,
>
> is attributable to his negligence.

It follows that an insolvency practitioner will in future be in danger of liability for land contamination under Part IIA only if it is caused by some negligent act or omission on his part. Provided the practitioner acts with reasonable care while in office, he should be safe.

Even where there is a negligent act or omission, the practitioner will only be liable 'to the extent' that the contamination is caused by that act or omission.

The main difficulty in the future will be that of determining causation – exactly which contaminant was contributed by the practitioner and when, and which was contributed by the borrowing company. This difficulty is likely to render actions against the practitioner a dead letter.

However, as stated above, the defence only applies to the contaminated land provisions contained in Part IIA which will be policed by the local authority, and not to other types of liability such as water pollution policed by the Environment Agency. Nor would the defence be available to any action at common law.

1.7   HOW CAN I PROTECT MY CLIENT?

The key to active environmental risk management, and all the advantages that flow from it, is knowledge.

The company, its individual participants and, come to that, a purchaser, lender or receiver, will need to undertake some form of environmental investigation or audit in order to assess the exact nature and extent of any polluting activities or contamination on its land, and the risks posed by its assets and operations.

For a further discussion of environmental investigations, see Chapter 7.

CHAPTER 2

Contaminated land

2.1   INTRODUCTION

2.1.1   General

Section 57 of the Environment Act 1995 (EA 1995) inserts a new Part IIA
into the EPA 1990, which contains new sections 78A–78YC. These require
local authorities to identify land which needs attention, and then serve
notice on the person liable to clean it up, non-compliance with which
would be a criminal offence.

The new provisions on contaminated land are remarkably complex, and
yet vague. Like so much legislation in this area, the governing legislation is
little more than a set of guiding principles, the detailed operation of which
is left to be specified by Regulations or Guidance Notes from the DETR.

The regime came into force on 1 April 2000, (see Contaminated Land
(England) Regulations 2000, SI 2000/227 and DETR Guidance on
Contaminated Land, April 2000).

2.1.2   Overall summary of procedure

The regulatory bodies are obliged to follow the sequence of steps set out
below:

1.   Inspect
2.   Investigate
3.   Identify/designate as contaminated land or special site
4.   Consider: Are works urgent?

If yes:

5A.   Do works and seek to recover costs

If no:

5B. Identify interested persons
6. Formulate proposed scheme
7. Notify/consult for three months
8. Finalise/Agree scheme
9. Consider exclusionary tests and apportion costs
10. Consider cost recovery/hardship
11. Consider: Can/must a remediation notice be served?

If no:

12A. Do works and seek to recover costs, insofar as possible

If yes:

12B. Serve remediation notice
13. Wait for the specified period [deal with any appeal]
14. Prosecute for non-compliance
15. Do works and recover costs insofar as possible

Each of these steps will be considered more fully in turn.

2.2   INSPECTION AND INVESTIGATION

The Act

Primary responsibility for identifying contaminated sites rests with local authorities, i.e. the district council or unitary authority. They must consult with the Environment Agency if water pollution is involved.

They are obliged to inspect land in their area from time to time for the purpose of identifying contaminated land, and such land as is liable for designation as a 'special site'.

In the case of the latter category – sites which may be particularly hazardous – the local authority must refer the site to the Environment Agency for a decision on whether it should be designated as a 'special site'. If it is so designated, only the Environment Agency has the power to determine when and how it should be remediated, and by whom.

When identifying sites, the enforcing authority is entitled to take into account the cumulative impact of two or more sites when assessing the 'significant harm' or 'pollution' (s.78X).

No further statutory assistance is given in defining the duty to inspect, but the application of the duty is again the subject of Guidance.

The Guidance

The authority is required to have a written strategy for the inspection process ensuring a consistent, ordered approach to the task, taking into account the information already in its possession and any additional matters brought to its attention by third parties.

Specifically, the authority is required to have established the likelihood of a pollutant linkage – the presence of a target, a source and a plausible pathway – before undertaking any intrusive ground investigations. It is required to obtain 'sufficient information' to enable it to form a judgment as to the extent of contamination. The authority need not produce a complete characterisation of the nature of the contamination, but only as much as is sufficient for it to make the determination that the land in question is contaminated.

The Guidance suggests that once land has been so designated, a remediation notice can be served requiring the appropriate person to carry out further, more specific investigations to determine where to go next.

In making the determination, the authority is required to indicate the basis on which the designation is made (significant harm being caused, risk of water pollution, etc.) and to specify what pollutant linkage gives rise to the designation.

Authorities are not to use numerical values of concentrations of pollutants to determine whether land is contaminated, unless those numerical concentrations are such as would justify a conclusion that significant harm is being caused in accordance with the new conceptual definitions.

Land shall not be regarded as contaminated in relation to water pollution risks if risk management arrangements are already in place to prevent such pollution.

Comment

The Guidance requires the local authority to be very specific in its reasons for designating land as contaminated, and this would give much scope for argument and appeal by the person served with the notice.

It will also require the authority to take much scientific evidence into account in order to be sure of its ground.

In view of the potential cost of investigation of sites it would seem that an authority would be quite keen to, and could, on reasonable suspicion of land being contaminated, designate it as such and then serve a remediation notice requiring further investigations to be carried out by the person served with the notice.

This would save the authority the cost of intrusive investigations into ground conditions and cast the burden of those expenses on to some other party.

In these circumstances, an appeal against the service of the notice would be appropriate as no landowner would want to bear the cost of investigations which may ultimately prove the land not to be contaminated after all.

2.3   DESIGNATION

The Act

Contaminated land is defined in s.78A(2) as being:

land which appears to the local authority in whose area it is situated to be in such a condition, by reason of substances in, on or under land, that

(a)   significant harm is being caused or there is a significant possibility of such harm being caused; or

(b)   pollution of controlled waters is being or is likely to be, caused

and in determining whether any land appears to be such land, the local authority shall act ... in accordance with guidance issued by the Secretary of State.

'Harm' is defined as 'harm to the health of living organisms or other interference with the ecological systems of which they form part and, in the case of man, includes harm to his property'.

There are several features to note about the new definition:

●   if there is no harm, land is not 'contaminated' within the meaning of the section, despite the presence of harmful matter;

●   land is 'contaminated' only if the harm, or risk of harm, to the non-aquatic environment is significant; it is 'contaminated' if there is any risk of water pollution, however small.

Each authority is under a duty to have regard to any Guidance issued by the DETR or the Environment Agency when assessing whether land in its area is contaminated. There is express provision within the Act for such Guidance to make provision for different weight to be attached to different descriptions of harm to health or property and other factors.

The definition of 'harm' and 'significant' – and therefore the practical impact of the whole provision – is the subject of Guidance.

The Guidance

The Guidance indicates the approach to be adopted. The definition is to be interpreted in the following way.

'Harm' is to be regarded as significant only if it is of the following types:

- death, disease, serious injury, genetic mutation, birth defects or impairment of reproductive function in humans (a 'human health effect'); this is further defined as including an 'unhealthy' condition of the body or part of it and can include, for example, cancer, liver dysfunction or extensive skin ailments, or even mental dysfunction attributable to some pollutant's effect on the body;

- irreversible adverse change in the functioning of an ecological system (or any species of special interest sustained by such a system) in a location protected under the Wildlife and Countryside Act 1981, European sites protected under Regulation 10 of the Conservation Regulations (Natural Habitats etc.) 1994, SI 1994/2716, sites afforded policy protection under para. 13 of PPG 9 or nature reserves estab-lished under the National Parks and Access to the Countryside Act 1949 (an 'ecological system effect');

- death, disease, other physical damage to livestock, crops, produce or domesticated or wild animals subject to hunting rights, amounting to 20 per cent or more of their value (an 'animal or crop effect');

- substantial damage to, or structural failure of buildings, or interfer-ence with rights of occupation, such that they can no longer be used for the intended purpose (a 'building effect').

An authority must confine its identification of targets to those likely to be present due to the current use of the site only.

In assessing 'risk', local authorities are to assess the possibility of harm, and its significance by reference to:

- the effects of the contamination; and

- fundamental principles of risk assessment.

Risk assessment involves an actual determination of the extent of contamination in a piece of land, i.e. the contaminants present and their concentration, their tendency to migrate, the geo-technical ground conditions in the locality (how might they contribute to the movement of the contaminant), the likely effects of an escape or migration and in particular, how quickly harm may be suffered after exposure to the contaminant.

The essence of the question for the authority is: how likely is it that an escape will actually occur, and what harm will follow if it does?

Substances, the routes by which they move and the entity which may be affected are described in terms of 'contaminant–pathway–receptor' or 'source–pathway–target', and when all three elements are present, a 'pollution linkage' is present.

In general, the more severe the harm, the greater its degree, the shorter the timescale for it to occur or the greater the vulnerability of the target, the more significant is the risk. When a pollution linkage gives rise to a significant risk of harm (as defined) a 'significant pollution linkage' exists. This is what can lead to a designation that land is contaminated.

In determining the risk of water pollution, the local authority is to liaise with the Environment Agency in the determination of whether a water pollution risk is present. There is a suggestion that the Environment Agency will in fact only take steps to deal with land which is polluting water where the pollution is 'significant'.

Comment

The operation of the new regime is profoundly curtailed by the formulation of the new definition, and the guidance on how it is to be interpreted.

Only the receptors mentioned are recognised by the legislation, and all others are to be ignored by the authorities.

One notable omission from the list is land itself – premises and buildings are recognised receptors but land itself is not. Subterranean migration of a contaminant from one site to another would not, of itself, give the recipient landowner any right to complain that his site is now contaminated under the new legislation (though he would have remedies in civil law). An authority would have to wait until a recognised receptor did emerge and then require the clean-up of that site giving rise to the problem. If this was the 'recipient' site, it would nevertheless be the polluter of the original site that would have to foot the bill. It seems, though, that the regime is not to be used to prevent the actual migration itself.

Likewise the recognised types of harm are very limited and this limits the use of the new powers (intentionally, no doubt) to those sites that give rise to real and imminent risks to health.

However, the definitions do pose problems of their own – for instance, with regard to human health effects, is asthma a disease in the same league as cancer or liver dysfunction? If so, land giving rise to such an impact on health is contaminated; if not, it is not. Thus, whether land is contaminated is as much a product of medical debate as it is a product of chemistry or geology.

Land is contaminated if there is any risk of water pollution, however small, and this presents the authorities with a tension between the wording of the legislation and the ethos of the guidance, which suggests that action be taken only in instances of real harm. This tension is due to the overlap with several provisions of the water legislation, and, whilst it may be overcome by recognising that, although a site may be 'contaminated' by reason of minimal amounts of water pollution, the amount of clean-up required may be small or non-existent, it is still an uneasy situation. So much so that the Government is intending to review the wording of the principal legislation, though whether this is of the water legislation or Part IIA is unclear.

2.4   CONSIDER – ARE WORKS URGENT?

If so, the authority will have power to do the necessary works and recover the costs of so doing from the appropriate person in due course.

If not, move on to the next stage.

2.5   IDENTIFY INTERESTED PERSONS

That, is anyone who is or may be:

- an appropriate person;
- an owner of the land;
- an occupier of the land;
- anyone who may have to give permission to allow entry to carry out works;
- anyone else affected by the remediation notice if it were to be served.

39

2.6 FORMULATE A SCHEME

The authority must put together a scheme using the best practicable means to cause the significant pollution linkage to cease to exist. Consideration must be given to the costs and the benefits at this stage.

2.7 NOTIFY AND CONSULT

The Act

The authority is under a duty to carry out a formal consultation exercise before the remediation notice is served (s.78H(1)).

This duty does not apply in cases where it appears to the authority that there is an imminent danger of serious harm or pollution of controlled waters (s.78H(4)).

Three months' notice of the intention to serve a notice must be given to:

- the appropriate person(s) on whom a notice would be served;

- the owner of the land; and

- any person who appears to be in occupation of the whole or part of the land.

2.8 FINALISE/AGREE SCHEME

The Act

A remediation notice 'must not' be served where the authority is satisfied that appropriate steps are being, or will be, taken without the service of a notice (s.78H(5)).

(In such circumstances, the person who would have received the notice is required to prepare, within a reasonable period, a remediation statement setting out what works will be carried out, and within what period.)

Comment

The consultation and waiting periods incorporate lengthy delays into the system.

A cynic may suggest that appropriate persons could delay the service of a remediation notice by engaging the authority in long, technical debates over the suggested measures, offering voluntary schemes or even applying for planning permission to redevelop the site. Such permission need not be implemented for five years, but the fact that planning requirements may be being negotiated may be taken to satisfy the authority that works 'will be' carried out, thus preventing it from serving a notice for the five years of the permission.

Pleading a plausible defence of poverty at this early stage may result in the authority being unable to serve a notice.

This period should also be used to identify other persons who should bear a share of the blame.

More realistically, it is certainly in the interests of all concerned to use the consultation period constructively and to resolve the steps to be taken and by whom, as the only alternative to an agreed strategy is the service of a notice, which would almost inevitably be appealed, benefiting no one except the legal profession.

2.9 CONSIDER EXCLUSION AND APPORTIONMENT

The Act

Under the legislation, the remediation notice must be served on the 'appropriate person', i.e.:

- the person(s) who caused or knowingly permitted the contaminating substances to be in, on or under the land in question (to be referred to as the 'original polluter'); or, if there is no such person, then

- the owner for the time being of the contaminated land; and

- the occupier for the time being of the contaminated land.

This is consistent with the 'polluter pays' principle, but has a number of defects in practice.

THE ORIGINAL POLLUTER

The identity of the original polluter may, of course, be complicated by a long history of contamination on the site. The difficulties of actually proving who put what chemicals into the ground, and when, will be

41

enormous, and impossible to judge without extensive and expensive intrusive investigations beneath the surface of the land in question, with all the attendant disturbance this would cause to the current occupier.

Having found a likely polluter, the primary issue is whether he or it comes into the category of 'causing' or 'knowingly permitting' the material to be present.

By analogy with a long line of criminal authorities interpreting the same form of words (see Chapter 1 for a fuller analysis), the concept of 'causing' pollution will require proof of some form of positive act on the part of the polluter.

'Knowingly permitting' amounts to allowing a state of affairs which one could have anticipated to continue.

Whereas 'causing' substances to be on the land obviously catches the original polluter of the land, the wider notion of 'knowingly permitting' substances to remain on-site also catches subsequent owners, lumping them into the same category of 'original polluters' and rendering them equally liable to service of a remediation notice.

THE OWNER

'Owner' is defined in s.78A as being the person who is or would be entitled to receive the rent for the property.

Section 78A(9) excludes from the definition of 'owner' a mortgagee not in possession.

THE OCCUPIER

There is no statutory definition of 'occupier'. Presumably it will be taken to be the literal definition of someone in physical presence on the land in question.

WHO IS NOT LIABLE?

The Act specifically exempts certain persons from the category of potential 'appropriate persons'. They are referred to as 'persons acting in a relevant capacity' (s.78X(3)).

This includes:

• licensed insolvency practitioners;

- the Official Receiver acting as a licensed insolvency practitioner (LIP);

- the Official Receiver acting as a receiver or manager;

- a receiver appointed by statute/court order.

In respect of clean-up costs, liability can be avoided by such persons except where the contamination is present as a result of any act done or omission made by the relevant person which it was unreasonable for a person acting in that capacity to do or make (s.78X(3)(a)).

There is no guidance on the concept of 'reasonable behaviour', but merely carrying on a business pending resale is unlikely to attach the LIP with liability.

Blatant, indeed negligent, disregard of contamination or deliberate dumping of material to make a site seem more attractive as a saleable item could still give rise to liability.

Criminal liability is not imposed unless there is a failure to comply with a requirement to do something for which the LIP is personally liable as a result of his unreasonable behaviour.

FINANCIAL INSTITUTIONS

The position of the banks and other lenders has still not been fully resolved although the policy statements are clear. They are not specifically excluded (cf. insolvency practitioners) but the position with regard to mortgagees in possession is clarified.

Section 78A(9) excludes from the definition of 'owner' a mortgagee not in possession. This means, however, that financial institutions could still be theoretically liable in two general cases:

- as original polluter, the person responsible for 'causing or knowingly permitting' the presence of the contamination if such person is in some degree of control over the day-to-day activities of the borrower; or

- as mortgagee in possession under the 'owner' category.

MULTIPLE APPROPRIATE PERSONS

As logic would dictate, different and separate remediation notices can require different things to be done by way of remediation by different appropriate persons in respect of different substances on the same site, or even the same substance in discrete locations where the separate depositors of the two 'lumps' of substance can be identified (s.78E(2)).

Each appropriate person may, however, only be served with a notice in connection with any remediation which is 'to any extent referable' to substances caused or knowingly permitted by that party (s.78F(3)).

It is not clear from the Act whether the same activity can be required of two persons by two notices in respect of the same substance in separate locations, but logic would dictate that it can.

Where the same remediation activity is required from different parties (e.g. presumably because the same substance has been put in the same location by a variety of people) the authority must first allocate responsibility for remediation to those persons who are potential appropriate persons, and then apportion the relative share of the cost of remediation to be borne by each.

The questions to be determined by the authority are, respectively, who is going to share the blame, and in what proportions?

In determining both these questions the authority must first decide whether anyone can be excluded from the 'liability group' (s.78F(6)), and then decide on the share to be borne by those who remain (s.78F(7)). The remediation notice must state the relative shares to be borne (s.78E(3)).

In this pursuit, regard must be had to Guidance, which is to set out the excludable parties, and how to apportion costs.

Although the Act is not clear on the point, it is submitted that, where it is clear that two or more appropriate persons have caused or knowingly permitted the presence of different substances in the same location, the costs should be shared between the parties in the relative proportions of the substances.

A summary of these complex points may look like this:

- *two persons, two substances, two locations*: two notices each speci-fying remediation activity, which may be the same for both, or different

- *two persons, two substances, one location*: one notice specifying activity and allocating proportions of costs of compliance

- *two persons, one substance, two locations*: one notice specifying same activity for both locations, and allocating proportions of costs of compliance, or (presumably, but this is not clear) two notices speci-fying different activities for each location

- *two persons, one substance, one location*: one notice specifying activity and allocating proportions of costs of compliance

The Guidance

It is in this area that the Guidance will be most controversial and complicated.

Chapter IV of the Guidance sets out a series of principles on the basis of which certain persons and categories of persons can be excluded from the definition of 'appropriate persons' (exclusions), and how costs can be shared between those who remain (apportionment).

The Guidance states that the first step is to define the 'liability group', i.e. all those who may be appropriate persons by the application of the definition in the Act. That means all those who 'caused or knowingly permitted' the contaminants to be present in the land (original polluters, or 'Class A appropriate persons') or all those who are owners and occupiers, liable as such because the original polluter cannot be found ('Class B appropriate persons').

The next step is to exclude from those groups anyone satisfying any one of a number of tests set out in the Guidance. The exclusionary tests are to be applied in the order set out in the Guidance. Only those who are not excluded are liable to receive the remediation notice. The exclusionary tests are to be stopped as soon as there is only one person left in the group.

The excluded categories are as set out below.

CLASS A LIABILITY GROUP (ORIGINAL POLLUTERS)

1. Anyone who is a member of the Class solely by reason of one or more excluded activities (*inter alia* lending to, insuring, licensing, consenting to the activities of, advising, carrying out work for, or leasing land to another person).
2. Any member of Class A who makes a sufficient payment to another member of Class A for particular remediation of land if that remediation is not carried out properly or at all, and provided the payer retains no control over the land.
3. Anyone who has sold freehold or long leasehold (more than 21 years) land on arm's length terms, the purchaser having sufficient information for him to be aware of the pollution risk which has led to the designation.

The Guidance specifically provides:

> 'in transactions since 1990 between large commercial organi-
> sations, permission from the seller for the purchaser to carry out
> his own survey should normally be taken as sufficient indication
> that the purchaser had the necessary information.'

4. Anyone who deposits a substance A, which is, on its own, inert and of
   no risk, but which, when combined with substance B, becomes a
   pollutant (in this case the depositor of substance B becomes liable).
5. Anyone who deposits a substance which will not escape without intervention, but which later escapes due to intervention (in this case it is
   the intervener who is liable).
6. Anyone who deposits a substance which is not a risk due to the lack
   of a pathway, but which later becomes a risk due to the subsequent
   introduction of a pathway (in this case it is the introducer of the
   pathway who is liable).

CLASS B LIABILITY GROUP (OWNERS AND OCCUPIERS)

Anyone occupying under licence with no value, or paying rent for the land
and having no beneficial interest in the ownership of it other than the
tenancy itself.

Having excluded persons from the liability group, it remains for the
authority to apportion liability amongst those who remain within the
group, as follows:

Class A persons: according to the relative degree of responsibility for the
presence of the linkage; whether they caused or permitted the presence;
whether they could have prevented or removed it; or in equal shares, if all
else fails.

Class B persons: in the proportions in which the owners or occupiers
share the capital value of the land.

The costs are to be calculated on the understanding that works should be
done which will be sufficient to remedy the risk of harm, but without
disturbing other contaminants or making any other problems on the site
worse. The costs are to include the cost of providing compensation to
occupiers for any disruption.

No member of a liability group can be called upon to pay more than his
share of the total liability, and if any of the costs are irrecoverable then the
authority must bear them.

Once the authority has apportioned the shares of responsibility within each liability group, the members of that group know the shares in which they must pay the costs of remediation allocated to that group – all of them if there is only one linkage and one group of persons responsible for it.

Matters become more complicated in relation to sites where a cocktail of substances and a host of polluters have all combined to create the significant pollution linkages on the site. This is the most likely scenario to occur in practice.

Where this is so, the authority should be considering serving one notice for the whole site (see 'Multiple appropriate persons' above), but having done so, it must:

(a) apportion costs within the liability group for each individual linkage, and then
(b) apportion shares of the total cost for the whole site between the various liability groups.

This is done as follows.

The notice may specify two alternative remediation strategies: the 'shared common action' (which is simply a combination of all the strategies that would have been appropriate for each pollution linkage lumped together in one notice) or the 'shared collective action' (which is the one strategy that best addresses all the linkages in one fell swoop and which is usually cheaper as a result).

For a shared common action, the Guidance says that liability for the total cost of the combined measures is to be apportioned between all the Class A liability groups equally.

For a shared collective action, the Guidance suggests that the costs should be borne by the Class A groups, but unequally, the costs being allocated insofar as possible by reference to the percentage share each polluter would bear of the aggregate total had separate strategies been specified for each linkage.

The result of both of these approaches is that wherever there is one Class A polluter for any linkage anywhere on the site, all Class B polluters are exonerated and removed from liability.

Example

A site gives rise to four significant pollution linkages (SPLs): SPL1, SPL2, SPL3 and SPL4.

The authority excludes and apportions liability within each SPL as follows:

SPL1   one Class A polluter (100)

SPL2   three Class A polluters (30:50:20)

SPL3   two Class A polluters (50:50)

SPL4   one Class B polluter (100)

The total cost of a shared common action (should the authority decide this is the way to go) is £250,000. This will be allocated between the three Class A groups equally (i.e. £83,333 each) and then shared within the groups:

SPL1   £83,333

SPL2   £25,000

                £41,666

                £16,666

SPL3   £41,666

                £41,666

The total cost of a shared collective action for the site may be only £200,000. This will be allocated between the groups responsible for SPLs 1, 2 and 3 (the Class A groups) but unequally as explained above. For example, if the sole cost of dealing with SPL1 had been £100,000, the sole cost of dealing with SPL2 had been £200,000 and the sole cost of dealing with SPL3 had been £50,000, the actual (more economical) cost of £200,000 would be shared:

SPL1 100/350, i.e. £57,143

SPL2 200/350, i.e. £114,286

SPL3 50/350, i.e. £28,571

Once allocated to the group, costs are then shared between individuals in the allocated proportions.

Comment

The exclusionary tests may seem fine in isolation, and the intention of removing from liability those who have no real connection with the contamination is laudable, but the practicalities of the system lead to several areas of concern.

TEST 1

This excludes those who are generally thought of as peripheral to the contaminating activity – advisers, lenders, landlords, surveyors and the like. Clearly, those who are offering services to a polluting business would not imagine that they could be made liable for the effects of the polluting business activities themselves. However, the fact that the exception exists at all indicates that in the government's view it is at least theoretically possible that such peripheral service providers could be held to have at least permitted the activities in some way.

If so, they are given an immediate exemption from liability, but the exemption can only operate at all if there are others who will be left in the Class A category after its operation. If there are no others, then the lender or the adviser can be made to pay the clean-up bill.

TEST 2

This excludes those who have, in some sense, already paid for the cost of a clean-up operation on the site and in relation to the pollution that is now giving rise to the problem. Having paid once, you will not be required to pay again, and this test gives the necessary exemption.

Note, though, that to benefit from the exemption, the payment must have been made expressly for the purpose of the relevant clean-up, and must have been of an adequate size to pay for that clean-up. Moreover, the clean-up must not have been carried out properly or at all. The size and purpose of the payment must be specifically set out in the contract under the terms of which the payment has come to be made.

That said, the payment could take a number of forms, and still qualify. It could be a specific payment made voluntarily or under court order, or, more likely, could take the form of a price reduction on a change of owner-ship of property, recorded fully and specifically in the contract.

Properly evidenced price reductions thus remove a seller from the Class A category. General price reductions, not specifically evidenced in the agreement, do not.

TEST 3

This excludes anyone who sells land to another member of the Class A group and who ensures that the purchaser had sufficient information about the nature and extent of the contamination to enable such party to decide whether to proceed and if so, with what price adjustments.

This is clearly an inducement to full disclosure on the part of the seller, and enables a buyer to make an informed choice on the purchase – knowing that if they proceed it will be at their own risk as to the cost of the clean-up, as the seller will be excluded from the Class.

The difficulty with this exclusionary test is in the detail. The Guidance states that the sort of transaction to which the test applies is not confined to property deals pure and simple, but can involve any network of transactions as part of which property changes hands – a company share or business acquisition being the obvious other instance.

Moreover, it states that in transactions between large commercial organisations (however they are to be defined) the mere offering of facilities for inspection, survey or investigation will be sufficient to fix the purchaser with all the knowledge they could have discovered had they undertaken such an investigation, whether they did or did not do so. This counts as full disclosure by the seller.

In addition, it should be noted that this aspect of the test is made retrospective and will catch any transaction entered into since 1990. This may cause considerable upset and dislocation as such transactions may not have made sufficient provision for indemnity, and recent purchasers may have to bear the full clean-up costs alone.

TESTS 4–6

These tests exclude the original polluter of the site in any circumstances where the pollution linkage is attributable to the intervention of some other factor, without which there would have been no problem.

Guidance seems to alter the operation of the Act on this point (see Exclusion Test 6, DETR Circular on Contaminated Land, Annex 3, Chapter D, Part 4, paras. D68–D.72). It provides that, if the migration of the contamination would not have occurred without the act or omission of some third party, then it is the third-party intervener who is the appropriate person for service of the notice, rather than the original depositor of the substance.

The Guidance proceeds on the basis that the third-party intervener must also be in the liability group to start with, i.e. they must themselves be said to have caused or knowingly permitted the substance to be present, so as between co-polluters, it is the person who causes the migration rather than the original pollution who has to remediate.

The Act proceeds on the assumption that, once you deposit a substance, you are liable for everything and anything which subsequently happens to it. For Guidance to change the express terms of the Act is a constitutional novelty, and it remains to be seen how the Courts will interpret these provisions.

TESTS A–B

These simply operate to exclude from liability those who only have a short-term interest in the land, leaving those with the long-term interest to bear the clean-up cost.

Agreements on liabilities

The parties may wish to agree between themselves how they wish to apportion any liability for contamination. Any such agreement will be honoured by the authority, and all its decisions regarding liability will be taken with the intention of enabling the agreement between the parties to have effect.

However, if the effect of the agreement would be to place an additional burden of expense on a person who would benefit from any relaxation of his responsibility to pay his full share, for example because of the hardship it would cause him, then the authority would, in principle, have to pay that share itself, at public expense. In such circumstances, the authority can ignore the whole agreement and apply the rules in the statutory guidance instead.

Such contracts therefore need to include mechanisms to ensure that, if the authority does not honour and implement the agreement as had been intended, the parties will indemnify one another to regulate the position between themselves. It would thus be the parties who bear the risk of one of them being unable to pay their share, rather than the public purse, and this is also intended as an anti-avoidance measure. For an example of such a clause, see Appendix 4.

2.9.1 The position of owners and occupiers

The Act

Although primary responsibility for remediation rests with the person who caused or knowingly permitted the substance to be present in land (the 'original polluter' or 'Class A appropriate person'), who may in certain circumstances not even himself be the original polluter on the ambiguous wording of the Act, there is a residual responsibility which falls upon owners and occupiers of land.

Where, after reasonable inquiry, the original polluter cannot be 'found', the owner or the occupier for the time being becomes the appropriate person.

The Guidance

No guidance has yet been given in respect of the definition of 'reasonable inquiry' and it is not altogether clear what is meant by the phrase. There is also some doubt about the meaning of the word 'found'. It would seem to mean 'identified, in existence and located'. An individual must still be alive, and a corporate entity must not yet have been dissolved, though solvency is not a requirement. If it 'exists', it matters not that it has no money – the authority will have to foot the bill.

The liability of owners and occupiers is restricted as regards remediation works in relation to the pollution of controlled waters (s.78J). Where a party finds itself responsible for remediation works solely as a result of its ownership or occupation of land (as opposed to being the original polluter) that party will not be liable for any works relating to the pollution of controlled waters (s.78J(2)). This brings the contaminated land provisions into line with s.161 of the Water Resources Act 1991, which allows the Environment Agency to serve works notices only on original polluters, and not on landowners purely by reason of their ownership.

2.9.2 Escapes of substances to other land

The Act

As contamination does not necessarily confine itself to boundaries of ownership or occupation there is provision for the service of remediation notices where substances have escaped from their original resting place on to other land.

The basic principle is that the original polluter of the first site (land A) is to be treated as the original polluter of any other land (land B, C, etc.) to which the substance migrates (s.78K(1)).

Owners and occupiers of lands A, B or C are not liable to carry out remediation works in respect of contaminating substances unless the original polluter cannot be found, and in any event could then only be made liable to clean up land within their ownership or occupation (s.78K(3),(4)).

The Guidance

As noted above, the Guidance seems to alter the operation of the Act quite significantly here. It provides that if the migration would not have occurred without the act or omission of some third party, then it is the third-party intervener who is the appropriate person for service of the notice, rather than the original depositor of the substance.

The Guidance proceeds on the basis that the third-party intervener must also be in the liability group to start with, i.e. they must themselves be said to have caused or knowingly permitted the substance to be present, so as between co-polluters, it is the person who causes the migration (rather than the person who caused the pollution) who has to remediate.

2.10 CONSIDER COST RECOVERY/HARDSHIP

The authorities must now consider what the consequences would be of serving a notice and then carrying out the works themselves.

Can they recover all the relative shares of the costs from all those identified as being liable to pay?

If not, no remediation notice can be served on anyone.

The authority must do works and recover the full amount from those who can afford it, and as much as possible from those who cannot afford it at all.

See ss.78H(5)(d), 78N(3)(e), 78P(1).

One of the problems here is that there is no appeal procedure available, as no notice has been served. Judicial review would be the only action open to any of the liable parties who wanted to dispute the designation or the steps taken.

Pending review of this point, the DETR is to encourage authorities to consult over liability issues and technical matters, to minimise disputes.

If there is no problem, proceed to serve the notice.

2.11   SERVE REMEDIATION NOTICE

The Act

Once a site has been identified as contaminated land (or a special site), the relevant authority is under a duty to prepare a 'remediation notice' specifying what must be done by way of remediation (s.78E).

In specifying the steps required under a remediation notice, the authority can only require reasonable steps to be taken having regard to the costs of carrying out the work and the seriousness of the harm/pollution caused (s.78E(4), (5)).

The definition of 'remediation' (s.78A(7)) includes:

- assessment of the condition of land;

- the doing of any works, carrying out of any operations or taking of any steps in relation to any land or waters for preventing, minimising, remedying or mitigating the effects of significant harm or pollution;

- the restoration of land or waters to their former state;

- inspections from 'time to time'.

It is expected that the content of remediation notices will reflect the existing content of abatement notices under the statutory nuisance system. The precise requirements with regard to content and procedure are to be dealt with by way of Regulation (s.78E(6)).

In addition to these Regulations, enforcing authorities are obliged to take into account any Guidance from the Secretary of State in relation to what is to be done, the standard to which it must be carried out and the definition of 'reasonable' in the context of the cost–benefit analysis.

There are, however, a number of circumstances where the duty to serve a remediation notice does not apply.

A remediation notice 'must not' be served where:

- the enforcing authority is satisfied that a site is contaminated but no remediation works can be specified to be carried out because they would be unreasonably expensive (s.78H(5)). In such circumstances it must publish a remediation statement setting out the grounds for taking the view that remediation works cannot be specified (s.78H(6));

- the authority is satisfied that appropriate steps are being, or will be

taken without the service of a notice (s.78H(5)). In such circumstances, the person who would have received the notice is required to
prepare, within a reasonable period, a remediation statement setting
out what works will be carried out, and within what period;

- the authority itself would be the recipient;
- grounds already exist for the exercise by the authority of its own
  clean-up powers in respect of the site.

These exceptions do not apply where there is imminent danger of serious
harm or serious pollution of controlled waters (s.78H(4)).

A further restriction is placed upon the authority in that it cannot issue a
notice where powers are available to the Environment Agency under s.27
EPA 1990 in relation to remediation of pollution caused by prescribed
processes (s.78YB).

The Guidance

Guidance suggests that the main purpose of notification and consultation is
to enable those affected by the notice to resolve technical and liability
disputes, to refine the requirements of the notice, and to agree voluntary
strategies. If such can be agreed, then no notice can be served at all,
provided that the authority is satisfied that works 'will be' carried out
within an agreed time-frame. The time-frame itself must be reasonably set
so as to enable the person to afford the works.

The restriction on serving a notice must also be read in conjunction with
the Guidance on cost recovery, as the powers for the authority to do works
can be exercised whenever it is satisfied that, at the end of the day, it
would not be seeking to recover from any appropriate person all of its
share of the costs of the work. In such a situation, no notice can be served
on anyone. The authority must do the work itself, if at all, and then recover
as much cost as possible from those responsible.

On the question of how clean is clean, the Draft Guidance suggests that the
remediation works specified should be such as to enable the identified
pollutant linkage which led to the original designation to cease to exist.
This may mean simply severing the pathway (e.g. by tarmacadaming a
surface) rather than cleaning the subsoil. It also means, of course, that land
is never given a clean bill of health as it may be redesignated as contaminated at a later stage should a new target or pathway emerge.

Comment

The circumstances where the duty to serve a remediation notice does not apply represent a major weakening of the regulatory powers under the Act.

2.11.1 Carrying out remediation works

The Act

A remediation notice can require an appropriate person to carry out works which they are not otherwise entitled to do, because, for example, they are no longer in possession of the site and have no rights of access to it.

In these circumstances, the owner or occupier of land has a statutory obligation to allow remediation works to be carried out on the land or waters that they own or occupy (s.78G).

Before the remediation notice is served, the enforcing authority has to use its reasonable endeavours to consult with all those parties who might be required to grant rights to the party carrying out the remediation works (s.78G(3)), though this requirement does not apply where there is imminent danger of serious harm, etc.

No provision is made in the Act for expediting the consent of those parties should they refuse.

In many cases the carrying out of remediation works will create an enormous amount of disruption to an occupier of land. Thus, where rights are granted, compensation will be payable by the appropriate person but detailed provisions for the payment of compensation have yet to be published. The cost of compensation could, of course, be significantly greater than that of carrying out the remediation works themselves.

The Guidance

The Guidance provides that the cost of compensating the occupier for rights of access is to be one of the costs to be identified by the authority in, and borne by the appropriate person receiving, the remediation notice.

2.12   WAIT

The Act

The authority must now allow the time specified in the notice to elapse.

There is a right of appeal against a remediation notice (s.78L). Where the notice is served by a local authority an appeal is heard in the magistrates' court and the appeal is to be made by way of summary application (in a similar fashion to the statutory nuisance provision).

Where the Environment Agency is the appropriate authority, the appeal is heard by the Secretary of State.

The time-limit is 21 days beginning with the first day of service.

The notice can be quashed if there is a 'material defect' in the notice. The notice can also be modified or confirmed.

The details of the appeal system will be the subject of further Regulations.

The Regulations

The Contaminated Land (England) Regulations 2000 provide the following grounds of appeal:

- the appellant is not the appropriate person;

- someone else is the appropriate person (the appellant must specify who and where they are);

- the authority failed to exclude the appellant from the definition in accordance with Guidance;

- the authority improperly apportioned the costs of remediation;

- there is some error in or connected with the notice;

- the authority served a notice when it was statutorily prevented from doing so;

- the notice requires works to be done in respect of controlled waters by an owner or occupier liable in that capacity only;

- the notice requires works to be done in respect of migrated matter on other land;

- the notice requires works to be done in respect of matters governed by other regulatory regimes (e.g. integrated pollution control (IPC));

- the land has been improperly identified as contaminated bearing in mind the relevant Guidance;

- the authority has unreasonably refused to accept that voluntary works are being or will be carried out;

- the notice's requirements are unreasonable having regard to the costs and benefits;

- the notice is served in circumstances where the authority had power to do the works itself;

- the notice's requirements fail to take account of Guidance from the Secretary of State or the Environment Agency (*inter alia* they are insufficiently precise, etc.);

- the period of time for compliance is insufficient;

- the notice requires an insolvency practitioner to carry out works, contrary to s.78X.

The Regulations provide that an appeal suspends the operation of a remediation notice.

Comment

Not even the most inventive litigator could have come up with a more comprehensive set of grounds on which to make the local authority's life a misery.

One hesitates to mention the American Superfund experience, but it is easy to see a decade of litigation marching towards the local authorities over the interpretation of these provisions.

2.13   PROSECUTE FOR NON-COMPLIANCE

The Act

Please see Chapter 1 for an analysis of the offences in context.

It is an offence to fail to comply with a remediation notice without reasonable excuse (s.78M).

The offence can only be tried in the magistrates' court.

Where the contaminated land is industrial, trade or business premises the maximum penalty is a fine of £20,000 with a further daily fine of up to £2,000 for every day before the enforcing authority has carried out any remediation.

In cases of other contaminated land, the maximum fine is £5,000 with a maximum daily fine of £500 (10 per cent of Level 5).

2.14 DO WORKS AND RECOVER COSTS

The Act

The relevant authority has the power to carry out remediation works:

- where it is necessary to prevent imminent serious harm being caused;

- where any requirement of a remediation notice is not complied with;

- where it is agreed that the authority should carry out the works;

- where a remediation notice could not have specified works of the type required;

- where the local authority would not be seeking to recover all of its share of the costs from any of the appropriate persons;

- where there is no appropriate person on whom to serve a remediation notice.

If works are carried out, the authority can recover the reasonable costs of the work (or at least a proportion of them) from the appropriate person(s), subject to Guidance and any hardship caused.

Costs may include interest if the appropriate person is both the original polluter and the current owner of the contaminated land.

In England and Wales the relevant authority also has the power to serve a charging notice on the owner which will constitute a charge on the premises which consist of or include the contaminated land in question. The costs of any charge may be paid by instalments over a maximum 30-year period.

A person served with the charging notice has a right of appeal which must be made to the county court within 21 days of the receipt of the notice.

The Government's intention behind these provisions is to avoid hardship, prevent the private sector from gaining from publicly funded improvements to land and 'to protect the public purse'. No provision is made in the

Act to deal with so-called 'orphan liabilities' (i.e. where no costs can be recovered).

The Guidance

First, the Guidance reminds authorities that they should not even consider serving a remediation notice if they already know that they have no likelihood of being able to recover all of their allocated share of the costs from the person served, due to the hardship caused. The only option then is for the authorities to do the works themselves, and recover as much as they can.

It suggests that hardship should be given its usual dictionary meaning of 'hardness of fate or circumstance, severe suffering or privation', and should be interpreted to include injustice, suffering and anxiety as well as financial impact. Threats to business solvency and the local impact of businesses becoming unviable are general considerations.

Authorities are allowed to develop their own policies on this point along other parameters – for example, whether the person served would be financially eligible to receive a housing renovation grant.

As far as original polluters are concerned, the Guidance suggests the following considerations as being relevant:

- whether they are businesses or private individuals;

- persons made liable in circumstances where co-parties cannot be found are to be called upon to pay only so much as they would have had to pay had the other party been found;

- whether any steps have been taken to mitigate the harm;

- the role played in, and the degree of responsibility for, the creation of the risk of harm by each person (subsequent interveners, occupiers, pathway introducers, etc.).

As far as owner/occupiers are concerned, the Guidance suggests the following considerations as being relevant:

- whether the owner/occupier knew of the contamination at purchase and whether the price was reduced accordingly;

- whether the costs are likely to exceed the value of the land, bearing in mind that windfall gains in value to the current owner at public expense should be avoided;

- where trustees may be called to pay costs, the value of any trust fund used to pay them.

None of these considerations is to override the tests for allocation and apportionment of liability set out above – the tests prevail.

Having determined who should pay what, where the recovery of costs is waived, the authority must bear the unpaid costs, and not reallocate them to other parties.

Comment

Again there are difficulties over the meaning and interpretation of these clauses.

Again the terms of a land transaction may come under scrutiny to determine the state of a buyer's knowledge, and whether there were any reductions in purchase price, to see whether any hardship would be suffered by owners in having to pay.

The fact that business solvency may be threatened would seem to enable smaller and medium-sized businesses to raise the defence of poverty, particularly in recessionary times. Even without creative accounting, many businesses are on the edge financially, and a clean-up bill may be the straw that breaks. The socio-economic costs of clean-up ('force me to pay and I'll sack the staff') are vital political considerations for a local authority.

There is also the perception that, where a local authority undertakes a clean-up operation, the 'reasonable' costs always seem to be very high.

2.15 REGISTERS

The Act

Every enforcing authority must keep a register whenever it decides to designate land as contaminated (s.78R). The register will contain the following details:

- remediation notices;
- charging notices;

- appeals against remediation and charging notices;

- remediation statements and declarations;

- designations of special sites;

- notices terminating the designation of special sites;

- notifications by owners/occupiers/appropriate persons of any voluntary works which they claim have been carried out on the site;

- convictions for relevant offences.

The fact that information is contained on the register which specifies what voluntary works have allegedly been carried out, is not to be taken as a representation by the authority that the works have in fact been carried out, or how successfully.

Access can be had to these registers by members of the public, free of charge, and copies provided on the payment of reasonable charges (s.78R(8)).

There are certain exclusions from the register (s.78S) for:

- information affecting national security; and

- commercially confidential information.

There will be an appeals system which will mirror the existing confidentiality appeals.

Comment

Just as we thought the contaminated land registers had been abandoned, here they resurrect themselves in different form. Surely the concerns about blight will be as real now as before, if indeed they were ever well founded.

The registers must be the first port of call in any conveyancing transaction from now on.

2.16   INTERACTION WITH OTHER LEGISLATIVE REGIMES

There are several other regimes which are intended to deal with many aspects of pollution and contamination and which could overlap with the operation of Part IIA. They are:

- planning law;

- radioactive substances legislation;

- food safety;

- health and safety;

- major accident hazards;

- landfill tax;

- integrated pollution control/pollution prevention and control;

- waste management;

- statutory nuisances;

- water pollution;

- sewer discharges.

What overlaps are there, and how are they resolved?

Planning law

Planning law is essentially focused on future land use, and all decisions regarding planning consent and conditions are taken with that future use in mind.

Contamination in the ground on any site coming up for redevelopment is a material consideration for the purposes of the planning legislation and conditions will therefore be set by the planning authorities which take the implications of that contamination into account and which require its remediation as part of the development work. It will thus be the developer who has the task of remediating the contamination as part of the development and who must therefore take such costs into account in any purchasing decision.

Any such remediation will be policed via the planning system and not Part IIA.

Remediation under Part IIA is intended to deal with current land use only.

Radioactive substances legislation

Radioactive substances and their effects are specifically removed from the normal ambit of Part IIA, but the facility is retained for the Secretary of State to apply parts of it to radioactive contamination by Regulation. A consultation process is currently underway on this topic.

Food safety

Authorities using Part IIA powers are to liaise with the Food Standards Agency and MAFF over any use by the latter bodies of their powers of control under Part I of the Food and Environment Protection Act 1985.

Health and Safety

Health and Safety issues under the Health and Safety at Work Act 1974 may arise on any site where workers may be at risk of exposure to contaminants. In any such case authorities under Part IIA are to liaise with the Health and Safety Executive (HSE) to ensure that no duplication of control takes place and that the most appropriate system of control is used to deal with the problem.

Major accident hazards

The Control of Major Accident Hazards Regulations 1999 (COMAH 1999), SI 1999/743 require action plans in relation to dangerous substances stored on sites, providing for the steps to be taken in the event of an escape. Authorities under Part IIA should again liaise with the HSE who oversee COMAH 1999.

Landfill tax

Landfill tax under the Finance Act 1996 will be payable on any wastes going to landfill. However, exemption is available for wastes from contaminated sites or those remediated as part of certain developments. This exemption will however *not* be available to anyone cleaning up a site as part of enforcement action under Part IIA, though it will still be available to those cleaning up a Part IIA site voluntarily. This is intended to be a fiscal incentive to voluntary clean-up.

Integrated pollution control/pollution prevention and control

Integrated Pollution Control (IPC) is a regulatory system of licensing for heavily polluting industrial processes. The IPC system contained in Part I of the Environmental Protection Act 1990 comprises a power of clean-up, exercisable by the licensing authority in the event of any breach of a licence condition. The EPA specifically provides that to the extent that any contaminant is already subject to control under Part I, it cannot also constitute contaminated land under Part IIA.

Integrated Pollution Prevention and Control (IPPC) is a similar system, introduced by the Pollution Prevention and Control Act 1999 (PPCA 1999) in response to a European Directive, which supersedes Part I of the EPA. Its essential components are identical, though, and the PPCA 1999 also provides that, to the extent that any contaminant is already subject to control under PPC, it cannot also constitute contaminated land under Part IIA.

IPC/PPC clean-up powers can be used to clean land up to any extent, and they are not subject to the restrictive operative provisions of Part IIA.

Clean-up operations ordered under Part IIA may constitute regulated processes under IPC/PPC.

Waste management

The waste management licensing regime contained in Part II of the Environmental Protection Act 1990 deals with the operation of waste-related processes. To the extent that material is already liable to be dealt with under Part II, it cannot also constitute contaminated land under Part IIA.

However, any material removed as part of a remediation operation under Part IIA may constitute waste (or even special waste), thus requiring a license or other compliance procedures.

Statutory nuisances

Statutory nuisances under Part III of the Environmental Protection Act 1990 are defined to include 'premises or accumulations' which could be a pollution or health risk, as well as the more routine examples such as smoke and noise.

However, this would have meant that Part III could have been used to require the abatement of any pollution risk arising on premises, which is exactly what the new regime in Part IIA is supposed to be for.

Moreover, Part III has been in force in one form or another for centuries and is familiar, quick and cheap.

In order to give Part IIA a fighting chance, the legislation has been amended to provide that no land in a 'contaminated state' can now be a statutory nuisance.

The definition of 'land in a contaminated state' includes any land on which contaminants are present and which may cause harm, and this is of course *not* the same as it being contaminated within the meaning of Part IIA, which requires additional criteria to be met.

Thus, one faces the situation where land may be in a contaminated state by virtue of the presence of chemicals on it, but is not yet so dangerous as to pose a real risk of significant harm to any recognised receptor. Such a site cannot be 'contaminated land', but nor can it now be a statutory nuisance either.

It seems that this lacuna in the drafting of the legislation is intentional – it is government policy, and now the law – that unless a site is imminently going to kill someone it should be left alone. Land is either 'contaminated' within the meaning of Part IIA, or it is nothing.

Deliberate this may be, desirable it is not.

Water pollution

Wherever and whenever water pollution occurs, however insignificant or harmless it may have been, the clean-up powers contained in the Water Resources Act 1991 ss.161A–161D come into play. These enable the Environment Agency as water regulator to serve a works notice on those responsible for the water pollution requiring them to clean it, and all its consequences, up. Moreover, the notice can be used to prevent anticipated water pollution before it occurs

There is a clear and undesirable overlap between these powers and those under Part IIA, which can also be used whenever water pollution occurs.

In any incident of water pollution, which set of powers should be used and by whom?

Logic would suggest that it should be the Water Resources Act powers that should be exercisable by the Environment Agency – they are, after all, the water specialists. Part IIA would thus be left to deal with land-based contamination only.

Sadly, logic has not guided government thinking on this matter and the Guidance suggests that it should be the Part IIA powers that should be used, the authorities liaising with the Environment Agency over the terms and conditions to be imposed in dealing with any water pollution.

It remains to be seen what point there is in having the works notice powers in the WRA, and the government has indicated a desire to amend primary legislation to clarify this overlap, which is, for the time being, dealt with under an Environment Agency policy statement on the use of the works notice procedure. It seems that the latter is of use only if and when Part IIA does not apply, but it is hard to envisage circumstances of water pollution emanating from land where it would not.

Sewer discharges

Discharges of trade effluent to sewer are regulated under the Water Industry Act 1991. That piece of legislation contains no statutory powers of clean-up and in that sense there is no overlap with the new regime in Part IIA. However, it is just about conceivable that leakages into the sewerage system from a contaminated site may amount to an unlawful trade effluent discharge.

2.17 CONTAMINATED LAND AND RELATED MATTERS – GENERAL CONCLUSIONS

The new provisions on contaminated land are complex, the Guidance even more so. Local authorities will take a long time to get to grips with some of the many subtleties and inconsistencies. Moreover, control via the planning process is more familiar and may be more effective.

The removal of the residual power to deal with polluted ground as a statutory nuisance may also give rise to some political embarrassment for local authorities.

Practitioners should note that the contaminated land provisions are not likely to become fully effective until July 2001 (the expiry of the 15-month strategic planning stage), so an early over-reaction would be unwise. However, practitioners must give appropriate advice on transactions occurring today – as the actual or constructive knowledge of pollution today, may make you liable to clear it up tomorrow, for having knowingly permitted it to remain.

In the author's view, the concept and lack of definition of 'knowingly permitting' – and its potential application to a range of people other than the person who first dumped the polluting material – is one of the key flaws in the system.

It is vital to understand that purchasers of land and their lenders can be Class A polluters, and will thus continue to inherit contaminated land liability on a purchase.

Other transactional considerations revolve around the concept of 'sales with information' and 'sufficient payments for particular remediation', which have the effect of exempting the parties from the paying category and may dictate the pattern of future dealings, depending on the final wording and interpretation of this crucial piece of Guidance. Much thought now needs to be given to the form of transactional documentation to gain maximum benefit from the exemptions in the Guidance.

CHAPTER 3

Property transactions

3.1 INTRODUCTION

Conveyancing practitioners have a difficult line to tread – providing a cost-effective service to the client, which deals with all the likely issues of concern without costing the client a fortune or leaving the solicitor guilty of negligence.

Of particular concern to solicitor and client alike are the potential environmental risks, that:

- a costly environmental liability may be inherited by a purchaser of a site; or

- the value of a property or site may be adversely affected, even to the point of it being unsaleable, as a consequence of some actual or perceived environmental problem with the site or neighbouring property.

As the previous chapters have explained, the network of environmental liabilities is complex, and the price that buyers will pay for sites which they know or believe to be polluted is very volatile. Purchasers with experience of foreign jurisdictions may be particularly sensitised to the issue. These risks should not therefore be ignored. The legislation applies with equal rigour to both commercial and domestic transactions, so all practitioners must take care.

The Law Society is intending to issue to all practitioners a 'Contaminated Land warning card' before end of December 2000 outlining the current position and suggesting an appropriate professional stance on these issues.

It is worth noting that more attention is being focused by other professions on the role of the solicitor in the giving of advice on pollution matters. Surveyors and valuers will often suggest to clients that 'their solicitor will advise' on such matters. In the Law Society's *Gazette* it was reported that:

'the attention of the Solicitor's Indemnity Fund has been drawn to valuation reports prepared for lenders which contain assumptions that there is no contamination in or from the ground.

For example, the Halifax Building Society's valuation report contains such a statement. Its practice is to forward the report to the purchaser's solicitors under cover of a standard letter asking the solicitor to 'check the valuer's assumptions are correct'.

Such requests place an onerous burden on conveyancers which they cannot always be expected to discharge. Furthermore, in the standard letter to solicitors, attention appears to be diverted away from assumptions with regard to contaminated land which are beyond the knowledge of the solicitor and towards more easily verifiable assumptions.

Again, in its standard letter the Halifax writes: 'In the report, you will see that the valuer has made certain assumptions about the property (for example, its tenure)'.

The Halifax is not the only lender adopting this practice; other lenders and privately-appointed surveyors are taking the same approach. This is an obvious attempt by lenders and valuers to shift responsibility for assumptions made in connection with the valuation of the property onto the solicitor.

Solicitors should specifically advise lenders in writing that they are unable to verify the assumptions concerning contaminated land and that their report on title is limited accordingly. The lay client also needs to be made aware that the valuer has made a number of assumptions which the solicitor cannot be expected to verify.

If no steps are taken and in the future it is discovered that the property has been built on contaminated land, a claim for damages could well be made against the solicitor. The property concerned may decline in value, become unsaleable, or be the subject of an expensive clean up operation.

The Environment Act 1995 [. . .] obliges local authorities to identify contaminated land and to serve upon the 'appropriate person' a 'remediation notice' setting out the work required to clean up the contamination. The 'appropriate person' is the polluter. In the absence of the polluter the owner or occupier of the land will be responsible. If the owner is insolvent, responsibility will fall on the lender who has taken possession, and who in turn will rely on the solicitor's report on title.'

[1998] Gazette, 16 April, 38. Reproduced with the permission of the Gazette.

Solicitors are further exhorted to 'exercise caution now to prevent future claims'.

This is a matter which the Law Society continues to discuss with both the RICS and the Council of Mortgage Lenders.

Solicitors and their clients should, however, take comfort from the fact that, with some relatively cheap and easy steps, an adequate view can be taken of the risks involved in any transaction, which can then be used to inform the decision whether to proceed at all, and, if so, with what additional protections.

The environmental liabilities potentially inherited by a purchaser of land are summarised in paras. 3.1.1 and 3.1.2. For a full discussion of these principles, see Chapter 1.

3.1.1 Environmental liabilities in commercial cases

Criminal liabilities include offences:

- under the INTEGRATED POLLUTION CONTROL REGIME, **replaced by** POLLUTION PREVENTION AND CONTROL **from 31 October 1999 [Pollution Prevention and Control Act 1999, Pollution Prevention and Control (England and Wales) Regulations 2000]** (conducting a prescribed process without or in breach of a licence) (**EPA 1990, s.23**; PPC(EW)R regs. 22 and 33)

  The offences under the IPC/PPC regime are related to carrying on 'prescribed processes' or activities, such as chemical and metal manufacture. It is an offence to operate such a process without or in breach of a licence to do so.

  For commercial buyers, it is essential to make an inspection of the public registers if one is taking over the site as a going concern and intending to carry on the process, but even if not, a run-down of the past track record of the site will assist in assessing the risk posed by the site, especially if any accidents or incidents are recorded.

- **relating to CONTROLLED WASTE (disposal or treatment without or in breach of a licence) (EPA 1990, s.33)**

  The waste offences largely involve the disposal of waste on a site without or in breach of a licence. This mainly, though not exclusively, relates to operative landfill sites.

  For commercial buyers of a closed landfill site, it is unlikely that any action would be taken against them in respect of historic events on the site, as there are defences to such prosecutions available for innocent occupiers. It would be a sensible step to make enquiries as to whether a site has been used as a landfill in the past, in order to assess whether any risks are ongoing, as other liabilities may emerge over time from the migration of gases or liquids from the site.

- **relating to CONTAMINATED LAND (failure to remediate when instructed to do so) (EPA 1990, Part IIA)**

This may come about as a result of substances already in the land at completion, which are giving rise to a risk of significant harm to persons or things nearby.

This may catch such commonplace matters as historic leakages of liquids from storage tanks, washings from site plant and equipment, spillages from delivery wagons, or wastes and liquids being deposited (deliberately or inadvertently) on site from an industrial process or other land-use.

If the original polluter of the land cannot be found, the current owner or occupier may be served with a remediation notice requiring the land to be cleaned up. An offence is committed if he fails to comply, and the authorities can do the necessary works themselves and recover the costs from the person served with the notice.

A further problem is that a purchaser can himself qualify as the 'original polluter'. This is because the original polluter is defined as 'any of the persons who [caused or] knowingly permitted the [contaminating substances] to be in, on or under the land'.

Allowing something to remain on land if you could remove it amounts to permitting it to be on the land.

Actual knowledge of the contamination, turning a blind eye to an obvious risk of contamination or failing to make enquiries for fear of discovering the truth would all amount to having the required knowledge.

Accordingly, if a buyer knew, or ought to have known or realised, or could have found out, that there was contamination on the site, he may be caught. This must be true in respect of most, if not all, commercial sites.

There may also be leakages of substances onto the ground after completion in respect of which the purchaser client may be deemed to be the 'original polluter' of the land.

The provisions relating to contaminated land are complex, but in essence, commercial purchasers should take comfort from the fact that:

- only the most seriously polluted sites are likely to be designated as contaminated;

- most remediation would have been addressed when the site was last developed (if this has occurred in the last two to three years), though this should not be taken for granted;

- remediation strategies must be cost-effective;

- liability is likely to be shared with others (e.g. predecessors in title).

On the other hand, a series of exclusionary tests to be applied by the authorities may result in the seller of property no longer being required to share the cost of remediation if the purchaser knew about the contamination of the site at completion. This provision may be interpreted as meaning that a purchaser is better off buying in ignorance of the state of the site, but this cannot be good practice.

Further exclusions take a seller out of the line of fire if a reduction in the purchase price was negotiated to take account of particular contamination and remediation.

- **relating to STATUTORY NUISANCES (failure to abate when instructed to do so) (EPA 1990, s.80)**

Statutory nuisances are noises, smells, dust, odour, premises or accumulations which may be a pollution or health risk. This could include dangerous structures as well as the sorts of matters already mentioned.

Buyers of land can be served with abatement notices in respect of any nuisances continuing after the date of purchase as it could be said that they are the person responsible for the continuing nuisance.

Otherwise, they may be liable as owner or occupier if the person responsible cannot be found.

An offence is committed if they fail to comply with any abatement notice, and clean up works can be undertaken and the costs recovered.

- **relating to the POLLUTION OF CONTROLLED WATERS (polluting water without or in breach of a licence, failing to clean up water when instructed to do so) (WRA 1991, ss.85, 161A)**

If any polluting matter gets into 'controlled waters' (virtually any watercourse other than a sewer), an offence is committed.

Any deliberate or inadvertent leakages of substances from a site which get into watercourses, either directly or via the drainage system, may give rise to a liability. No intention to commit the offence need be shown, only a causal chain of events from the activities of the owner on-site leading to the emission into the waters.

The same problems afflict buyers with regard to water pollution offences occurring before completion but persisting afterwards, as it may be said that the buyer has knowingly permitted the offence to continue.

So if a buyer ought to have known or realised, or could have found out, that there was a possibility of water pollution occurring from the site, they may be caught.

- **relating to SEWERS (discharging trade effluent to sewer without or in breach of a licence) (WIA 1991, s.118)**

This offence relates to ongoing discharges of trade effluent to a sewer for an operative site and would only really be relevant when buying a business as a going concern, though it is conceivable that if substances are getting into the sewerage system by migration or leakage, an offence could be committed.

Civil liabilities include the tort of:

- **nuisance (*Cambridge Water* v. *Eastern Counties Leather* [1994] AC 264)**

Purchasers of land giving rise to a nuisance will be liable for continuing nuisances created by predecessors in title if they knew or ought to have known of the nuisance, could reasonably have foreseen it causing harm, and could have taken reasonable steps to prevent or abate it, but failed to do so.

Purchasers must therefore take any such reasonable steps to stop ongoing pollution if they are to avoid such liability at some point in the future.

Clean-up liabilities include those for:

- integrated pollution control (EPA 1990, s.27), pollution prevention and control (regs. 22 and 33);

- controlled waste (EPA 1990, s.59);

- contaminated land (EPA 1990, Part IIA);

- statutory nuisances (EPA 1990, s.81);

- water pollution (WRA 1991, s.161A).

All these powers apply in circumstances where an offence has been committed, a notice has been served on the owner of the land, and he has failed to comply with it. The authorities may enter onto the site and undertake any necessary works, and recover the cost from the person served with the notice.

3.1.2   Environmental liabilities in residential cases

Criminal liabilities include offences:

- **relating to CONTAMINATED LAND (failure to remediate when instructed to do so) (EPA 1990, Part IIA)**

   This may come about as a result of substances already in the land at completion, which are giving rise to a risk of significant harm to persons or things nearby. This may catch such commonplace matters as leakages of oil from storage tanks for domestic heating systems, or waste oils from car engines, or other polluting matter disposed of on the land from DIY activities.

   If the original polluter of the land cannot be found, the current owner or occupier may be served with a remediation notice requiring the land to be cleaned up. An offence is committed if he fails to comply, and the authorities can do the necessary works themselves and recover the costs from the person served with the notice. Again, the problem is that a purchaser can himself qualify as the 'original polluter'.

   If a buyer knew, or ought to have known or realised, or could have found out, that there was contamination on the site he may be caught, as the definition of 'original polluter' includes anyone who knowingly permits contamination to remain.

   There may also be leakages of substances onto the ground after completion in respect of which the purchaser client will likely be the 'original polluter' of the land.

   Residential purchasers should, however, take comfort from the fact that:

   - only the most seriously polluted sites are likely to be designated as contaminated;

   - most remediation would have been addressed when the site was last developed (if this has occurred in the last two to three years), though this should not be taken for granted;

- remediation strategies must be cost-effective;

- liability is likely to be shared with others;

- regulators are more likely to want to target the developers of a site than the current owners;

- in considering the recovery of costs, the authorities must take potential hardship to the owner into account.

On the other hand, a series of exclusionary tests to be applied by the authorities may result in the seller of property no longer being required to share the cost of remediation if the purchaser knew about the contamination of the site at completion. This provision may be interpreted as meaning that a purchaser is better off buying in ignorance of the state of the site, but this cannot be good practice.

- **relating to STATUTORY NUISANCES (failure to abate when instructed to do so) (EPA 1990, s. 80)**

Statutory nuisances are noises, smells, dust, odour, premises or accumulations which may be a pollution or health risk. This could include dangerous structures, loose roof tiles and the like, as well as the sorts of matters already mentioned.

Buyers of land can be served with abatement notices in respect of any nuisances continuing after the date of purchase as it could be said that they are the person responsible for the continuing nuisance.

Otherwise, they may be liable as owner or occupier if the person responsible cannot be found.

An offence is committed if they fail to comply with any abatement notice.

- **relating to the POLLUTION OF CONTROLLED WATERS (polluting water without or in breach of a licence, failing to clean up water when instructed to do so) (WRA 1991, ss.85, 161A)**

Any leakages of oil from storage tanks, any washings or other deposits from garages, etc. or any fertilisers from the garden shed which get into watercourses, either directly or via the drainage system, may give rise to a liability.

The same problems afflict buyers with regard to water pollution offences occurring before completion but persisting afterwards, as it may be said that the buyer has knowingly permitted the offence to continue.

So if a buyer ought to have known or realised, or could have found out, that there was a possibility of water pollution occurring from the site, they may be caught.

Civil liabilities include the tort of:

- **nuisance (*Cambridge Water* v. *Eastern Counties Leather* [1994] 2 AC 264)**

  Purchasers of land giving rise to a nuisance will be liable for continuing nuisances created by predecessors in title if they knew or ought to have known of the nuisance, could reasonably have foreseen it causing harm, and could have taken reasonable steps to prevent or abate it, but failed to do so.

  Purchasers must therefore take any such reasonable steps to stop ongoing pollution if they are to avoid such liability at some point in the future.

Clean-up liabilities include those for:

- contaminated land (EPA 1990, Part IIA);

- statutory nuisances (EPA 1990, s. 81);

- water pollution (WRA 1991, s. 161A).

All these powers apply in circumstances where an offence has been committed, a notice has been served on the owner of the land, and he has failed to comply with it. The authorities may enter onto the site and undertake any necessary works, and recover the cost from the person served with the notice.

3.1.3 Other risks in both commercial and residential cases

Of equal importance to the buyer of any site is the risk that at some point in the future the property may be rendered unsaleable, or its valuation significantly reduced, if it becomes known that a pollution problem exists, or has existed, on the site or on one nearby.

This is an unquantifiable risk, and is dictated by perception as much as by actuality, and, as the perception of environmental risks is often worse than the reality, it is difficult to cater for.

In the residential sphere, one might expect purchasers to take a view, and simply withdraw, or proceed depending on their perception of the problem, and its relative priority in their buying decision.

One would, however, expect any future, cautious buyer of land to be expecting to negotiate a reduction in price to take account of environmental risks, so anticipating the problem as best one can now, and adjusting the price one pays now, must be better than buying at full value now and then realising a loss later.

Price reductions would have the effect, on the basis of current law, of relieving a seller of liability for contaminated land, leaving only the buyer exposed to the costs of clean-up. Correspondingly, price concessions on a future resale would have a similar effect for the current buyer.

Nevertheless, an accurate assessment of price effects should be undertaken as soon as possible, preferably in conjunction with valuers.

Generally, in conducting and determining valuations, surveyors will not be taking actual or potential pollution aspects into account. If a buyer wanted specific assistance on this matter, specific instructions would need to be given to the surveying and valuation team. Solicitors will also specifically state that they are giving no advice on contamination matters to buyer or lender.

A solicitor's failure to deal adequately in appropriate cases with the risks associated with buying land may well be classed as negligent.

3.2 COMMERCIAL FREEHOLD TRANSACTIONS

3.2.1 The steps to take

Generally

All land is second hand, so when buying property, it is essential to bear in mind – and provide for – the possibility that the buyer will inherit some or all of the liabilities attaching to the site, or suffer a diminution in value in the future. It is not always the polluter who pays, but occasionally the current owner, so purchasers have to be vigilant; *caveat emptor* is still the watchword.

The worst thing a buyer – or his legal adviser – can do, is ignore the environmental issue. Ignorance of the law has never been a defence; ignorance of the fact of pollution, or the consequences of it, may not be a defence either.

Many professional advisers called in to advise on environmental aspects of a transaction may not be covered for such advice under their professional indemnity policies. This is especially true of the surveying profession, who would need specific instruction (and top-up professional indemnity cover) before they are able to assist in advising on environmental matters.

To avoid allegations of negligence, therefore, one should:

- alert the client to the fact that there may be problems associated with a site (whether in the form of liabilities or just decreased valuation);

- discuss with the client the steps which can then be taken to assess further the scale of the problem, and to solve it in the most cost-effective way.

Often the perception of the environmental risks on a site is worse than the reality, and steps to alleviate or remove the problem may actually be less costly than imagined, and thus a less significant matter.

A choice will need to be made by the client as to how much to spend on the investigations, though commercial search organisations will now provide informative studies quite cheaply, and these should perhaps now be routinely suggested to a purchaser.

Such searches will comprise a desktop study of past land use in the area, a search of public records and a prima facie indication of levels of potential risk associated with the site. This information is collated from old Ordnance Survey information and other database sources. Average cost is in the order of £75–100 but may be cheaper (see para. 3.2.5).

Information revealed by these steps will give a much clearer idea of the potential risk, which can then be pursued in a much more targeted way with the seller. The buyer can then decide whether the transaction will proceed, and if so, with what terms, assurances, price adjustments or pre-completion remediation works.

3.2.2   Step 1: Advise the client of the potential for problems

It is essential not to overstate the environmental risks, but to ignore them completely is potentially negligent. The possible follow-up steps that could be taken to investigate any likely risks further – and possible cost implications – should be discussed with the client at the initial stage.

The client may not wish to pursue the point at all, in which case solicitors should confirm the initial advice (and the fact that no investigations have been made) to the client and any lender.

Practitioners may like to have some sort of rudimentary risk-rating system for property to enable them to gauge the likely risks and the steps which would be appropriate by way of further investigation (see para. 3.4).

3.2.3 Step 2: Make full enquiries of the seller

Solicitors should include specific environmental enquiries in their standard pre-contract enquiries. Some suggested forms of enquiry are shown in Appendix 2.

Too many clearly irrelevant enquiries will merely induce the seller to issue a blanket response indicating that the purchaser should 'rely on his own enquiries'. Specifically targeted enquiries generally get a better response.

The extent of the enquiries may well depend on the relative bargaining strengths of the parties, indications from pre-contract site surveys, and last (but not least), the client's budget. From the practitioner's point of view it is essential that the client be told how much pollution investigation (if any) is covered by his budget at the outset.

As a reasonable minimum, enquiries should deal with:

- the need for, and compliance with, all consents, licences, authorisations and permits in relation to any activities or processes conducted on the site, etc.;

- any disputes with the regulatory bodies;

- details of any pollution incidents or accidents affecting the site and copies of any reports, correspondence, court orders, notices (including in particular remediation, charging or works notices) or recommendations relating to such accidents or incidents and details of any remedial work carried out including certificates of satisfactory completion;

- details of any environmental impairment liability insurance or any application therefor (whether or not the proposal was accepted by the insurers);

- disclosure of any consultants' or other report on the environmental risk assessment of the property or the vendor's business;

- whether the seller is aware of any potentially contaminative current or previous use of the site or neighbouring sites. (The list of potentially contaminative uses set out in the first DoE Consultation Paper (3 May 1991) also provides an excellent checklist for the solicitor when perusing the title to a property. The list is set out in Appendix 1);

- whether the site or any adjoining sites have been used for landfill or waste disposal;

- details of previous owners or occupiers and activities carried on by them;

- what (if any) planning consents have been issued in respect of the site, what conditions they contained regarding contamination and its remediation, and details of any works carried out in compliance with it.

There are a number of possible responses to these enquiries:

(a) Replies are forthcoming: The replies may need specialist interpretation by surveyors or environmental consultants. Further, more detailed investigation may be needed of specific areas of concern.

(b) The seller stonewalls: If the seller issues the blanket 'not so far as the seller is aware, please rely on own investigations and surveys', the client must consider whether to undertake alternative investigations of his own.

3.2.4 Step 3: Make enquiries of the statutory and regulatory bodies

The main bodies to contact are:

- Environment Agency (licences, registers and prosecutions);
- local authority (registers and information on contaminated land);
- Health and Safety Executive (incidents and accidents);
- sewerage undertakers (consents and registers);
- British Coal (mining activities and abandoned mine leakage issues);

making full searches of any public registers regarding the site and adjacent land.

A greater awareness of the geology, and hydrogeology, of the area may be called for – if groundwater abstraction is commonplace then the risks are greater. Mining activity can also substantially affect the levels of chemicals on land and migration – both to and from. Details of all planning consents affecting the property should be obtained from the planning authority, not just those revealed by the local search which will only cover post late-1970s.

One should make enquiries of these bodies regarding any:

- information held by them about the site, any investigations or inspections made of it or adjacent land, details of any accidents, incidents or complaints and an indication of whether there is any intention to serve any notices in respect of the land;
- accidents, incidents and complaints by regulators or others relating to adjacent land.

Searches from commercial search companies (see para. 3.2.5) will usually include details obtainable from the public registers.

Enquiries of the Environment Agency

Development work is continuing between the Law Society and the Environment Agency on the drafting of a standard form of enquiry for use when making searches of that body.

Recent concerns for the Environment Agency surround difficulties in relation to the Data Protection legislation which, in the Environment Agency's view, restricts them from releasing any information which contains personal data relating to a site or its occupants, without the consent of those occupants. This would mean delay and inconvenience if consent is not given.

The Environment Agency is intending to offer a 48-hour turnaround for any enquiries made to it on the agreed standard form. To achieve this the areas subject to enquiry have been substantially reduced, rendering the search of much less (some might say negligible) value. Consultation is continuing at the time of going to press.

Local authority searches

New enquiries have been added to form Con. 29 as a result of consultations between the Law Society and local authorities which seek to identify all the information that a local authority is required to compile for the purposes of the official registers that they have to maintain under Part IIA.

However, such information need only appear on the register if land is actually designated as contaminated, and it may be arguable that if land is not so designated, no information need be revealed in answer to the new enquiries.

However, information regarding the actual state of the land (albeit not yet 'contaminated') may be in the possession of the authority and may be of interest to a purchaser. In such cases, consideration should be given to widening the scope of the enquiry and the wording of the new questions.

Information, in the widest sense, is to be made publicly available under the terms of the Freedom of Access to Environmental Information Regulations 1992, SI 1992/3240.

The Environmental Information Regulations 1992, SI 1992/3240

It is possible to ask local authorities and the Environment Agency, under the Environmental Information Regulations 1992, whether they hold any information relating to the possible contamination of sites. However, surveys of authorities by Friends of the Earth suggests that many authorities are ill-equipped to answer such enquiries.

These Regulations, in force from 31 December 1992, override any other, more restrictive, rights of access.

They require that relevant persons holding past or present information relating to the environment make that information available to anyone who requests it, within two months maximum at a charge of no more than is reasonably attributable to the supply of the information.

Any grounds for a refusal to give the information must be given.

'Relevant persons' are:

- public authorities;
- bodies with public responsibilities for the environment and under the control of public authorities (this may include privatised utility companies).

'Information' means records, registers, reports, etc. available in an accessible form (i.e. written, visual, oral or database).

'Relating to the environment' means relating to the state of any water/air, any flora/fauna, any soil, any natural site or other land or to any 'measures or activities' which may harm, or which may be intended to protect, anything so mentioned.

The Regulations need not allow access to information which may or must be treated as confidential. Information which may be 'confidential' is that affecting national security, pertaining to legal or similar proceedings, internal communications of an organisation, in the course of completion or relating to matters of commercial confidentiality. These categories give many instances where information can legitimately be refused.

Information must be treated as confidential if disclosure would entail breach of contract/law, it is personal information and the person concerned does not consent, information is given to the relevant person voluntarily and the donor does not consent or its disclosure may harm the environment.

Information need not be given if the request is too vague or manifestly unreasonable.

Thus the Regulations may allow access to information held by relevant persons regarding:

- physical/biological state of any environmental media at any time;

- conditions in and around man-made structures;

- living and dead organisms;

- UK, EU or worldwide matters;

- human health issues;

- activities having a potentially damaging impact;

- steps/activities taken with aim of improving the environment.

Primarily this information will be in the form of:

- IPC or Local Authority Air Pollution Control (LAAPC) registers of applications, authorisations, conditions, requests, variations and certain monitoring data;

- details of emissions, incidents, etc. required to be furnished to the Environment Agency/local authority;

- information compiled by the Environment Agency/local authority inspectors;

- Environment Agency registers of applications, licences, authorities, consents, conditions, variations and monitoring and sampling data;

- sewerage undertakers' registers of discharge consents;

- HSE reports, investigations, etc.;

- Environmental Impact Assessment statements by planning authority;

- waste regulators' records relating to waste management licences and waste carriers;

- local authority information and registers relating to statutory nuisance, especially noise, litter, sewer and drainage maps, etc.

In practice it can be difficult to enforce the Regulations. The exemptions are wide and easily arguable; debates rage about whether certain types of organisation are caught by the Regulations at all; information is occasionally presented in a form which is meaningless to the lay person or even lawyers and the cost may be prohibitive. Access to the information may be free, but the cost of copies may be high bearing in mind that bodies can charge the reasonable cost of 'supplying' the information – and there are differing interpretations of the meaning of that phrase.

The recent case of *Maile* v. *Wigan Metropolitan Borough Council* [1999] C99/0212, QBD also underlines the difficulties of access, the judge in that case refusing access to information relating to contaminated land on the basis that the investigations by the local authority were incomplete, and that the Regulations allowed access to 'information', not 'speculation'.

3.2.5 Step 4: Undertake independent site history investigations

If little or no meaningful response is forthcoming from the enquiries and searches, then one must take a view on whether to take any further investigatory steps.

These may include:

- desktop studies of the site involving consideration of old maps, plans, photographs and local physical and anecdotal evidence, to evaluate potential risks;

- consideration of contaminated land profiles issued by the DETR, which outline the usual types of contamination associated with certain types of land use (e.g. landfill, railway yards, gasworks, munitions factories, etc.);

- obtaining a site investigation report from a commercial search company.

Commercial search companies and value-added data providers: the Environmental Data Association (EDA)

The Environmental Data Association's stated mission is to establish and maintain high professional standards in supplying accurate site-specific environmental information to property owners, property buyers and all those professionally involved in advising on property transactions in the United Kingdom. To this end, the EDA has adopted a Code of Practice, which its members have agreed to observe.

The intention is that commercial searches of this type will be offered in standard form for around £100. Some products are already available at £39.

For more information about the Association, the contact address is:

> Environmental Data Association,
> Environmental Auditors House
> Redhouse Farm
> Newtimber
> West Sussex BN6 9BS
>
> Tel: 01273 857500
> Fax: 01273 857550

The founding organisations behind the EDA and the market-leading providers of such products are:

Landmark Information Group Ltd

    7 Abbey Court

    Eagle Way

    Exeter EX2 7HY

    Tel: 01392 441700

    Fax: 01392 441709

    E-mail: cbearm@landmark-information.co.uk

Environmental Auditors Ltd

    Environmental Auditors House

    Redhouse Farm

    Newtimber

    West Sussex BN6 9BS

    Tel: 01273 857500

    Fax: 01273 857550

The British Geological Survey also provides similar information as do several other smaller organisations, some offering an internet-based service. Practitioners will need to evaluate the comparative strengths of each product. At the time of writing work is being undertaken with the insurance sector to offer insurance products designed to guard against unforeseen environmental risks associated with a site.

3.2.6 Step 5: Initiate a full site investigation by environmental consultants

This should be commonplace in most commercial cases, as the nature or value of the transaction, and the size of the potential liabilities, would usually justify the cost involved.

Clearly, the scope for detailed surveys of potentially contaminated sites is enormous. Clients naturally wish to avoid unnecessary additional costs in relation to their acquisition. Nevertheless, the risks can be great and the costs of the detailed site investigation may well be justified in certain circumstances. It is estimated that full site investigation costs around £15,000 per hectare, but this is a very rough guess and the cost will depend on the precise problems.

As it may be in the seller's interests that the purchaser knows the state of the site at completion, an investigation at joint expense may be negotiable.

Where there is a substantial risk of contamination, the investigation costs may well be acceptable to an intending purchaser or lessee. For sites with a lower degree of prima facie risk the client may prefer to limit the investigation to a 'desk survey'. If the desk survey reveals problems that need further investigation, then a thorough site survey involving test boreholes and sampling may be advisable (particularly on 'hot spots'). For previous landfill sites, methane monitoring over a reasonable period of time may be required to ascertain whether the site or watercourses flowing from or under the site are carrying methane.

In these events, the solicitor should be consulted regarding the terms of engagement of the environmental consultant to ensure that the client gets a report which is useful and reliable as a basis for risk assessment. This is covered further in Chapter 7. It is important that the client is made aware of the risks of having no survey, or one that does not cover contamination issues.

Cost may not be the only factor limiting the extent of surveys and investigations on-site which may be possible; if the site is in current use and occupation and is covered by buildings, there may be difficulties in obtaining complete access for the purpose of carrying out the necessary physical examinations.

It is now increasingly common for indemnities to be sought by a seller – or by the investigating consultant – against any liabilities triggered by the investigation itself.

3.2.7   Step 6: Consider contractual protections against seller

These may include:

- requiring the seller to make a specifically quantified and earmarked payment or price reduction, to take account of the potential liability;

- requiring the seller to provide full information about the contamination to the buyer in the contract;

- agreeing a formula whereby remediation costs are shared between potential polluters;

- seeking appropriate warranties as to the state of the site at completion;

- seeking an indemnity against future liabilities or reductions in value due to the state of the land at completion;

- requiring remediation by the seller before completion;

- obtaining assignment of any environmental insurance policies which may cover the site (or obtaining fresh cover).

This is a matter for the relative bargaining power of the parties. It is increasingly common for buyers or lessees to insist upon warranties and indemnities in respect of contamination issues. The liabilities that can arise on pollution incidents can be heavy and therefore the value of such contractual terms may be limited by the financial means of the seller or any guarantor.

Specific payments or price reductions

The buyer may seek a reduction in the price (as opposed to a retention) to cover the cost of remediation or clean-up, or any perceived blighting effect on value. Alternatively, the buyer may want the seller to make a payment towards the cost of remediation.

The buyer should be aware that if such payments are made, this may have the effect of removing the seller from the category of persons eligible to receive a remediation notice in respect of contaminated land. If this occurs, the buyer would have to foot the seller's share of any clean-up costs, in addition to any liability of its own.

Buyers may not wish this to occur (though a seller will) and should therefore note the following points.

For a price reduction to be sufficient to count as a 'relevant payment' for remediation so as to exclude the seller from the category of appropriate persons for receipt of a remediation notice it must be explicitly stated in the contract to be for the purpose of particular remediation in respect of specific contamination. Indeed it must relate to the specific 'significant pollution linkage' identified by the regulator, and not some other problem or issue.

Further conditions which must be met for this exclusion to apply are that:

- the payment would have been sufficient at the date it was made to pay for the remediation in question;

- the remediation specified would have been effective to cause the land to cease to be contaminated by the specific significant pollution linkage in question;

- the remediation has not been carried out effectively or at all.

If, for lack of compliance with these specific requirements, a payment does not have the effect of removing the seller from the relevant category, any payment made would likely be taken into account in any decision on the apportionment of the costs of any clean-up works.

Requiring the provision of full information

This may seem to add little to the information-gathering process already undertaken. However, it is a way in which a seller can establish precisely that full information has been given to a buyer in relation to the presence of contaminants on the site, their nature and concentration.

The provision of this information would have the effect of removing the seller from the category of person eligible to receive a remediation notice in respect of contaminated land, thus leaving the buyer to foot the seller's share of the cost in addition to any they would already have to bear. There is thus a clear incentive for a seller to give the information and a corresponding incentive for the buyer to know exactly the state of the site and take decisions about whether to proceed and if so, at what price.

Clauses however provide that the mere offer of inspection facilities may be sufficient to fix the buyer with all the relevant knowledge necessary to exempt the seller, so the seller may take the view that there is no need to go into print on the point in the contract, other than the evidential reason mentioned above.

It should be noted that this exclusion only allows a seller the exemption if:

- the sale was on arm's length terms;
- no material misrepresentation was made;
- the seller retained no interest in the land after completion.

Agreements on liabilities

The parties may wish to agree between themselves how they wish to apportion any liability for contamination.

When considering the extent of any indemnities to be given, not only is it essential to decide who must take the risk of all existing contamination, but also the effect of any future contamination, the effects of any future development of the land, which may release earlier contamination and the risks of changes in environmental legislation. Standards of clean-up need to be agreed, as do the respective contributions. A sliding scale over 3–5 years may be appropriate as may threshold and cap arrangements for levels of expenditure.

Any such agreement will be honoured by the authority, and all its decisions regarding liability will be taken with the intention of effecting the agreement.

However, if the effect of the agreement would be to place an additional burden of expense on a person who would benefit from any relaxation of their responsibility to pay their full share, for example because of the hardship it would cause them, then the authority would, in principle, have to pay that share itself, at public expense. In such circumstances, the authority can ignore the whole agreement and apply the rules in the Guidance instead.

Such contracts therefore need to have mechanisms contained in them to ensure that, if the authority does not honour and implement the agreement as had been intended, the parties will indemnify one another to regulate the position between themselves.

It would thus be the parties who bear the risk of one of them being unable to pay their share, rather than the public purse, and this is also intended as an anti-avoidance measure.

For a suggested precedent, see Appendix 4.

Earlier insurance cover: assignment of the policy?

The availability of insurance cover in respect of past polluting events should also be considered and investigated with the seller in preliminary enquiries.

Although the current practice of insurers is to limit or exclude liability for such events, older public liability and third-party liability policies were wide enough to cover them and there may still be residual cover under old policies.

If this is possible or likely, specialist brokers might be called in to carry out an investigation into past insurance policies. If cover is available to the seller under these older policies, the indemnity clause in the contract should be coupled with an assignment of the benefit of this policy.

New insurance

New insurance cover may be available to the buyer against the risks of liability resulting from contamination or pollution. This will usually only be granted following an environmental risk assessment by specialist consultants appointed or approved by the insurance companies. It will generally be a requirement that any contamination found be cleaned up and an annual environmental audit of pollution control procedures carried out.

The specialist insurance market is limited, but cover is available, albeit at significant rates of premium.

Retention by buyer

Alternatively, the buyer may prefer to complete on the basis of a retention from the price sufficient to cover any likely costs of remediation or clean-up. This will enable the buyer to carry out the remediation works rather than rely upon the seller and this has advantages in terms of quality control and project management.

Indemnities

The seller might be required to indemnify the buyer against the costs of remediation or clean-up or against any damages, loss or injury resulting from any past contamination or pollution of the soil or any water courses or aquifers.

Caps on the level of indemnity are common, and they are only as good as the credit of the person giving them.

Phased indemnities are becoming more common – an arrangement whereby the seller remains liable for the first year, but the buyer gradually assumes part of the risk as the years go by until after, say, 10 years, the buyer is wholly liable.

3.2.8 Withdrawal from the purchase

At any stage in the above process, a buyer must be prepared to walk away from the deal if:

- the risks are too great;

- the information is too hard to find; or

- the seller is too resistant to negotiation.

American and continental purchasers in particular are not prepared to accept the environmental risk associated with the contamination of sites.

This will become a more common occurrence as public awareness of the issues grows and the courts and public authorities impose more and more liability on property owners and occupiers.

Where there is a portfolio of properties comprised in the assets of a company, it may be necessary to hive off the clean ones for disposal purposes.

3.3　RESIDENTIAL FREEHOLD TRANSACTIONS

Inheriting a costly environmental liability is unlikely in most typical residential conveyancing cases, but may be of significance for larger sites.

Of equal, if not more, importance to the buyer of residential property is the risk that at some point in the future the property may be rendered unsaleable, or its valuation significantly reduced, if it becomes known that a pollution problem exists, or has existed, on the site.

This is a risk which is dictated by public perception as much as by actuality, and it is therefore difficult to cater for or quantify, as the perception of the risk is often worse than the reality.

Interpreting how future events may affect the valuation may then have to be a matter of inspired guesswork, but anticipating the problem as best one can now must be better than buying at full value now and then realising a loss later.

Close liaison with the valuation profession is required, and here there may be problems, given that the Royal Institution of Chartered Surveyors (RICS) do not require their members to take into account the fact or potential for pollution in conducting inspections or determining valuations. The surveyor may not even be covered under their professional indemnity policy for such matters, and will not therefore be giving any advice on pollution issues.

As already noted, surveyors and lenders may try to pass the burden of advising on such matters on to the solicitor, often by oblique means. Solicitors need to check what assumptions they are being asked to make in reports on title, and qualify them accordingly.

If advice is required, specific instructions would need to be given to the valuer in the terms of engagement, and specific top-up insurance cover purchased.

In the absence of meaningful assistance from valuers, a full investigation of historical problems and of what, if anything, has been done to alleviate those problems, should put the current client's mind at rest, and provide some evidence to give to future purchasers by way of comfort.

3.3.1 Step 1: Advise the client of the potential for problems

It is essential not to overstate the environmental risks, but to ignore them completely is potentially negligent. The possible follow-up steps that could be taken to investigate any likely risks further – and possible cost implications – should be discussed with the client at the initial stage. Having brought up the issue, it may be taken no further, but at least it has been discussed.

Practitioners may like to have some sort of rudimentary risk-rating system for property to enable them to gauge the likely risks and the steps which would be appropriate by way of further investigation (see para. 3.4).

3.3.2 Step 2: Make specific enquiries of the seller

Solicitors should consider raising specific environmental enquiries of the seller, though it is recognised that this rather cuts across recent refinements aimed at speeding up the conveyancing process. Some suggested forms of enquiry are shown in Appendix 2.

The extent of the enquiries will depend on the client's budget and attitude. From the practitioner's point of view it is essential that the client be told how much pollution investigation (if any) is covered by his budget at the outset.

As a counsel of perfection enquiries could deal with:

- whether the seller is aware of any potentially contaminative current or previous use of the site or neighbouring sites. (The list of potentially contaminative uses set out in the first DoE Consultation Paper (3 May 1991) also provides an excellent checklist for the solicitor when perusing the title to a property. The list is set out in Appendix 1);

- whether the site or any adjoining sites have been used for landfill or waste disposal;

- details of previous owners or occupiers and activities carried on by them;

- what (if any) planning consents have been issued in respect of the site, what conditions they contained regarding contamination and its remediation, and details of any works carried out in compliance with it. It would be essential to check any such information whenever acting for a purchaser of new property from a developer. They will offer facilities for inspection of the documentation. Take the chance to read it.

There are a number of possible responses to these enquiries:

(a) Replies are forthcoming: The replies may need specialist interpretation by surveyors or environmental consultants. Further, more detailed investigation may be needed of specific areas of concern.

(b) The seller stonewalls: If the seller issues the blanket 'not so far as the seller is aware, please rely on own investigations and surveys', the client must consider whether to undertake alternative investigations of his own.

3.3.3 Step 3: Make enquiries of the statutory and regulatory bodies

The main bodies to contact are:

- Environment Agency (licences, registers and prosecutions);

- local authority (registers and information on contaminated land and any relevant planning consents);

- sewerage undertakers (consents and registers);

- British Coal (mining activities and abandoned mine leakage issues);

making full searches of any public registers regarding the site and adjacent land.

One could make enquiries regarding any:

- information held by them about the site, any investigations or inspections made of it or adjacent land, details of any accidents, incidents or complaints and an indication of whether there is any intention to serve any notices in respect of the land;

- accidents, incidents and complaints by regulators or others relating to adjacent land.

Make use of Freedom of Access to Environmental Information Regulations 1992, SI 1992/3240 where no information appears on public registers, but may nevertheless exist.

Searches from commercial search companies will usually include details obtainable from the public registers.

At the time of writing, development work is continuing between the Law Society and the Environment Agency on the drafting of a standard form of enquiry for use when making enquiries of that body and Con. 29 is being revamped to take on board questions regarding contamination (see para. 3.2.4).

3.3.4 Step 4: Undertake independent site history investigations

If little or no meaningful response is forthcoming from the enquiries and searches, then one must take a view on whether to take any further investigatory steps.

These may include:

- desktop studies of the site involving consideration of old maps, plans, photographs and local physical and anecdotal evidence, to evaluate potential risks;

- consideration of contaminated land profiles issued by the DETR, which outline the usual types of contamination associated with certain types of land use (e.g. landfill, railway yards, gasworks, munitions factories, etc.);

- obtaining a site investigation report from a commercial search company. As the cost of such searches falls, the obtaining of such a document may become commonplace, and should be routinely considered. Commercial data providers (see para. 3.2.4) will provide site information on a target property at moderate cost (approximately £40). The most popular products are the 'Home Envirosearch' offered by Landmark Information Group and 'Contamicheck' offered by Environmental Auditors Ltd, but others are available. Related insurance-based products are expected on the market soon (see para. 3.2.4).

3.3.5 Step 5: Initiate a full site investigation by environmental consultants

This would be rare in most routine residential cases, as the nature or value of the transaction would not usually justify the cost involved. It may, however, be relevant on larger sites. Additionally, the client may prefer to take the risk and proceed regardless.

Where there is a substantial risk of contamination, the investigation costs may well be acceptable to an intending purchaser or lessee. For sites with a lower degree of prima facie risk the client may prefer to limit the investigation to a 'desk survey'. If the desk survey reveals problems that need further investigation, then a thorough site survey involving test boreholes and sampling may be advisable (particularly on 'hot spots').

In that event, the solicitor should be consulted regarding the terms of engagement of the environmental consultant to ensure that the client gets a report which is useful and reliable as a basis for risk assessment.

In the vast majority of cases, if the risk is so great as to justify expense of this type, the client would be better advised to withdraw.

3.3.6 Step 6: Consider contractual protections against seller

These may include:

- amending conditions in National Conditions of Sale, especially conditions 3 and 5 (regarding compliance by the buyer with public requirements, and accepting land in the state it is at completion, respectively);

- reducing the price to take account of the potential liability;

- requiring remediation by the seller before completion.

Clearly this is a matter for the relative bargaining power of the parties, but it would be rare indeed for any of the more sophisticated commercial drafting devices – warranties, indemnities, capped and phased indemnities – to find their way into domestic conveyancing documentation.

3.3.7 Withdrawal from the purchase

At any stage in the above process, a buyer must be prepared to walk away from the deal if:

- the risks are too great;

- the information is too hard to find; or

- the seller is too resistant to negotiation.

This may well occur earlier in the process than in the commercial world.

3.4 PROPERTY RISK RATING

To assist practitioners in gauging what steps should be taken, and in what circumstances, a risk-rating system is offered in Tables 1.

Table 1 Risk-rating system

Key:
***   Essential
**   Not essential but ideal in most cases, 'good practice'
*   Probably not worth bothering with

Commercial cases	Steps to take/priority
HIGH RISK any site or location conducting a prescribed process under EPA 1990, Part I; any sites conducting any other process, or on which any activity is occurring, known or suspected of giving rise to appreciable contamination of land, water or air; any site used for a potentially contaminative use; any site within proximity of a watercourse; any site within proximity of another obviously contaminated site from which migration may occur; any site within proximity of residential properties; any site within an area of known past industrial use any site intended for redevelopment (commercial or residential)	Step 1 *** Step 2 *** Step 3 *** Step 4 *** Step 5 *** Step 6 **
MEDIUM RISK any site used for a potentially contaminative use in an area not known for its past industrial use	Step 1*** Step 2*** Step 3*** Step 4*** Step 5** Step 6**
LOW RISK sites on which activities have only recently begun (say, since 1993) or which have undergone recent redevelopment where contamination has been dealt with as part of the redevelopment	Step 1*** Step 2*** Step 3*** Step 4** Step 5* Step 6*

Residential cases	Steps to take/priority
HIGH RISK any property built on a site known to have been used for a potentially contaminative use; any property within an area of known recent or current industrial use; any property or site within proximity of another obviously contaminated site from which migration may occur;	Step 1 *** Step 2 *** Step 3 *** Step 4 *** Step 5 ** Step 6 **
MEDIUM RISK any post-war property in an area of suspected past industrial use	Step 1 *** Step 2 ** Step 3 ** Step 4 ** Step 5 ** Step 6 *
LOW RISK properties built on greenfield sites; properties built on land developed since, say, 1993 where contamination has been dealt with as part of the redevelopment; old-established properties in rural areas; old-established properties in urban areas (say, more than 50 years old); flats in blocks or converted properties; any property in an area of known non-industrial history	Step 1 *** Step 2 ** Step 3 ** Step 4 * Step 5 * Step 6 *

3.5 RELATIONS WITH LENDERS

3.5.1 Certificates of title

Some common difficulties have already been noted (see paras. 3.1 and 3.3).

Some lenders are increasingly requiring practitioners to certify that all issues of contamination have been fully investigated, and that the property gives rise to no environmental risk. Clearly, in most cases it will be impossible to give such an unqualified indication, and practitioners are advised to contact the lender and renegotiate the terms of the certificate if they do not feel happy with the wording.

Difficulties may be experienced when acting for buyer and lender. In particular, can one certify 'good and marketable title' to the land in the report on title if one is aware of contamination problems?

The title may be fine legally, but will it sell, and is it good security?

Some qualification may be needed to the wording of the certificate, indicating in particular that the site has not been inspected and the certificate therefore does not comprise environmental matters and gives no assurances as to the physical state and condition of the land, nor of its value and marketability.

The Council of the Law Society has approved an alteration to Solicitors' Practice Rule 6, regarding acting for purchaser and lender in a land transaction. The new Rule 6 spells out with effect from 1 April 1999 the terms of a solicitor's retainer in such circumstances, clearly stating that it is for the lender to satisfy itself on matters of contamination and the consequent effect on valuation.

3.5.2 Conflicts of interest

Solicitors may feel they have to cease acting if the buyer refuses to allow them to draw appropriate matters to the lender's attention in this way.

3.6 ADVICE TO SELLERS

This chapter has so far concentrated on the position of a purchaser and his solicitor.

From the seller's point of view, achieving a clean break from the liabilities attaching to a site may not always be possible.

In particular, liability may continue for:

- breaches of the consents committed while the seller was the site-owner and operator (commercial sites only);

- breaches of waste legislation while in possession (commercial sites only);

- contaminated land (on the person who originally caused or knowingly permitted substances to be on the site pre-sale) (commercial and residential sites);

- statutory nuisances caused or continued (commercial and residential sites);

- water pollution offences caused or knowingly permitted (commercial and residential sites);

- sewerage discharge offences (commercial sites only);

- civil liability (as co-defendant for damage caused or continued during the period of ownership (commercial and residential sites).

In respect of most of these liabilities (all save for contaminated land) there is no easy way to shift liability on to a purchaser other than by getting it to give indemnities, which is unlikely.

A more important strategy is to ensure (perhaps by incoming and outgoing audits) what the state of play is when the site is sold on, so as to be able successfully to determine who did in fact cause a pollution incident, should there ever be a dispute.

As far as contaminated land is concerned, sellers should take close note of those clauses in the Guidance Notes that would exempt a seller from liability if:

- contract documents specifically reject the payment (often in the form of a price reduction) of a specific sum for remediation (see para. 2.9);

- the land is sold in circumstances where full information is provided to the buyer about the contamination on the site (see para. 2.9);

- the seller and buyer agree on a contractual formula for dealing with any liabilities which emerge;

and ensure that the paperwork is drafted in such a way as to maximise the chance of exemption.

3.7   LEASEHOLD TRANSACTIONS

3.7.1   Standard lease

Existing leases

As currently drafted, most full repairing and insuring (FRI) leases will not contain provisions specifically requiring the tenant to clean up or remove any contamination which may from time to time exist on the site. For many sites it may well be inappropriate to suggest that the tenant should be responsible for handing back to the landlord demised premises which have been cleaned up to a polished earth standard as this would render the lease extremely onerous. Onerous leases have knock-on effects in terms of assignability and rental growth.

The case law currently relating to repairing covenants in leases is confusing enough as it stands – particularly in the area of inherent defects. The added dimension of contaminated land will certainly not help to clarify issues.

The relative lack of sophistication of older FRI leases is likely to mean that the question of liability for clean-up is between landlord and tenant will have to be debated within the context of the repairing covenant. The temptation for the judiciary to produce a just result in individual cases is likely to produce a body of law which is inconsistent and difficult for practitioners to apply with any certainty.

Cases like *Post Office* v. *Aquarius Properties* [1987] 1 All ER 1055, CA would suggest that landlords are going to have great difficulty in imposing obligations upon tenants to make good any contamination existing prior to the start of the lease.

There must, therefore, be doubt as to whether the repairing covenant would cover contamination of the site during the term, where the premises remain fit for occupation and use for the permitted user.

It has been suggested that a covenant to keep the demised premises 'clean' may add weight to the landlord's contention that contamination of the premises is the responsibility of the tenant. It is unlikely that such a covenant would be interpreted as being intended to refer to, e.g., the subsoil of the property, and therefore it would probably not add weight to the landlord's argument.

It is not uncommon for leases to require the tenant to comply with statutory and other regulations relating to the premises and to comply with notices served by the appropriate authorities. Such clauses would indicate that the tenant and its successors in title would be responsible for any contamination that had arisen during the term as a result of any such breach. It would also indicate as between landlord and tenant that the tenant will be responsible for pollution or clean-up notices received from public bodies (although this would not fetter the ability of the authorities to serve such notices on the landlord also).

Some leases will contain a tenant's covenant not to commit waste. In the absence of an express covenant, the ancient law of waste creates obligations in tort rather than contract and will exist alongside the tenant's obligations in the lease. This would mean that only the tenant committing the waste will be liable in respect thereof. The right to sue for damages in respect of the tort of waste may not be assignable, on the grounds of public policy, and so the successor in title to the reversion may be unable to recover damages from the tenant in respect of earlier torts.

In many leases, covenants not to commit waste have been superseded by covenants not to carry out alterations or additions. In view of the derivation of such clauses, they may be sufficient to enable the landlord to recover damages from the tenant in respect of contamination arising during the term. Widely drafted alterations (and waste) clauses may also impose responsibility on the tenant in respect of contamination caused by third parties or migrating from adjoining property.

Clauses dealing with the permitted user of the property will usually be expressed in general terms (often by reference to the relevant use class) and are likely to add little. Provisions relating to nuisance and annoyance are more likely to give the landlord an effective lever where there is a risk of migration of contamination from the site.

If premises are being demised for a use where there is a substantial risk of contamination, then the standard alienation clause is unlikely to provide adequate comfort to the landlord. Provisions can be inserted dealing with the experience and competence of assignees. To put the matter beyond doubt, however, 'offer back' clauses may be appropriate. Again, in situations of high risk it is appropriate for the alienation provisions to be invoked where there is a change in the control of the tenant company.

Perhaps the most significant clause in most modern leases will be the indemnity clause, which is often drafted very widely indeed and will frequently require the tenant to indemnify the landlord in respect of all losses as may arise directly or indirectly out of the state and condition of the property. Whilst this may not necessarily require the tenant to be responsible for a full clean-up, it is quite possible that it could face a claim for loss of profits – if at the end of the term the landlord would otherwise be able to sell the property for, e.g., residential redevelopment.

It is apparent that the modern FRI lease does not deal with the issue of contamination in a satisfactory way. The extent to which additional clauses are required will depend primarily upon the condition of the property at the commencement of the term, the intended use of the property and the likelihood of contamination arising.

Whilst some provisions may sit relatively easily alongside existing lease clauses, e.g., aftercare conditions contained in any consents obtained by the tenant – it is generally most appropriate to consider pollution control and environmental protection as a separate and self-contained issue within the lease. For one suggested clause, see Appendix 3.

This separate section of the lease will need to deal with:

- compliance by the tenant with pollution control legislation and all the terms of any consents, licences, etc.;

- prior to implementation, obtaining consultant's report (approved by landlord) and fully complying with all recommendations;

- provision of a bond (if applicable) to cover aftercare/proper performance;

- procuring surrender of licences before end of term, alternatively transferring to or at the direction of landlord (if required);

- notification of all contaminating events at the site and carrying out of remediation programme as recommended by the landlord's consultant;

- notification of any proceedings in relation to pollution control legislation brought against the tenant/employees;

- obligations to maintain environmental impairment liability insurance;

- indemnity for state and condition/operations/contaminating events plus cost of remedial action/preventative measures to protect the demised premises/neighbouring property;

- rights for landlord to enter and carry out works (and recover cost);

- continuation of liability of the tenant under this clause beyond the expiry of the term.

The landlord retains an interest in the property so it inevitably risks liability in respect of the actions of its tenant. Because of the 'deep pocket' syndrome, the landlord needs to be fully satisfied as to the quality of the tenant's covenant and the degree of control that it can exercise over the way in which processes are carried out on the property if there is any material risk of contamination.

Landlords may be excluded from the categories of appropriate person for receipt of remediation notices in respect of contaminated land if they are not in 'effective control' of the activities of the tenant. Guidance Notes currently provide that one is not in effective control merely by leasing land to someone else.

Equally, tenants are not to be treated as appropriate persons in their capacity as 'occupiers' if they pay rent, but have no beneficial interest in the property. See Chapter 2 for a fuller discussion.

New leases

Having considered the effects of more familiar terms it is appropriate to look at negotiating a new lease for the acquisition of land which may be contaminated. The lease is a useful mechanism for allocating the risks associated with past or present contamination between vendor and purchaser; operating company and holding company; lender and borrower. It may therefore be appropriate to adopt a leasehold structure where a free-hold sale cannot proceed because contamination is discovered as part of pre-contract investigations.

The lease may allow the existing owner of a contaminated site to get an income from it even if it is not disposable on a freehold basis, and if there is an existing liability for clean-up and total clean-up is not practicable (so that there will be a residual legal liability after the remediation has been carried out) the rent-stream may be able to fund or support the cost of remediation.

In the traditional lease arrangement, the tenant takes a lease of the whole site with no special arrangements to exclude the contaminated sub-soil. The tenant is therefore potentially an 'owner' of the contaminated land and as such may be liable for clean-up and other liabilities arising out of the contamination. Before setting up such an arrangement careful pre-lease investigations are vital.

Moreover, the lease should contain:

- covenants by the landlord (or the tenant) which identify specifically the responsibility for carrying out any remediation works, the standards to be applied, the notification, inspection and reporting procedures as between the landlord and the tenant and the obligations in respect of compliance with all relevant legislation;

- provisions dealing with containment, interception, dissipation and monitoring of the contamination, depending on the appropriate engineering solutions;

- rent suspension if contamination prevents the tenant from using and enjoying the site;

- break clauses;

- guarantees and sureties;

- covenants to maintain employment impairment liability (EIL) and other insurances.

3.7.2 'Pie-crust' leases

The purpose of the 'pie-crust' lease is to leave the contaminated soil out of the demised premises so that the tenant does not become the owner of the contamination and therefore has no liability to third parties for its escape. The demised premises will consist of everything (buildings and airspace) above the surface of the ground, plus the layer or layers of clean soil, hard core and surfacing material above the impermeable capping layer.

As noted above, tenants are not to be treated as appropriate persons in their capacity as 'occupiers' if they pay rent, but have no beneficial interest in the property. As regards the contaminated sub-soil, they have no beneficial interest in it and pay no rent either, so it is doubly difficult to see how they could be classed as its 'occupier' under the terms of the Guidance. Common sense may, however, suggest a different view. See Chapter 2 for a fuller discussion.

Whilst this is not a complete panacea as the landlord retains control over the sub-soil and the tenant loses a degree of flexibility for future use and development, it has provided considerable comfort to banks taking security. This is particularly so where continuity of occupation is essential to the value of the business.

Where the landlord is the original polluter, it may be advisable to retain control and ownership of its pollution for two reasons:

(i)   it may yet be primarily liable for that pollution and thus benefit from greater control over the clean-up costs; and

(ii) as polluter, the likelihood is that it will be more familiar with the contaminants thereby being better able to quantify the risk. The cost to the landlord of assuming that risk should be significantly lower than the premium required by any purchaser, tenant or insurer.

There is still a need for the covenants in the lease to be carefully drawn to reflect the contamination of the sub-soil (e.g. landlord to comply with all requisite standards; indemnify tenant against the claims and liabilities arising; suspension of rent if the tenant's use and occupation is interrupted; right for the landlord to enter and remain to carry out the remediation works; possibly a break clause; guarantees and sureties; restrictions upon alterations by tenant or anything that may affect the pollution control measures taken by the landlord).

In addition, the easements and rights reserved and granted need to be very carefully drawn to ensure that both the landlord and the tenant are able to use and enjoy or control the respective parts of the land held by them.

3.8   PLANNING IMPLICATIONS OF PROPERTY TRANSACTIONS

This handbook is not intended to deal with planning law, so the comments below are merely a brief indication of some of the planning-related issues that may be relevant to environmental matters, and of which practitioners should be aware.

In the various policy documents issued in conjunction with the Environment Act 1995 provisions on contaminated land, it became clear that the government still sees planning control of development as one of the major ways of dealing with contaminated land in the years ahead. It is familiar, it deals with less dangerous sites at a time when works would be being carried on anyway, and arguably works in a more 'just' fashion – the person who gets the profit from the site has to spend the money tidying it up – than the new contaminated land regime threatens to.

Recent indications are that the planning system will play an ever larger role over the next 20 years with estimates of the number of new homes required ranging around the four million mark. Much of this development will have to take place on brownfield sites, raising the spectre of how to deal with contamination as part of the redevelopment.

3.8.1   Contamination: a 'material consideration'

The presence of contamination on land is a 'material consideration' for planning purposes and, in very serious cases, may restrict or prevent the development of the land; for instance, if the development cannot be carried out without tangible and serious harm to the environment.

In less serious cases, the local planning authority may impose stringent conditions to protect the environment (including current and proposed occupiers of the land in question) or neighbouring residences.

3.8.2 An opportunity as well as a threat

There may be circumstances when a distinction is drawn between different categories of occupier and the perceived level of sophistication.

For example, supermarkets may be regarded as sufficiently sophisticated to warrant planning permission for a supermarket development on a former landfill site with methane migration problems with which the proposed building will cope by technologically advanced monitoring and ventilation controls (see *Wm. Morrison Supermarkets* v. *Wakefield MDC* [1991] JPL 985).

On the other hand, development of a similar site for residential purposes might be considered inappropriate because the residential occupier is less likely to ensure that the buildings and outbuildings are adequately maintained and operated to avoid the risk of methane accumulation.

The existence of contamination problems on a site may in fact militate in favour of development which would otherwise be unacceptable – for an example, one need only look at the Secretary of State's decision on a called-in application by British Airways for planning permission for a corporate headquarters and business centre on 5.1 hectares in the metropolitan greenbelt at Prospect Park near Harmondsworth. In this case, planning permission was granted mainly because the development would lead to remediation of methane problems which were affecting a nearby residential estate ([1993] JPL 268).

3.8.3 Requirement for notification – Article 18 of the GDO 1988

Article 18 of the Town and Country Planning General Development Order 1988 requires the local planning authority to consult with the relevant waste disposal authority in respect of any application for planning permission within 250 metres of existing or past waste disposal sites.

3.8.4 DoE/DETR Circulars

DoE Circular 17/89 provides guidance on the special precautions needed to guard against the hazards of developing landfill sites and adjoining areas, especially migration of gases.

Solicitors should also have regard to the provisions of Planning Policy Guidance notes, especially PPGs 23 and 24, for which see para. 3.8.11 below.

3.8.5 Planning obligations, aftercare and restoration conditions

Even before the Environmental Protection Act 1990, it was not uncommon for local planning authorities to impose 'aftercare conditions' to ensure the safe clean-up and landscaping of a site used for environmentally harmful uses.

In particular, in relation to mining and landfill sites, these frequently require the land to be graded and landscaped at the end of the works, but may (especially in relation to land-filled sites) include remediation works, e.g. methane venting or capping and grading.

Anyone who buys a site which is subject to these conditions may unexpectedly find themselves saddled with expensive obligations. It is therefore essential to check all planning consents carefully to ensure that any aftercare conditions in existing consents have been complied with fully.

Under s.21 and Sched. 1 to the Planning and Compensation Act 1991 the powers to impose aftercare and restoration conditions were increased in the case of mineral and waste-tipping operations.

Practitioners should be aware of the power to serve breach of condition notices contained in s.187A Town and Country Planning Act 1990 (TCPA 1990). Such notices are enforceable by planning authorities through the magistrates' courts, and there is no right of appeal.

3.8.6 Environmental impact assessment

Environmental assessment is largely governed by the Town and Country Planning (Assessment of Environmental Effects) Regulations 1988, SI 1988/1199 (as amended) and is explained in DoE Circulars 15/88 (WO 23/88) and 7/94 (WO 20/94).

An environmental assessment is required by the 1988 Regulations in all cases of development proposals falling within Sched. 1 to those Regulations and also in cases of development proposals falling within Sched. 2 if that development would be likely to have significant effects on the environment due to factors such as its nature, size or location.

Schedule 1 development covers major industrial developments such as crude oil refineries, thermal or nuclear power stations, certain iron, steel, asbestos, chemical and waste disposal installations and certain road, railways, aerodromes and ports.

Schedule 2 lists 13 categories of development, all but two of which list at least six types of development within that category. The categories cover agriculture, the extractive industry, the energy industry, metals processing, glass making, the food industry, textile, leather, wood and paper industries, the rubber industry, certain infrastructure projects such as industrial or urban estates or tramways, and certain other projects such as holiday villages and hotel complexes.

To guide developers and local authorities as to when Sched. 2 development proposals might require an environmental assessment, Circulars 15/88 and 7/94 set out both general tests and also specific indicative criteria and thresholds for each of the categories of development in Sched. 2. The three main categories of Sched. 2 project which will require an environmental assessment are:

- major projects which are of more than local importance;

- smaller-scale projects in a particularly sensitive or vulnerable location;

- in a small number of cases, where the project has unusually complex and potentially adverse environmental effects and where detailed analysis of those effects would be desirable.

Development which would otherwise be permitted development (e.g. under the GPDO (General Permitted Development Order) or an SPZ (special planning zone) scheme) will not be so permitted if it constitutes Sched. 1 or Sched. 2 development. Developers can apply to the LPA for an opinion on whether a proposed development which would have constituted permitted development requires an environmental assessment: see the Town and Country Planning (Environmental Assessment and Permitted Development) Regulations 1995, SI 1995/417.

Because of the uncertainty as to whether Sched. 2 development requires an environmental assessment and because the preparation of an environmental statement involves a lot of time and expense, there is provision in the Regulations for a developer to ask the LPA whether, in its opinion, an environmental assessment is required. If the LPA states that one is required and the developer is not happy with this, he can apply to the Secretary of State for the Environment (SSE) for a direction on the matter. The procedure for requesting an opinion is set out in reg. 5 of the 1988 Regulations.

There is no prescribed form as such for an environmental statement. However, Sched. 3 of the Regulations specifies what it must contain. The contents are too long to list here but it should be noted that the information required is very detailed and will require much time and expense to prepare.

Where an environmental statement is submitted with a planning application, the applicant must observe special rules regarding additional documentation and publicity for the application. In addition, the LPA is under a duty to send the application and environmental statement with accompanying documents to the SSE and must consult with various bodies specified in reg. 8(5).

Where an environmental statement is not submitted with the planning application but the LPA considers that one is necessary it must notify the applicant within three weeks. If the applicant disagrees, he can, within three weeks of the notification, apply to the SSE for a direction on the matter.

Where an environmental statement is required the LPA or the SSE cannot grant planning permission until it has been supplied and an environmental assessment has been carried out (reg. 4).

In reaching a decision on the planning application the LPA has 16 weeks (instead of the usual eight) in which to notify the applicant of its decision.

3.8.7 Enforcement powers

Under s.215 Town and Country Planning Act 1990 (TCPA 1990) (formerly TCPA 1971, s.65) the local planning authority have power to serve notice on the owner and occupier of land if it appears to the LPA that the amenity of a part of their area (or of an adjoining area) is adversely affected by the condition of land in their area.

The notice shall require such steps for remedying the condition of the land as may be specified in the notice to be taken within such period as may be specified (being not less than 28 days from service). There are criminal penalties for failing to comply with the notice and under TCPA 1990, s.219 the LPA may enter on to the land and take the necessary steps to comply with the notice and recover from the person who is then the owner of land any expenses reasonably incurred in so doing. In the past, this power has rarely been used but recent amendments have made it easier to use and there are suggestions that local authorities may be prepared to use these powers in the future for the improvement of the environment.

Practitioners should also note the power, contained in TCPA 1990, s.187B, for a planning authority to obtain an injunction if it considers such action to be necessary or expedient to prevent any actual or apprehended breach of planning control.

Unlike under previous legislation, an authority need not show that it has exhausted all other possibilities before following this line.

3.8.8 Powers of revocation and modification

Local planning authorities have power to revoke or modify planning consents under TCPA 1990, s.102.

These powers are very rarely used because they involve rights of compensation but it is possible that pollution problems arising from contamination may give rise to the exercise of these powers.

3.8.9 Planning obligations

Under TCPA 1990, s.106 the planning authority can enter into contractual arrangements with the developer, which will bind the land and all subsequent owners.

This is a useful delivery mechanism to ensure that a remediation package for a contaminated site, say, is appropriately designed and implemented and that there are adequate arrangements for monitoring and testing, maintenance, insurance (insofar as it is available), repairs and renewals.

3.8.10 Grant aid

Financial assistance towards the costs of clean-up may be available from English Partnerships (the Urban Regeneration Agency), though recent policy statements suggest that it may favour joint venture approaches rather than straight grants. In addition, its emphasis will be on a strategic approach to the regeneration of whole areas rather than support for isolated ad hoc projects.

3.8.11 PPG 23 (Planning and Pollution Control) and PPG 24 (Planning and Noise)

PPG 23

This Note was issued on 1 June 1994, and gives policy guidance on the intended interaction between planning authorities and other pollution control bodies such as the Environment Agency. To what extent should a local authority attempt to police pollution control through the planning system?

Paragraph 1.3 states that 'the planning system should not be operated so as to duplicate controls which are the statutory responsibility of other bodies'. The aim is therefore to encourage close consultation and to prevent unnecessary duplication of effort.

The LPA may take into account potential pollution, but only to the extent that it may affect current and future uses of land, and they must work on the assumption that 'the pollution control regimes will be properly applied and enforced. They should not seek to substitute their own judgment on pollution control issues for that of the bodies with the relevant expertise and the statutory responsibility for that control'.

Planning applications which may give rise to pollution must still be determined in accordance with the development plan, unless material considerations indicate otherwise.

Annexes 1–4 of the PPG outline the type of conditions that an LPA can impose in the context of integrated pollution control, air quality, water quality and waste management. Further guidance is given on contaminated land and waste disposal, the relationship between LPAs and the Environment Agency in the planning process and restoration aftercare and after-use of landfill sites for agricultural amenity or forestry use.

PPG 24

This Note gives guidance to LPAs on the use of planning powers to minimise the adverse impact of noise. In particular, it outlines the considerations to be taken into account in determining planning applications both for noise-sensitive developments and for those activities that will generate noise; it introduces the concept of noise exposure categories for residential development, encourages their use and recommends appropriate levels for exposure to different sources of noise; and advises on conditions to minimise the impact of noise.

CHAPTER 4

Corporate transactions

4.1   INTRODUCTION

Companies are now wise to the fact that there is a need to consider environmental issues arising in relation to specific transactions which involve the acquisition of an interest in an existing business. They may have implications for the future operation of the business, and the purchaser's bankers will no doubt wish to make further enquiries before they will be prepared to fund the acquisition.

The risks and liabilities must first be fully assessed. This may involve the commissioning of an environmental audit or investigation by either party to the transaction or both of them, ideally at an early stage of the transaction, and the disclosure of potential liabilities by the vendor.

The risks will then be allocated between the purchaser and the vendor and the result will be dependent on who has the commercial upper hand. This will involve the negotiation of warranties and indemnities, a consideration of whether insurance can be obtained to cover the relevant risks or possibly the performance of remedial work by the proposed vendor before completion of the transaction.

4.2   THE QUESTION OF LIABILITY

As discussed in Chapter 1, breach of environmental statutes carries criminal sanction. Commonly, few defences are available for offences under such legislation so even companies which regard themselves as blameless can still find themselves penalised. In addition, there may be responsibility for clean-up costs, which may be significant, and civil liability may be owed to other third parties.

The legislation also allows for officers of a convicted company to be held personally liable where the offence is proved to have been committed with the consent or connivance of, or is attributable to, any neglect on the part of any director, manager, secretary or other similar officer of that company. It is not yet clear whether the standard of care usually required by a director in relation to his civil liability (i.e. that set out in *Re City Equitable Fire Insurance Co. Ltd* [1925] Ch. 407, CA) which is that he must exhibit such skill as can reasonably be expected from the person with that director's knowledge and experience, will be applied in this situation, though indications in cases such as *Norman* v. *Theodore Goddard* [1992] BCLC 1028 would suggest that those with particular expertise in environmental matters should show higher standards.

Solicitors should note the case of *Williams* v. *Natural Life Healthfoods Ltd* [1996] 1 BCLC 288 which indicates that directors can be liable for the torts of their companies if they 'direct or procure' the commission of the tort by the company.

In most instances it is the person who causes or knowingly permits pollution to occur who is potentially liable. However, owners/occupiers of land may be liable under certain provisions and principles. Therefore, it is not simply a question of the polluter paying.

The key point for a purchaser is to appreciate the costly and complex liabilities flowing from operating a process, or even merely from owning or occupying land, and which he may be buying in a corporate acquisition.

4.3   PRACTICAL STEPS

When advising a purchaser or vendor, the solicitor must ensure that he understands the nature of the business and the processes that are being, and have been, carried on at its sites and, accordingly, that he has the appropriate questions in mind in order to identify problems at the outset.

He should also have the necessary contacts on call in the event that the questions of insurance or the appointment of environmental consultants are raised.

The following issues should be considered:

1. **The product** – just because the product itself does not appear to be polluting this must not be the end of the enquiry.
2. **Raw materials** – it is necessary to consider the components used in the production process since in any of these there may lurk the

potential for an environmental breach. If toxic materials are used in the manufacturing process how are they being dealt with? A prospective purchaser should seek details of the current environmental policy operated by the company together with details of its implementation and how compliance is monitored. Under the IPPC regime (in force from October 1999), operators are required to monitor raw material and other input usage (such as electricity and water). It may be the case, over time, that certain conditions are attached to the use of such materials which may affect the operation of the process in the future.

3. **The process** – the onus is on the purchaser as part of its due diligence exercise to find out whether the process will result in emissions to environmental media and if so, what steps are being taken to minimise their effects. At the end of an IPPC process, the operator will have to remove any contamination not discovered in the land assessment done at the start of the process, so a copy of that assessment should be made available and suitable indemnities obtained.

4. **Disposal of waste** – the waste management responsibilities (especially the duty of care) dealing with its storage, transportation and disposal must be complied with.

5. **Historical use of the site** – old processes may give rise to current liabilities and a clear understanding of historical use may give warnings as to whether or not the land is currently contaminated.

6. **Licences** – it is important to check that all appropriate environmental permits, consents and licences have been obtained, to note the conditions attaching to them and to determine whether these conditions are being complied with. Certain licences are subject to review by the relevant regulatory authority and it is important to identify whether this is pending.

It is also helpful to see copies of correspondence with the regulators and others to assess the local climate of opinion regarding the industry in question.

7. **Site and local inspection** – a significant concern is the risk of discharge or loss of fluids to groundwater via, for example, cracked concrete or soakaways. The position of the drains and the route of rain water run-off will also need to be considered. The local sub-surface hydrogeology and uses of groundwater are also of significance. Site inspections should be carried out by reputable specialists.

4.4 PROBLEMS IDENTIFIED – WHAT APPROACH TO TAKE

The first issue is whether a purchaser should acquire the assets or the entire issued share capital of a company. A purchaser may choose to take certain of the assets off-site and limit the liabilities it assumes by not acquiring a contaminated property.

A process that is licensed or authorised by the appropriate regulators is permitted (subject to conditions) to operate in that location and no other. To relocate such a process is to risk difficulties with fresh licence applications. In practice, therefore, this may not be a real option to achieve the desired objective of being able to continue the business but leave behind environmental contamination. This will be especially difficult in relation to IPPC processes, where land assessments will have to be carried out on any relocation. For this reason, in essence, all of the issues relevant to a share purchase apply equally to an assets transaction where the purchaser intends to carry on the existing business.

If the purchaser wishes to acquire the company, perhaps for tax reasons, the company is acquired with all of its liabilities (subject to any reorganisation which the vendor can be persuaded to undertake prior to completion of the transaction). The practical solution for a purchaser faced with a large environmental liability which has been properly identified, whether on an assets transaction or share purchase, is to negotiate suitable warranties, to seek an appropriate indemnity and to feel that the price paid reflects the acceptance of potential liabilities.

There may be difficulties in limiting the acquisition to an 'assets' purchase, as it may be the site that is licensed, and the land may therefore have to be acquired in any event. If this is so, then some sophisticated conveyancing solution may be needed (a pie-crust lease, for example) to leave contaminated ground out of the transaction.

It is worth noting that the tests of exclusion relating to contaminated land exempt from liability anyone making a sufficient payment for remediation in the contractual documentation.

The exemption relating to 'sales with information' relates to any deals as part of which land portfolios may change hands, and would, therefore, apply to a share purchase transaction. Full contractual apportionment and indemnity is, however, still the best way to proceed to eradicate any ambiguity, and to ensure that the liabilities fall where the parties expect and provide.

Any agreement which apportions responsibility for the cost of contaminated land within the meaning of Part IIA of the EPA 1990 must be honoured by the regulatory authority. (For an example of such a clause see Appendix 3.)

If acting for the vendor, you will obviously try to avoid giving an indemnity to the purchaser. This may not be possible if a specific problem has been identified and in these circumstances you should seek to put a ceiling on the vendor's liability under the environmental warranties and/or indemnities. The vendor will also want a time-limit on his potential exposure and the ability to control the conduct of any claims.

Insurance is a theoretical alternative, either for the purchaser in respect of future claims, or for the vendor in respect of liability under warranties and indemnities. This is expensive and there will be difficulty in finding an appropriate product on the market. To the extent it is available at all, it is likely to cover only events of future contamination and is likely to be expensive. The availability of environmental insurance is discussed further in Chapter 6.

Finally, it may be possible for either the purchaser or the vendor to carry out remedial work to resolve or reduce the problem. This will, however, depend on the nature of the contamination, the intended use of the land, the cost of the work required and the negotiating strengths of the parties.

4.5   DOCUMENTING THE TRANSACTION

A form of share purchase agreement containing sample environmental warranties and indemnities is set out in Appendix 5. These have been provided for illustrative purposes only and are not intended to be used as a precedent.

The definitions in the sample warranties and indemnities have been extremely widely cast. That of 'environmental contamination' is aimed at catching all types of contamination whether accidental or gradual, toxic or merely excessive in quantity.

The definition of 'waste' also repays careful attention. Waste can give rise to a liability without being toxic or dangerous. Excess quantities of any substance can generate a disposal cost, which, if appropriate and commercially possible, should be shifted to the other side.

4.5.1   Environmental warranties

The purpose of the warranties is to elicit as much information about the operations of the business as possible. They also supplement the right of recourse against a vendor under the environmental indemnity, by providing a network of contractual promises which can be sued upon if they turn out to be false.

Where there is to be a sale of shares of a company, the purchaser cannot avoid taking the company subject to all existing liabilities and continuing commitments. This is to be contrasted with the purchase of a business where liabilities do not pass unless specifically taken over.

It has therefore always been the custom for the purchaser to receive some form of assurance from the vendors as to the liabilities attaching to the target company or assets in a business sale. The process of checking the warranties will bring out potential problems and provide information on the business to be purchased and the parties will be able to negotiate as to what impact these should have on the transaction.

However, another purpose of the warranties is to allocate risk as between the vendors, the parties giving the warranties, and the purchaser, in relation to the possibility of the target company or assets being subject to undis-closed liabilities or obligations. To the extent that warranties are given, the warrantors accept the liability; in so far as the warranties are not given or are restricted in their scope by limitations or disclosures in the disclosure letter, the purchaser takes the risk.

The remedy normally sought by a purchaser where there is a breach of a warranty is compensation by way of payment of damages which may be difficult to quantify. The basic rule is that the purchaser should be compen-sated for its loss of bargain; however, it will be under an implied duty to mitigate any loss suffered and he will not be able to recover for any losses which are too remote. In contract, under the indemnity, the purchaser can claim for a specified sum in certain circumstances on a pound-for-pound basis, subject to any cap or limitations placed upon this.

Warranty 1.1 seeks to obtain details of all permits, licences, authorisations, consents or other approvals required under the relevant environmental legislation in order to carry on the business of the company or to use the property where it is located and to gain an indication of the costs of such compliance. This is also dealt with in Warranty 1.11.

The definition of 'environmental law' is deliberately made very broad, and is intended to catch laws not yet in force but which may have retroactive effect – particularly, the contaminated land provisions in Part IIA EPA 1990. It is intended to cover both statutory and common law liabilities of all types and to catch health and safety laws.

Warranty 1.2 has the aim of eliciting details of any breach of the environ-mental law or environmental licences or the conditions attaching thereto. This is expanded in Warranties 1.5–1.9. The key concern of the purchaser here is to ensure that the company or business is capable of carrying on its processes or manufacturing its products in compliance with its licences and consents and without annoyance to its neighbours. The important areas to be borne in mind here are discharges to air, water and sewer, storage and disposal of waste (whether by third parties or otherwise), noise and odours. These are all the subject of 'environmental law'.

Warranty 1.3 is included to glean information as to the state of knowledge of the vendor in respect of recently granted consents and licences and in respect of periodic rights of review by the relevant regulatory authority. It also requires the vendor to confirm, in effect, that the licences and consents relating to the business or the company are held on acceptable terms.

Warranty 1.4 deals with environmental assessments and investigations. Currently, a statutory 'assessment', pursuant to the Town and Country Planning (Assessment of Environmental Effects) Regulations 1988, SI 1988/1199, is only required for the purposes of certain particularly significant planning applications, but this warranty also aims to discover whether a private voluntary investigation, or remedial work, has been undertaken by the vendor. Any such assessment or investigation report will assist a purchaser's understanding of the site.

When acting for the purchaser, there are a number of consulting organisations who can give competent technical advice in relation to environmental problems and can undertake an environmental investigation. You should consider instructing one of these consultants personally so that their report is privileged. If your client company deals direct with them, they may run up against disclosure problems, for example, to inspectors appointed by the regulators.

All environmental reports must be private to the purchaser and a common argument put forward by the purchaser is that the report should not be disclosed to the vendor. The vendor – if it obtained a copy – would usually attempt to disclose any such report back to the purchaser by way of the formal disclosure letter to limit its liability under any indemnity. The contents of the disclosure letter serve to amend or contradict the warranties and possibly the indemnity and therefore if an environmental report is annexed to it, the purchaser will take the risk of liabilities revealed therein and will not be able to claim for such losses under the warranties or the indemnity. Clearly disclosure of the report is a matter for commercial negotiation between the parties.

Warranty 1.5 is designed as a catch-all warranty to enable the purchaser to discover facts relating to latent environmental problems within the knowledge of the vendor but not yet the subject of actual or threatened proceedings.

Warranty 1.6 is self-explanatory and could be one to give away in the course of negotiations.

Warranties 1.7, 1.8 and 1.9 all relate to waste management. Warranty 1.8 is onerous and consequently would usually be qualified by the vendor's awareness.

Warranty 1.10 seeks to repeat certain of the warranties in respect of persons occupying adjoining land. A vendor will obviously seek to exclude this warranty and you would be extremely successful to win this. Chapters 1 and 2 deal with the potential liabilities arising from migration in some detail, against which the operation of these warranties becomes clear.

4.5.2 Environmental indemnity

It is not uncommon for a purchaser to seek an indemnity from a vendor in connection with environmental liabilities. The purchaser will be concerned that it is buying a contingent liability that results from the fault of the vendor or its predecessors in title. As a first step it is necessary to identify what liabilities this will cover. For example, if the vendor is to pay only the 'costs of clean-up', what does this actually mean? Should this involve merely removing the affected material to landfill elsewhere, or does it also include making good the land, i.e. remediation? The vendor will be concerned that such an indemnity might be a blank cheque and that it will suffer if environmental legislation grows more strict.

It is sometimes argued that the purchaser should only be indemnified against costs and damages that it is actually ordered to pay and that the vendor should have conduct of any such claims. This may affect the purchaser's ongoing relationships with the environmental regulators and its neighbours. Possible compromises include the appointment of an independent environmental consultant whose opinion binds both parties and stipulations that the purchaser must take all reasonable steps to mitigate the liability.

If an indemnity against clean-up costs is given, the vendor will want to ensure that this provision is not used by the purchaser to effect some sort of betterment of the property.

In the draft, there is a suggestion for a 75 per cent/25 per cent split of liability between vendor and purchaser. This is a suggested compromise which attempts to deal with a vendor's concern over the betterment argument. Whether an apportionment is included is a matter of negotiation. The limitations in the indemnity are for illustration only.

The provision for a 75 per cent cap on the vendor's liability also aims to prevent the purchaser from using the indemnity as an excuse to upgrade the site at the vendor's expense. Such costs as are recoverable from the vendor ought to represent the bare minimum necessary in order to bring the property into a state of compliance with environmental law. Again, an independent environmental consultant may be useful in order to give effect to provisions of this sort.

Environmental indemnities commonly give protection for longer than would be normal for other kinds of indemnity: 10 years is by no means unusual. This of course results from the long lead-time between environmental incidents and their effects.

Environmental law is likely to change during the lifetime of a reasonable environmental indemnity. The question of whether the vendor should be liable under an indemnity in respect of liabilities payable pursuant to laws not in existence at completion is frequently the subject of debate and is rarely won by the purchaser's adviser. This means that the purchaser will be at risk from future unquantifiable liabilities.

Possible sources of compromise in other areas include the cap on liability, a requirement for the purchaser to bear a certain percentage of costs (thus meaning the purchaser will bear some of the pain in an attempt to discourage it from making frivolous claims), provisions apportioning liability in respect of certain kinds of problem, phased indemnities which provide for the progressive take-over of responsibility by the purchaser (say, at the rate of 10 per cent per annum for 10 years), duration of the indemnity, *de minimis* provisions and requirements to notify the vendor in certain ways.

The sample indemnity also seeks to indemnify the purchaser in respect of civil and criminal actions brought against the purchaser on the basis of facts associated with acts/omissions of the vendor. It is important to include legal costs in such clauses. It should be borne in mind that an indemnity in respect of criminal sanctions is not enforceable.

4.5.3 Effect of new contaminated land provisions in EPA 1990, Part IIA

The principles applicable on a corporate transaction are largely unaffected by the Part IIA provisions, in that, on an assets transaction, contaminated land would often be left out of the acquisition anyway.

If included, all the considerations enumerated in Chapter 3 should be borne in mind in relation to full investigations (possibly at joint cost), specific payments (in the form of price reduction) and sales with information.

On a share acquisition, there is no land acquisition as such – the buyer steps into the shoes of the seller and inherits all their potential liabilities. However, it is provided that the exemption from liability for those making full disclosure of any contamination (or offering the facility for inspection) does apply to any series of transactions as a result of which property portfolios change hands. Thus share transfer deals should include full investigation of the target's property portfolio – a standard step in any event – and protection with fully drafted warranties and indemnities redrafted to include some of the new terminology.

Moreover, the regime does provide that any 'agreements on liabilities' should be honoured by the regulators, see Chapter 2 and Appendix 4.

CHAPTER 5

Funding and borrowing transactions

5.1 ENVIRONMENTAL IMPACT ON FUNDING AND SECURITY

The toughening of the environmental regulatory regime has affected lenders as well as polluters. In particular, lenders are concerned about environmental risk for the following reasons:

- it can reduce the creditworthiness of the borrower by imposing additional costs on its business, for example liability for clean-up costs, or the tightening of environmental systems by the introduction of new technology;

- it can reduce the value of the security held by the lender;

- it can, in certain circumstances, create direct liability on the lender.

In the first two examples, the impact of the environmental regime may serve to put the borrower in breach of its bank agreements (perhaps non-compliance with financial covenants) which will put lenders on notice of problems with the borrower's financial stability.

Lenders will have at the forefront of their minds the possibility that their security may be jeopardised, not only by direct pollution, but by indirect contamination; for example, where an adjacent site is contaminated or the property is in an area of high pollution where the mere possibility of creeping pollution is usually sufficient to depress the market value of a property. Disposal of a site (even though it is 'clean') in these circumstances may be extremely difficult (see the two recent cases of *Blue Circle Industries plc* v. *Ministry of Defence* [1998] 3 All ER 385 (a judgment in excess of £6 million), and *English Partnerships* v. *Mott MacDonald*, reported in ENDS Report, April 1999, (a judgment in excess of £18 million, turning on the interpretation of the term 'clean')).

The subject of direct liability faced by lenders in respect of contamination has already been discussed in Chapters 1 and 2.

5.2 PROTECTION FOR THE LENDER

What steps can lenders take to restrict the impact of the environmental regime and the other liabilities discussed earlier?

5.2.1 Risk evaluation

Most lenders have addressed the issue of environmental risk in their lending criteria and sanction authority.

Lenders will consider issues such as:

- the environmental record and standing of the borrower;

- environmental auditing and control systems;

- environmental planning and continuing measures;

- the extent to which pollution (particularly known risks) would impact on the value of the security;

- assessment of the risk of pollution or contamination in the light of the nature of the business and the locality in which it operates.

Lenders will generally factor into the lending decision the environmental risk and the terms of the loan will reflect it, perhaps by taking increased security, a higher interest rate margin or tighter covenants and monitoring.

(a)   Environmental investigations or audits

Risk evaluation cannot take place without information. If a proposal involves a contaminative industry, lenders will often require an environmental investigation. The lender's satisfaction with the investigation report should be a condition precedent to the drawdown of the facility. The choice of environmental consultant is discussed in Chapter 7.

(b)   Certificate of title

Provisions may be included in a certificate of title produced by the borrower's solicitors dealing with the environmental condition of the land. An example is set out in Appendix 6. However, the solicitors acting for the business may be reluctant to include it in the certificate. Nevertheless, if instructions require it, it must be provided.

In these circumstances the lender may require the management of the business to confirm that the business is not subject to environmental problems or enforcement actions. This type of confirmation will usually be qualified to the best of the management's knowledge.

(c)   Consents and licences

The lender should investigate, particularly in relation to facilities granted to contaminative industries, whether all consents and licences have been obtained, whether they are all in full force and effect and are being complied with, and whether any notices (prohibition, enforcement, remediation, abatement, works, etc.) have been served.

(d)   Environmental management systems

The lender should ensure that adequate management systems are in place to cope with pollution or contamination problems, and more importantly, to try and prevent environmental problems arising. Increasingly, this means an externally verified and accredited system such as ISO 14001 or EC Eco-Management and Audit Scheme (EMAS).

(e)   Representations and warranties

The inclusion of appropriate representations or warranties in the facility letter should ensure that further information is disclosed to the lender against those warranties. This is a very useful source of information and is discussed in further detail below.

5.2.2   New proposals and ongoing protection

New proposals create an opportunity for lenders to face environmental issues head on and deal with them in any manner which gives them some protection and comfort for the duration of the facility. The facility agreement and security documents should make provision for the lender's protection. The following are some rudimentary steps which can be taken to safeguard the interests of the lender.

(a)   Conditions precedent

Prior to any funds being drawn down the lender should have sight of and be happy with all environmental reports, consents and licences. Appendix 6 sets out the issues which should be on a lender's list of conditions precedent from an environmental point of view.

(b)   Representations and warranties

The representations and warranties, if drafted thoroughly, should provide a lender with information about environmental risks at an early stage.

The representations and warranties are first given by the borrower immediately before drawdown. Certain representations and warranties (relevant to environmental problems) are set out in Appendix 6. Briefly these warranties are:

- a warranty that the environmental report (if one has been produced) is true and the borrower is not aware of anything material omitted from the report of anything else which would be likely to give rise to any material liability on the part of the borrower under any environmental legislation;

- the borrower complies with all environmental laws;

- the borrower has all the necessary consents and licences to operate the process, that no notice has been served on the operator relating to any breach of licence or consent condition and that such consents can be transferred;

- the borrower has maintained all necessary assets;

- the borrower is not subject to any compliance or enforcement orders;

- the borrower is not subject to any claim, demand or notice alleging responsibility for any clean-up or other costs or property or personal damage or fines or penalties arising out of the presence of any hazardous or polluting matter or violation of any environmental law.

As mentioned, the representations and warranties should be certified by the borrower to be true immediately before drawdown of the facility. They should also be repeated at regular intervals to ensure continued compliance and so that the lender obtains swift warning of any problems. If acting for the borrower, annual repetition is satisfactory; daily repetition is preferable when acting for a lender. A compromise position is repetition of the representations on the days upon which interest is paid under the loan.

The impact of the representations is diluted if they are not monitored and policed properly. Lenders must ensure that the information is provided punctually.

(c)   Covenants and undertakings

Representations and warranties provide a snapshot of the borrower at any particular moment. Covenants are ongoing obligations of the borrower which usually persist for the entire period of the facility.

There is a degree of overlap between the representations and warranties and the covenants, particularly if the representations and warranties are repeated on a regular basis. Appendix 6 sets out some illustrative covenants that the lender might ask for.

There is a provision for the production of a certificate, within 60 days of the financial year end, from an officer of the company confirming that there have been no changes to any of the matters set out in the environmental report and if that certificate is not given the lender has the right to undertake a further environmental investigation.

Where the lender receives notice of a claim under any environmental law, there is a covenant requiring a more comprehensive delivery of information. This should ensure that the lender is kept fully aware of the potential problem enabling it to assess its position fully.

The insurance covenant in the facility letter should be expanded to ensure that it covers environmental risks to the extent that such cover is available in the market place. Environmental insurance can be a difficult issue and is discussed in Chapter 6.

It may be prudent to restrict the borrower from acquiring assets or commencing a new business which may be an environmental risk. The difficulty here is that the lender does not wish to get involved in relatively minor asset acquisitions, but there cannot be a *de minimis* exception because the potential liability for the company could be large, even though the consideration for the asset is insignificant.

(d)   Events of default

A specific event of default may not be necessary as a breach of a representation, warranty or covenant will usually be a default anyway. But a specific environmental default may be required due to the fact that the full impact may be difficult to assess and the liability to the borrower may not be calculable for some considerable time. This may give rise to arguments about whether a general event of default clause is applicable. In these circumstances, a specific default clause would be preferable.

The occurrence of an event of default under a facility agreement will generally give rise to the right to demand repayment of the facility and enforce security. Lenders must be wary about enforcing security unless they are fully aware of the environmental problems with land over which they have security. As discussed in Chapters 1 and 2 the lender risks direct liability in respect of contaminated land in certain restricted circumstances. If a site over which the lender has security is particularly contaminated the lender may be forced to release the tainted security.

Uniquely in respect of contaminated land under EPA 1990, Part IIA an insolvency practitioner is released from potential liability save in respect of his own negligent acts. Appointing a receiver over tainted security would seem to be preferable to entering into possession, but the receiver may still be liable for other matters and may not therefore be willing to take the risk of appointment.

(e)   Recovery of clean-up costs

The greatest concern for lenders is the direct liability for clean-up in respect of contaminated sites over which they held security. Chapters 1 and 2 discuss the circumstances where this may arise. Even if the lender is not automatically responsible for clean-up, a sale of a contaminated site will be unlikely unless clean-up occurs. The lender may have to bear this cost. Therefore, it is essential that the lender's facility or security documents incorporate an appropriate clause to enable it to recover such costs. An illustration is set out in Appendix 6.

5.2.3   Existing facilities

Lenders may be restricted in the options available by the terms of existing facility letters most of which will not address the issues of environmental default.

Facilities which are uncommitted may be withdrawn and demand made for outstanding liabilities. Practically, the lender will not be able to take this course without jeopardising the customer relationship. Term facilities which are not in default are even more of a problem.

Once again it is important for the lender to acquire information. The existing information covenant contained in the facility letter should be carefully examined to see whether it can be used to demand the relevant information. If not, it will often be possible to agree with a borrower to expand certain terms of the facility agreement to incorporate more extensive information covenants. This can be formalised very readily by the signature by the lender and borrower of an amending agreement.

The flow of information is crucial. If, for example, the borrower is operating in a highly contaminative sector, the lender may decide that despite a desire to enforce its security, it will not do so because, on the basis of its intelligence, there is a significant potential direct liability for clean-up and other issues.

Armed with the relevant information at an early stage, lenders have sufficient weapons in their armoury to protect themselves. It is the unexpected major problem which sends lenders scurrying for their security documents.

CHAPTER 6

Environmental insurance

6.1   WHICH LIABILITIES CAN YOU INSURE AGAINST?

The environmental liabilities for which insurance cover is available are limited to third-party claims (civil claims by a third party whose person or property is injured by a pollution incident), and first party claims (claims for the recovery of clean-up costs – the expense of cleaning up one's own land, often under court order).

Generally, insurance is not available for criminal fines or penalties, and most insurance policies will contain an exclusion clause relating to such fines. This is unfortunate, as criminal liabilities are undoubtedly the greatest risk for the time being.

This exclusion applies both to companies, and the officers and managers of those companies.

6.2   PUBLIC LIABILITY POLICIES

In the past, environmental liabilities have been covered under the wording of general public liability policies. Such policies are still widely available, and indeed may be the only form of cover taken out by many industrial and commercial operations.

Such policies are generally written on what is known as an 'occurrence' basis, i.e. the policy will cover and pay for the consequences of an event provided that it occurs within the policy period. This is so, no matter when the claim arising out of that event is actually made against the company by the person who suffers the loss. This may be some years later.

This should be compared to policies which are written on a 'claims made' basis, which require an event to take place, and the claim arising from it to be made against the company within the policy period, as conditions of cover. Usually, the claim must be notified to the insurer within the period as well, for the insurer to bear the cost. Most professional indemnity policies are written on this basis.

Since April 1991, however, as a result of suggestions from the Association of British Insurers, public liability policies have excluded pollution liability, except for the consequences of 'sudden, identifiable, unintended and unexpected incidents which take place in their entirety at a specific time and place during the Period of Insurance'.

Under such policies, therefore, a company is covered for one-off pollution incidents and catastrophes only, and there is seemingly no cover for gradual pollution, taking place over a number of years.

There may even be disputes with insurers over what is an 'unexpected' or 'unintended' incident, and whether the consequences of such an incident can nevertheless be gradual, making it unclear what is and is not covered by a policy.

It is likely that insurance companies will include a total pollution exclusion clause in such policies in the near future. Accordingly, companies will need to buy specific environmental insurance in order to get cover for the real risks mentioned in Chapter 1.

6.3   SPECIFIC ENVIRONMENTAL POLICIES

Specific environmental policies are available, but take many forms and names. They are essentially very similar and offer similar cover.

They include:

- third-party, gradual, creeping pollution damage policies covering damage to persons or property off-site. These are usually known as environmental impairment liability (EIL), or pollution legal liability (PLL) policies;

- first party policies covering clean-up costs on-site. These are known as environmental remediation insurance (ERI), or first-party liability (FPL) policies;

- newer policies on offer seek to combine both first- and third-party cover into one policy document;

- recent entrants to the market can offer more specialised and restricted cover for much reduced, and therefore more attractive, premiums.

131

6.3.1   EIL/PLL policies

These policies cover liability to third parties arising from gradual pollution seepage, as well as sudden incidents, and will pay the amount of any damages awarded for bodily injury or property damage, together with any costs, charges and expenses incurred in the investigation, adjustment or defence of such claims.

Bodily injury will include illness, sickness, disease, psychiatric damage and shock. Property damage will include physical damage or destruction of land or property, clean-up costs and in some cases loss of business.

6.3.2   ERI/FPL policies

These policies are intended to cover one's own losses, in particular the costs of cleaning up the site from which the pollution originally escaped.

Clean-up costs include expenses for the removal, neutralisation and remediation of contaminants on-site, but often do not include costs, charges or expenses associated with the defence of any administrative or legal proceedings brought in respect of clean-up obligations.

6.4   LIMITATIONS ON POLLUTION INSURANCE POLICIES

Pollution insurance policies have many limitations, and many of the preconditions to cover are very restrictive. Some of the conditions may be negotiable, depending on the circumstances. The main conditions and limitations are as follows.

THE POLICIES ARE SITE SPECIFIC

The policy will often only cover liabilities flowing from a specific site or installation, which is specified in the policy. Specialist insurers will not take on liabilities from a portfolio of properties owned by a company, as they will generally insist on an environmental investigation before giving cover.

The insurer's key-word is 'knowledge'; only if the insurer knows the full extent of the risk associated with a property or piece of land will he give cover. Blanket cover over a range of poorly specified and uninvestigated properties is inconsistent with this approach, and such cover will not be given.

THE POLICIES WILL GENERALLY ONLY GIVE £10 MILLION COVER PER CLAIM, AND IN AGGREGATE

Against the potential costs of an environmental clean-up, £10 million may not go very far. The insurers' view is that some reasonable limit is required. If £10 million is inadequate, top-up cover can be bought from reinsurers, but at an additional premium.

The limitation on aggregate cover may cause problems – particularly for environmental consultants – as one claim already made against them may exhaust their cover for other clients.

Newer policies on offer give lower aggregate cover (often £2 million) but for a reduced premium. This may prove more attractive for smaller, better-managed or already remediated sites.

THE INSURER WILL REQUIRE AN ENVIRONMENTAL INVESTIGATION BY APPROVED CONSULTANTS

Inevitably, the company will be required to undertake a full environmental investigation (see Chapter 7) as a condition of cover. This will usually be at the company's expense, and will be undertaken by the consultant appointed by the insurer.

This is because the insurer will want to be able to assess fully and accurately the precise nature and extent of the environmental risk posed by a particular piece of land or factory.

The policy will frequently require follow-up investigations from time to time, but often these will be at the insurer's expense.

THE POLICY WILL USUALLY REQUIRE THAT THERE BE NO PRE-EXISTING CONTAMINATION

Clearly, this is not a practical limitation, in that virtually all industrial and commercial land will have some sort of contamination present. The way insurers deal with this likelihood is to include in the policy a condition which excludes liability arising from conditions which exist prior to the start-date of the policy, if those conditions could have been expected to give rise to a claim. They will also insist on an investigation, and the remediation of any conditions found as a result.

This has the advantage that both the insurer and the company will know the state of the installation at the start of the policy period, and no pollution incident should arise as a result of anything which took place before that time.

If something does occur, it is likely to be as a result of something covered under the policy, i.e. an escape taking place during the policy term, or one arising from something occurring beforehand, but entirely unforeseen and unexpected.

CLAIMS MUST BE MADE AND REPORTED WITHIN THE POLICY PERIOD

Clearly, this is a severe limitation on the usefulness of an insurance policy.

A policy written on this basis requires an event to take place, the claim arising from it to be made against the company and that claim to be notified to the insurer within the policy period, for the insurer to bear the cost. Unless all these things occur within the policy period, no cover will be given.

In cases where the pollution damage is gradual, and the effects are not immediate, but only become noticed some time after the original event, this is a significant problem, in that cover may not be available.

The problem is made worse by the fact that the policy period is usually only 12 months from the start-date (though terms of up to five years are available), and the further into the period the time runs, the less likely it is that all the conditions will be met.

The problem is further exacerbated by the fact that, for personal injury claims, an injured person has three years from the date of the injury in which to bring a claim, and for property damage, six years from the date of damage.

In cases where injuries are not immediate, but gradual, the injured person has three years from the date on which they knew they had suffered a significant injury in which to bring a claim. In relation to property damage, the damage is suffered when the contamination reaches the claimant's property, which may be a considerable time after the polluting event itself. The Latent Damage Act 1986 would not apply to impose a long-stop on claims of 15 years as it applies only to actions for negligence. Most environmental claims are for nuisance, not negligence.

It can therefore be difficult to decide when a company is no longer in danger of a claim being brought. Some insurers would only require the injured person to notify the company of the potential claim (or 'assert a legal right' in the wording of the policy) and the company to notify the insurer, for this to amount to a 'claim made' for the purposes of cover. An insurer will then accept this claim, even though legal proceedings based on it may not be brought for some years.

This is something to clarify specifically with any insurer, as the meaning of the words 'assert a legal right' is unclear.

As an option to many policies, the period within which the claim must be made and notified can often be extended after non-renewal or cancellation of the policy.

This is occasionally referred to as the 'extended discovery period'. This will require an additional premium and is of little comfort as the company still cannot control when the claim is actually brought against it, and the extension itself is usually only for 12 months, although it can be for as long as three years.

THERE IS OFTEN NO COVER WITHOUT A COURT ORDER

Particularly in ERI/FPL policies, there is a clause which states that the policy will only cover clean-up costs which the company is 'ordered' to pay. This means liability under a court order.

It is often cheaper to undertake clean-up steps voluntarily, without waiting to be ordered to do so. Such voluntary costs would not be covered under the terms of the standard policies.

However, most insurers see the sense and logic in saving money where possible, and will usually agree to pay for such expenses. This will have to be specifically negotiated.

RETENTIONS

There will be an 'excess' on the policy, a sum which the company will have to bear as a contribution to the loss. Typically, these retentions will be in the region of £25,000, which is insignificant in percentage terms, but not to be ignored in small claims cases.

POLICIES ARE EASILY CANCELLABLE

Policies can usually be cancelled by the insurer simply by service of 30 days' written notice, with an adjustment of premium.

This means that a company which has spent significant sums persuading an insurer to write a policy, may find itself without protection if the insurer's confidence is shaken by an event or incident which shows that the risk of a claimable incident is higher than desired.

Rather than continue cover and risk exposure, an insurer may cut and run, just by cancelling the policy.

This emphasises the need for good environmental management systems –

devices and mechanisms which are designed to minimise the risk of an incident. Such systems will go a long way towards reassuring the insurers, as well as being a useful discipline for the company.

IMPLEMENTATION OF ENVIRONMENTAL MANAGEMENT SYSTEMS

In order to reduce the risk of an incident occurring, and a recoverable claim being made, insurers will usually also insist on the company implementing a management system, to ensure continual monitoring of the company's environmental performance.

Such a system should have the benefit of imposing the discipline necessary to ensure that no incident occurs, or if it does, to identify it in good time, reduce its impact and ensure no repetition.

The majority of claims in the past have arisen out of slack management, and this is one area on which insurers are now especially keen to crack down.

A company may feel that an insurance policy on these terms is not appropriate, and that some other alternative method of funding the risk needs to be found.

6.5   OTHER OPTIONS

The other main alternatives to buying an insurance policy are self-insurance; finite risk programmes; captive insurance companies; or mutual benefit companies.

6.5.1   Self-insurance

Often, premiums for insurance cover can be so large as to cause a company to rethink whether it is worthwhile. Instead of buying a policy, the company could consider simply making provision out of its own resources for the occurrence of an environmental incident.

The main problem is caused by the very nature of an environmental incident – low in frequency, but high in severity. Like earthquakes, they may not happen often, but when they do, the effects can be devastating.

Funding of self-insurance schemes can be obtained from internal or external sources. Internal sources are usually inadequate, as few companies can afford a capital reserve or a diversion of income on the scale necessary to fund an environmental claim. It is usually only the very largest corporations for whom this is a viable option.

External funds would normally be provided by an insurer or reinsurer, but banking facilities – such as contingency loans, standby credit and overdraft facilities – would be another source. It is likely that such facilities may be expensive to service if called upon.

Self-insurance is also only really effective as a way of offsetting, over a period of time, the large unit cost of a claim.

Finite risk packages are similar in their aim.

6.5.2 Finite risk insurance

Such insurance is known by a plethora of titles – 'financial reinsurance', 'chronological stabilisation plans', and 'banking plans', being some of the more familiar.

In essence, the nature of the schemes is to spread the cost of a claim over a pre-determined period of time – usually three, five or ten years. This is achieved by the payment of a fixed annual premium over the life of the policy. The total premiums payable may well come close to the level of the aggregate cover under the policy, with relatively little being contributed by the insurer in the traditional sense. However, the company achieves a form of credit, in that if a claim is made early in the life of the policy, the insurer will pay, and the company has the rest of the term to pay the premiums – a shifting of the credit risk, in effect.

In addition, the company may enjoy the return of the unused premium and the investment income from it (less the management fee), in the event that no claim is made at all.

It would also be possible to combine this sort of scheme with a conventional policy, the finite scheme providing top-up cover, over and above the basic cover provided by the conventional policy.

6.5.3 Captives

A captive insurance company is a wholly owned subsidiary of the parent. It is created purely to provide insurance cover for the parent's activities. Because it is wholly-owned, it acts on the orders of the parent, and will be used to provide cover for risks and in circumstances which a normal insurer would not touch.

It is funded by substantial capital investments by the parent, which may benefit from beneficial tax treatment, like a conventional premium, but unlike normal provision out of capital by a self-insuring company.

Usually, the captive will need to find some supporting funding, either in the form of a chronological stabilisation plan or financial reinsurance to swell its ability to pay for an incident.

6.5.4 Mutual benefit companies

These devices are conventional insurance schemes, but with the advantage that, on inception of the policy, the company has the opportunity to take shares in the mutual company set up for the benefit of the various insureds.

After non-renewal of the policy and over time, participating companies derive dividends from the mutual benefit company, which go some way towards repaying the initial premium.

The profits to be divided in this way are derived from the premium pool, and the fewer claims that are made, the larger is the dividend.

6.5.5 Structured settlements

These are not an alternative method of insurance, but merely an alternative way of paying any compensation which may be ordered as a consequence of an environmental incident.

Familiar in personal injury claims, there is no reason in principle why structured settlements, arranged through the insurance industry, cannot be applied to environmental compensation payments. A company interested in any of these schemes or options should take specialist advice, before deciding which route to take.

6.6 OTHER INSURANCE POINTS TO WATCH

Because of the limitations on environmental policies, and the variable wording of the various policies on offer, a company should also watch out for other exclusions.

Legal costs may not be covered, so a company may consider taking out legal expenses insurance. Depending on the wording of the policy this cover may also extend to the expenses incurred in defending criminal proceedings.

An employer's liability for injury to its employees may be excluded, so the company should check its employers' liability policy to ascertain whether injury caused to employees by an environmental incident is covered.

Liability arising from carriage, or the loading and unloading of vehicles, aircraft and ships is usually excluded. Environmental problems and incidents may come about as a result of spillages from tankers, so the company should check its motor and other insurances to ascertain whether such incidents may be covered under those policies instead.

Liability from products may be excluded, so the company should check its product liability policies, in appropriate cases, to ensure that cover is provided for the environmental impact of the company's products.

6.7   OTHER TYPES OF SPECIFIC ENVIRONMENTAL POLICIES

Other specific 'niche' policies are available to cover environmental risks which are normally excluded even from the normal run of specific environmental policies. They cover the following risks.

6.7.1   Underground storage tanks

Underground storage tanks (USTs) pose a particular risk for pollution and contamination, partly due to their contents (usually petroleum products), and partly due to their susceptibility to corrosion. Leakages or other incidents surrounding such tanks are therefore normally excluded from cover.

6.7.2   Directors and officers

Directors and officers' (D&O) cover is intended to protect a company director against personal liability for environmental incidents arising as a result of the company's activities.

A director can be made personally liable for the criminal acts of the company, and prosecuted, convicted and fined as if he had personally committed the offence. Such liability is not covered under conventional policies, and such penalties are not usually insurable.

However, certain insurers do now offer cover of this type to indemnify any personal losses sustained by directors in actions for breach of duty, etc. in the performance of their duties as directors.

6.7.3 General environmental protection

Most policies are site specific, but some insurers do offer a multi-site package of cover which combines pollution liability insurance with risk funding, though it is likely that only larger corporations would be able to sustain the level of premium expected under such schemes.

6.7.4 Contractors' pollution liability

During an environmental investigation, or during reclamation, remediation or construction works, it is possible that the contractors on-site may upset some long-dormant problem, and create a pollution incident, for example, by activating the migration of contamination that had lain stagnant.

It is unlikely that their own general liability policies would cover this risk, and an employer should consider insisting on the contractor taking out specific environmental cover, which is available from some insurers.

6.7.5 Consultants' liability

The position, as discussed above, may be doubly true of environmental consultants, who may be engaged to design and execute a remediation programme. Policies covering their liability both in the design and in the works phases are available.

Policies are also now available on a project basis for up to five years. Cover can be arranged by employers in respect of a range of consultants and contractors working on their behalf on one policy.

6.7.6 Landfill sites

Because of the particular nature of the problems caused by landfill sites, some specialist insurers offer specifically tailored policies geared directly at waste disposal contractors and site operators.

6.7.7 Professional liability

Similarly, professional advisers called in to advise on aspects of the company's environmental performance may not be covered for such advice under their professional indemnity policies.

Specific environmental cover may be needed. This is especially true of surveyors and engineers, both of whose professional insurers have withdrawn cover for environmental risks totally.

So far, this has not happened with the legal profession, but there is an immediate prospect of it being so withdrawn as solicitors go to the open market for their cover from September 2000. However, the Law Society is in the process of arranging comprehensive cover for practitioners for liabilities arising out of conveyancing transactions.

It should be noted also, that most professional indemnity policies are written, and have for many years been written, on a 'claims made' basis, meaning that claims must be made against the professional concerned within the policy period for cover to be available.

This leaves a professional adviser exposed if a claim is made within the claimant's limitation period (of, say, six years) but after expiry of the policy period itself.

As far as the legal profession is concerned, the Solicitors' Indemnity Fund has in the past operated rather differently, in that the effects of a solicitor's negligence will be indemnified by the Fund whenever the claim occurs.

Since this may be many years after the initial deficient advice (transaction in 1991, incident in 1995, damage to claimant in 2000, client sued by claimant in 2005, solicitor sued in 2006), the Solicitors' Indemnity Fund may be called on for some years to come – with the consequent drain on resources and increased claims against the rest of the profession in the form of contributions.

Since the lawyer would be sued in negligence if the contractual limitation period had expired or was inapplicable, the limitation period would be three years from the date of knowledge of loss (2005) subject to the long-stop period of 15 years from the date of the advice (1991) under the Latent Damage Act 1986.

The fact that the lawyer may be the only professional in a transaction with worthwhile cover, may mean that lawyers become the target for those aggrieved by poor advice and left with an unforeseen liability.

It remains to be seen what attitude the commercial professional indemnity insurance market takes now that the solicitors' profession has gone to the open market for its indemnity cover (from September 2000).

6.8   RECENT DEVELOPMENTS

Policy terms are changing constantly in response to the demands of the market and new products are starting to enter the market, especially in anticipation of the contaminated land regime.

Recent initiatives include cheaper policies with lower levels of cover, joint ventures between insurers and consultants, new brokerage services and a greater willingness to write bespoke policies which deviate from standard wording.

CHAPTER 7

Use of environmental consultants

7.1 ENVIRONMENTAL INVESTIGATIONS AND AUDIT

The necessity and desirability of carrying out environmental investigations and audits has grown rapidly in recent months and years. Lenders, insurers, purchasers and enlightened managers all perceive the need for knowledge relating to a particular company's environmental situation, and its potential exposure to incidents, accidents and claims.

Broadly, an environmental investigation or audit involves a full assessment of a company's sites, operations and installations with the intention of evaluating the potential environmental risks posed by those installations, and to monitor corporate environmental performance.

It is important to appreciate the distinction between what shall be referred to in this chapter as an 'investigation', and an 'audit'.

An 'investigation' is an investigation for the purposes of general information gathering – maybe as a preliminary to a purchase – and will normally consist of a paper, or desk study, possibly followed by site visits, of a more or less detailed type.

An 'audit', on the other hand, involves a thorough site investigation, together with detailed monitoring operations, so that a company's performance can be measured against clearly defined criteria, which have already been determined and set by the company. It is a quantitative exercise, intended to gauge in precise terms how a company measures up to its own standards, and if not, by how far it is falling short.

This concept of 'measurability' is what distinguishes an audit from an investigation. This distinction will be adhered to in the rest of this chapter.

7.1.1 Types of investigation

There is no standard form of investigation. They are almost infinitely variable according to the circumstances and the purposes which they are required to serve.

The most common manifestations of investigations are usually said to include:

- investigations of the whole of a company's activities or operations;
- investigations of specific activities or operations;
- investigations of specific assets (e.g. prior to purchase, sale or development);
- analysis of specific environmental risks to ensure compliance with the regulatory framework;
- investigations of waste facilities;
- risk assessment investigations;
- waste minimisation strategies;
- environmental impact assessment in connection with planning consents;
- investigations as a preliminary to environmental impairment liability insurance; or
- investigations designed to assist in the production of a corporate environmental policy statement (CEPS), and management system, as part of the company's 'green' image.

It is vital to the success of the investigation to have identified its objectives, and what it is intended to achieve. Setting objectives can seem like a waste of time and effort, but a lot of money can be wasted getting a report which analyses the wrong aspects of a company's operations, or which tackles the job from a wrong perspective.

The management team, with the help of appropriate professional advice, must decide on the objectives, and inform the professional investigation team what it is they are expected to produce, how and when. Time spent setting out the terms will be time saved having to seek clarification and further information later.

The general objectives of an investigation, however, are also variable according to the company's circumstances and requirements, but will often include a combination (or even all) of the following considerations:

- introducing a proactive approach to the management of environmental aspects of the business;
- the avoidance of criminal and civil liabilities and clean-up costs;
- reporting to shareholders, bankers/lenders, insurers, employees and regulatory bodies;

- the enhancement of the company's public image;

- to safeguard authorisations, permits, licences and insurance policies;

- to avoid disruption to production or trading arising out of environmental hazards and the extraordinary costs associated with it;

- the avoidance of the devaluation of assets due to contamination; and

- to establish and maintain good relations with the local community and neighbouring residents.

There are two basic types of environmental investigation:

- the 'compliance' investigation, to look at the whole business, and its operations and processes; and

- the 'transactional' investigation, undertaken in connection with specific transactions, such as purchase or disposal of assets, or funding arrangements.

Underlying this diversity, there is a fairly common procedural approach which can be applied and adapted to meet the differing needs of the investigation and the circumstances in which it is carried out. It consists of a three-part process.

Phase I – desk study and historical review

A Phase I study involves a paper exercise to discover the past land-use of the site, in order to determine whether there is the potential for contamination. Study of old Ordnance Survey maps, interviewing local residents, aerial photographs and visits to the site to pick up visual clues are all sensible steps to take.

Phase II – site inspections/walk through the production process

Having identified the potential for contamination and other environmental problems, the study can move on to the next stage – a full site visit. This visit will usually involve the drilling of boreholes and trial pits and trenches to find out what is actually beneath the ground. It may involve geological analysis, groundwater modelling, and chemical testing of contaminants to give a final indication of the level of contamination, and degree of risk, involved.

Phase III – implementation of recommendations and remediation programme; further sampling if necessary, monitoring and follow-up

The final, Phase III section is the basis of the environmental 'auditing' process – the continuing investigation and measuring of a company's performance, and the comparison of the actual with the intended performance as set out in the company's environmental policy, which itself is derived from the results of the earlier investigation phase.

7.1.2 Types of audit

As explained in para. 7.1, there is a distinction between investigations and audits. Strictly, an audit is merely a comparison of corporate performance with stated policy criteria. Once a company has formulated a policy, and set specific targets for certain emissions to air or water, for example, it is essential to good management of the risks that the company keeps track of how it is performing. This will entail monitoring emissions in quantitative terms, and comparing actual performance with the stated performance targets in the corporate policy.

Of course, many companies may have policies which do not bind the company to any particular set of targets or measurable standards, and whilst this is less effective as a way of checking real performance, it is nevertheless less onerous for the company.

It means, though, that any later investigations which are carried out are not compared with specific targets, because there are none, and the process is not therefore an 'audit' in the true sense.

7.1.3 Risks of having an investigation

One of the main risks of an environmental investigation is that it may provide damaging information which could be the basis for civil or criminal liability, or write-downs on the values of assets.

Such results may have a damaging impact on public perception and confidence, which may in turn affect the company's share price. It may also affect a company's position with its bankers, in that loan facilities may be withdrawn or renegotiated.

The problem is that investigation reports commissioned by a company from, say, an environmental consultant, and the reports submitted by the consultant to the company, would not be secret, confidential or in any way protected from having to be shown to inspectors and officers of the regulatory agencies.

Nor would it be possible to avoid having to show these documents to an opponent in any civil court proceedings which may be brought. It would be highly embarrassing to have to reveal the contents of a damaging investigation report in court.

Many clients do not appreciate that the concept of 'confidentiality' is not protected by English law. Merely calling a document 'confidential' does not make it secret in the way that the company might want.

A typical investigation report is almost inevitably going to contain potentially damaging information about the company's site operations and installations, and may even point out specifically the potential danger for a pollution offence or explosion.

Most formal environmental management systems, like ISO 14001, will require not only the documentation and recording of the corporate environmental policy, but also the monitoring of records and results of later audits, which will spell out the ways in which company performance is inadequate, and in breach of stated policy.

Clearly, the company may wish to keep this information confidential, particularly from public-interest groups, regulatory authorities or opponents in a civil action.

7.1.4   Can consultants' reports be privileged?

There are ways in which protection for this documentation can be maximised, though never fully guaranteed, by the use of legal professional privilege.

The only documents protected from disclosure to any of these parties or bodies, is documentation which is protected by legal professional privilege. Only if a document attracts legal professional privilege can it truly be called confidential or secret, because it is only such documents which are protected from disclosure.

The main category of privilege is solicitor–client communications, which breaks down into two sub-categories:

- communications passing between a solicitor and his client; and

- communications between third parties and a solicitor, which are privileged only if they are made in anticipation of contemplated or pending litigation and the dominant purpose of the communication was to prepare for the proceedings.

Communications between a lawyer and his client will be privileged

147

provided they are confidential, made between a lawyer in his professional capacity and his client, and made for the purpose of either seeking or giving legal advice. No opponent or inspector can have access to them or use them in subsequent proceedings.

Clearly, this is a very valuable protection for a client, but it is available only if the client instructs the solicitor to give 'legal advice'.

In the context of an environmental investigation, therefore, the ideal situation would be for the client to contact the solicitor and instruct the solicitor to advise the client on compliance with legal environmental duties and responsibilities.

Particular problems arise in dealings with third parties, such as environmental consultants, in that an investigation report commissioned by a company without involving its lawyers would not be privileged, as it would not be 'legal advice', nor would it be prepared 'for the dominant purpose of anticipated or pending litigation', unless, of course, criminal or civil proceedings had already been started against the company by the time the report was commissioned.

However, there is some authority (see the case of *Getty* v. *Getty and Treves* [1985] QB 956) for the proposition that privilege extends to information which a solicitor receives in his professional capacity from a third party, for onward transmission to the client as part of the legal advice which the client has sought.

This suggests that there is some mileage in arguing that if a solicitor is engaged by a company to give legal advice, and that solicitor feels it necessary to take further advice from other consultants and specialists in order to advise the client of the full and true legal position, then the advice by the third-party consultants to the solicitor should be privileged, just as much as the solicitor's own advice to the client would be.

In the context of an environmental investigation, one would seek to argue that the technical consultants and, maybe, the management consultants or accountants, were merely undertaking investigations and expressing opinions in order that the solicitor could fully and accurately assess the legal position, in particular, the requirements for the company's compliance with its legal obligations.

To be able to argue this point successfully, it would be necessary for the solicitor to engage the third-party consultants, whether they be technical engineering consultants or accountants and management consultants, as it would be, in effect, the solicitor who required their services.

Such reports would therefore be commissioned by the solicitor, and be addressed to the solicitor to ensure consistency with this approach. The solicitor would then collate all the information, and provide the necessary advice to the client company.

By this means, the consultants' reports to the solicitor, and the ultimate advice to the client from the solicitor, may attract legal professional privilege and thus be safe from disclosure.

However, this approach has not been tested in court, and cannot be guaranteed to be successful. Moreover, there are severe dangers for any solicitor who is in the 'hub of the wheel' in this way. In particular:

- solicitors may be liable in negligence for the quality of the advice they are passing on, and if the consultant gets it wrong, it may be the solicitor who is sued by the client;

- there may be insurance difficulties in passing on information in this way.

It may be thought best, therefore, for the solicitor to engineer the appointment of the consultant by the client direct, subject to suitable advice on the terms and conditions of that appointment. A draft set of terms and conditions is set out in Appendix 7.

In addition, precautions should be taken as to the storage of any such report, so that it is not inadvertently handed over to an inspector by a member of staff, as part of an official investigation.

7.2   CARRYING OUT AN INVESTIGATION

7.2.1   Internal matters

It is assumed, for the following discussion, that a company undertaking a compliance investigation genuinely wishes to take proactive steps to manage its risks, and is therefore committed to implementing the suggestions made in the final report.

A company without such a commitment is wasting its money undertaking the investigation in the first place.

For compliance investigations, conducted with a view to introducing (or improving) the management of businesses in respect of environmental issues, ISO 14001 sets out the practices to adopt.

Whilst not all compliance investigations are commissioned with a view to

ISO accreditation, it nonetheless provides a helpful guide to the sort of issues that should be addressed in a compliance investigation.

The essential elements of an investigation are numerous and involve, as a fundamental condition, full management commitment to the process – and the implementation of the findings and recommendations.

Accordingly, the company should appoint a main board director with specific responsibility and accountability for environmental issues, and the implementation of the environmental policy. This individual will be charged with the responsibility for commissioning the investigation, and implementing its recommendations in due course. The same individual will be responsible for the follow-up audits in due course also.

There must be a dedicated team (accountable to the responsible director and the board) to formulate and implement the company's environmental policy, comprising any relevant internal or external technical and scientific experts, line managers and legal advisers, whether internal or external.

The investigation itself should produce a written document setting out the findings of the investigation and any recommendations.

The investigation should include a careful environmental impact study of each area of production activity in the business and should set out specific, measurable objectives and targets, and a timetable for achieving them.

Facilities for monitoring and investigation should be programmed in as part of the policy, as should systematic records of performance, so that achievement can be monitored and investigated effectively.

The investigation itself, and perhaps the follow-up audits, will very often be undertaken by an external, independent environmental consultant.

7.2.2 Using environmental consultants

Environmental investigations have for some time been a growth area and the number of consultancies has mushroomed. There are now in the order of 400 consultancies in the UK, and choosing one should not be difficult. However, picking one at random is unlikely to be the best solution, and close thought must be given to the selection process.

Shop around – not all consultancies do the same things, charge the same fees, or are of a comparable standard.

The term 'environmental consultant' covers a vast range of technical and scientific disciplines, e.g. geology, hydrogeology, acoustics, chemistry, biochemistry, ecology, etc.

There are a wide variety of consultancies available, ranging from the very common, small domestic consultancy (turnover £100,000 or less) at one end of the market, to UK divisions of large foreign engineering and environmental consultancies at the other. In addition, many of the UK engineering companies are setting up dedicated divisions within their overall operating structure to provide these services.

7.2.3 Do I need to appoint a consultant at all?

There is no need to appoint a consultant to achieve the purposes of an investigation. Companies may well be able to solve their environmental problems and achieve their aims by developing their own in-house expertise.

However, appointing a specialist consultant is certainly the easiest and commonest way of addressing the issues, and almost the only option in a purchase transaction.

7.2.4 Selecting and appointing consultants

Prior to appointing a consultant to carry out an investigation, the business should have a clear idea of the objectives which it wishes to achieve in the investigation. Some of the possibilities are mentioned above.

It should then select and appoint the investigation team which will best provide the service required by the company. This may sound obvious, but only when the company has addressed this question will it be able to choose the right consultancy for the job. Without such analysis, the company only stands a 1:400 chance of getting the right product. Using consultants is too expensive to take that sort of risk.

Solicitors can often provide useful advice at this stage in helping to specify the investigation service required and the quality standards that will need to be achieved.

Choosing a consultancy can be done by the tried and trusted method of word-of-mouth recommendation, though this is not always a fail-safe and speedy method.

Various directories are now available which list the consultancies, and specify their level of expertise and technical coverage. The *ENDS Directory of Environmental Consultants* (published by Environmental Data Systems Ltd (ENDS), Finsbury Business Centre, 40 Bowling Green Lane, London EC1R 0NE, Tel: 020 7278 4745, Fax: 020 7415 0106) is the obvious publication to consult, though the Institute of Environmental Assessment (IEA) would be another useful contact.

151

Inviting a selection of consultants to attend a 'beauty parade', and to tender for work is another method favoured by many.

Contacts through parent companies, trade associations, seminars, professional advisers and, increasingly, through civic initiatives such as local business clubs and fora are all useful sources of information and contacts.

Some banks and other lending institutions – as well as the EIL insurers – tend to have their own panel of approved consultants, and will insist on the report being compiled by one of them. A client may not therefore have a totally free choice.

7.2.5   Considerations on appointment

There are a number of considerations which need to borne in mind in the appointment of the consultants. A non-exhaustive list of the more important ones would include:

(a)   Type of consultancy

An early decision needs to be taken as to what type of consultancy is required. Does the company need engineering or analytical advice, or does it need management consultancy? Consultants from both ends of the spectrum are available, and the answer to this question will limit the options.

The history and background of the consultancy, and what the core business of its parent company is will also affect the angle taken by the consultant on the project, and again will limit the options.

(b)   One large consultant, or many small ones?

In the vast majority of cases, the company will want the whole investigation process and the whole project handled by one consultant.

With this in mind, employing a multi-disciplinary practice will be preferable to employing a series of specialists, particularly when one bears in mind the logistical difficulties in getting all the reports in the right form, at the right time, at the right price and on the right terms from a variety of different suppliers.

On the other hand, it would be foolish to employ a consultancy on the grounds of convenience, if they do not have the specific expertise required, and in any event, the larger consultancies tend to be more expensive.

(c)   Previous experience and details of relevant projects

The ability of the consultancy to do the job is what counts. There are few better indicators of this than experience. However, due to the relative newness of the profession, not everyone has it. This is not to say that those who do not are bad. Far from it. Key personnel in a consultancy may have significant experience and reputations, not shown in any analysis of the consultancy itself. Foreign companies may have technological back-up from abroad which makes up for their lack of project experience in the UK.

Moreover, in professional and business life there are those for whom practice does not make perfect, and who may still perform badly despite plenty of opportunity to improve.

One could consider taking references from previous clients.

(d)   Membership of professional bodies

One should ideally choose a consultant that has some independent accreditation of quality. The Institute of Environmental Assessment launched a quality standard in 1991.

The Association of Environmental Consultants has membership criteria which require quality standards to be maintained, and a certain level of expertise to be acquired.

Registration with the National Environmental Auditors Registration Association should also carry a degree of confidence in the quality of the consultancy.

These bodies have no official status, however, so membership is no guarantee of quality.

There is, of course, the possibility of accreditation to ISO 9000 or equivalent standards, though this is not necessarily an indication of the quality of the investigating, merely of the management of the business. One can perform a bad investigation very effectively.

(e)   Professional indemnity insurance – are there any restrictions on cover?

Adequate insurance coverage should be insisted upon. Bad advice from a consultant may expose a company to huge potential liabilities, and recourse may be had against the adviser. It would be unfortunate if there were no fund with which to pay the bill.

Sadly, many insurers are including pollution exclusion clauses in professional indemnity policies, and the surveying profession have had their professional indemnity cover removed for such risks.

It should be routine to check the cover available to the consultant. Even if they are insured, there may be limits on the level of cover offered which may be too low for the comfort of the employer company. In addition, exclusions in the policy may result in the specific project not being covered, the specific contaminant not being covered, or an excess being required.

If a claim has already been made against the consultant by another client it may have exhausted the aggregate limit of funds available under the policy – leaving no funds for the next claimant.

Has the renewal date passed?

These points need to be checked direct with the insurer, if possible.

Many large consultancies carry perfectly adequate cover because of their size and reputation in other fields, and many take a responsible view of their obligations – some have a more cavalier attitude.

In any event, cover can usually be purchased on a project-specific basis.

(f)   Beware of 'standard contracts', as some do not give adequate protection to the client company

Many consultancies work on standard terms of engagement, and those terms are frequently biased in favour of the consultant.

Often, they are based on foreign versions, often American, and are vaguely worded to the point of being meaningless, and unenforceable.

Particular restrictions to be wary of are:

- clauses which restrict the amount that can be claimed to a set sum (often £50,000) or to a sum equivalent to the contract price. These limitations are inadequate, as the value of the decisions taken on the strength of the advice is significantly greater than the price paid for the initial investigation report itself;

- clauses which limit the limitation period within which claims can be brought. The normal period of six years can be reduced by agreement between parties of equal standing to a contract. Many standard contracts reduce the period to three years, two years or even one year;

- clauses which require the client to indemnify the consultant against all liability whatsoever for all matters arising in connection with the investigation.

(g) Giving a precise specification of works required

Having decided what is required by the investigation, the company and its advisers must ensure that the message is adequately and clearly communicated to the consultant.

In particular, depending on the purpose behind the investigation, the methodology adopted by the consultant may be required to correlate with that required to be adopted by local authorities in the identification of contaminated land.

(h) Requiring detailed information on costs

It is essential to ensure complete understanding of the basis on which the fees are to be assessed and paid. This would include finalising details of any fixed cost preliminary investigations, the provision of regular progress reports with costs limits, or the delivery of interim invoices linked to specific tasks, and time sheets and a final account with a full statement of work done.

(i) Assignability of rights

If the client has engaged the consultant direct it is essential to insist, if possible, that the right to use, and sue upon, the report is transferable to anyone else involved in, or affected by the project.

Normally, only the company which engaged the consultant would be allowed to sue, as it is only the company which has a contract with the consultant. There may be times, however, when others (purchasers of a reclaimed site, tenants, funders, or potential shareholders for example) are affected by the inadequacy of the service offered by the consultant, and want to sue. They would need to have the right to sue assigned to them specifically.

The right of the employing company to assign this right should be retained in the contract with the consultant.

This is frequently resisted, and the matter dealt with on an ad hoc basis by means of collateral warranties between the consultant and the person purportedly relying on the report.

(j)   Readable reports produced in a form accessible to the company

One problem often encountered with investigation reports is that they are produced in a technical way, using graphs, read-outs and technical language which is incomprehensible to a company manager.

The consultant should be aware of the need for clear, simple language, and clarity of expression.

Nevertheless, the company should make clear its requirement for clear and readable presentation, perhaps confining technical documentation to an appendix.

(k)   Copyright and other 'intellectual property' rights associated with the investigation to be owned by the company

The terms of engagement should provide that any technical information disclosed to the consultant remains the property of the company, and also that any novel or inventive discoveries made by the consultant in the process of the investigation also belong to the company.

Likewise, there should be company access to all source material and data generated by the consultant.

This is to ensure that any inventions, trade marks, designs, patents and other confidential information is not misused.

(l)   Confidentiality

All matters relating to the investigation must be treated with the strictest confidentiality by the consultant, and not revealed to anyone without the express authority of the company.

Discipline of this nature is essential to ensure that there is no undue reliance on the contents of the report by anyone to whom it is not directed, and also to ensure that copies of the report do not fall into the wrong hands, thus waiving any privilege which may otherwise have attached to it.

(m) Privilege

All correspondence, draft documents and other papers including the final report, all technical or other confidential information learned by the consultant in the course of the investigation about the company's business, and all correspondence between solicitors and the consultant and other documents should be retained by the appointing solicitor in order to maximise the protection afforded by the solicitor–client privilege.

A suggested set of terms and conditions dealing with most of these issues is reproduced in Appendix 7.

CHAPTER 8

Current developments in the EU

8.1   EU POLICY

In 1986, Articles 130r–130t were inserted into the Treaty of Rome and these provisions are the source of the various EU directives that implement the broad policy of the EU's Environmental Action Programmes.

The day-to-day responsibility for ensuring implementation lies with Directorate-General XI (DG XI) in Brussels. There is an embryonic European Environment Agency in Copenhagen, set up under the provisions of Regulation 1210/90, but it does not have enforcement powers, and its main function for the time being is to gather information about environmental issues across the EU for comparative purposes.

8.2   KEY ASPECTS OF EU LEGISLATION

8.2.1   Waste Framework Directive

75/442/EEC: Council Directive of 15 July 1975 (OJ L194 25.07.75 p. 39).

Amended by 91/156/EEC (OJ L078 26.03.91 p. 32.) and 91/692/EEC (OJ L377 31.12.91 p. 48).

The Framework Directive seeks to harmonise aspects of waste management legislation throughout the Member States in order to prevent producers of waste from taking advantage of inconsistencies in national law and differentials in disposal costs. The Directive establishes community-wide definitions of significant terms, in particular 'waste' and 'disposal', requires Member States to establish waste disposal authorities, and lays down the essential elements of a waste management licensing system to be adopted by all Members States. The Directive as amended underlay Part II of the Environmental Protection Act 1990, the Controlled

Waste Regulations 1992, SI 1992/588 and the Waste Management Licensing Regulations 1994, SI 1994/1056 as amended by the Waste Management Licensing (Amendment) Regulations 1997, SI 1997/2203 and the Waste Management Licensing (Amendment) Regulations 1998, SI 1998/606.

The amended Directive includes a stricter definition of waste, greater emphasis on recycling, strengthening of controls on disposal sites, encouragement for Member States to become self-sufficient in waste disposal capacity and a requirement for the registration of waste carriers.

8.2.2 Fresh Water Directive

78/659/EEC: Council Directive of 18 July 1978 on the quality of fresh waters needing protection or improvement in order to support fish life (OJ L222 14.08.78 p. 1).

Amended by 91/692/EEC: Council Directive of 23 December 1991 (OJ L377 31.12.91 p. 48).

Latest position

A Communication from the Commission to the Council and the Parliament on European Communities' water policy has been issued (COM (96)59). It proposed a Framework Water Resource Directive to supersede existing and proposed Directives. The Communication was heavily criticised by the European Parliament on 23 October 1996 for failing to impose uniform discharge limits and allowing Member States too great a freedom to set their own water-quality standards (OJC 347.18.11.96 p. 80 and Opinion of the Economic and Social Committee OJC 30 30.1.97 p. 5). In the meantime, the Commission has proposed an action programme to protect groundwater supplies. (COM (96)315 OJC 355 25.11.96 p. 1). A revised draft proposal for a Council Directive establishing a framework for European Community water policy was considered by the Council of Ministers on 19–20 June 1997 (COM (97)49 OJC 184 17.6.97 p. 20) and has been amended (COM (97)614 OJC16 20.1.98 p. 14). The Economic and Social Committee has given its opinion (OJC 355 21.11.97 p. 83). The Commission has amended the draft framework Directive to strengthen controls over discharges to water from small- and medium-sized industrial plants (COM (98)76 OJC 108 7.4.98 p. 94). A common understanding on the draft Directive was reached at the Council of Ministers held in Luxembourg on 16–17 June 1998 (COM (99)271). The Parliament approved the Directive with amendments (OJC 150 28.5.99 p. 388) and a political agreement was reached by Ministers at Brussels on 11–12 March

1999. A Common Position was reached by the Council of Ministers on 22 October 1999 (Common Position No. 41/1999 OJC 343 30.11.99 p. 1) and the proposed Directive has been amended (COM (2000)219). In February 2000 the Commission proposed a priority list of 32 water pollutants to be regulated under the new Water Framework Directive (COM (2000)47).

8.2.3 Existing Municipal Waste Incinerator Directive

89/429/EEC: Council Directive of 21 June 1989 on the reduction of air pollution from existing municipal waste-incineration plants (OJ L203 15.07.89 p. 50).

The Directive introduces tougher emission limits and operating standards for incinerators. A Directive is expected to extend the emissions standards prescribed by the Hazardous Waste Incineration Directive to existing incinerators.

Implemented by Part I of the Environmental Protection Act 1990.

Latest position

The Commission has produced a draft Directive on the incineration of all non-hazardous waste which will replace the 1989 Directive (COM (98)558 OJC 372 2.12.98 p. 11). A political agreement was reached at the Council of Ministers in June and a Common Position in November 1999. The Commission has provided an opinion on the Parliament's amendments to the Common Position (COM (2000)280).

8.2.4 GMO Directives

90/219/EEC: Council Directive of 23 April 1990 on the contained use of genetically modified micro-organisms (OJ L117 08.05.90 p. 1) and 90/220/EEC: Council Directive of 23 April 1990 on the deliberate release into the environment of genetically modified organisms (GMOs) (OJ L117 08.05.90 p. 15).

Amended by 94/51 (OJ L297 18.11.94 p. 29), 94/15 (OJ L103 22.4.94 p. 20), 97/35 (OJ L169 27.6.97 p. 72) and 98/81 (OJ L330 5.12.98 p. 13).

The Directives provide for a system of notification of operations and containment, dealt with accidents and waste management and provided safeguards for research and development.

Implemented by Part VI of the Environmental Protection Act 1990; the Genetically Modified Organisms (Contained Use) Regulations 1992, SI 1992/3217; the Genetically Modified Organisms (Deliberate Release) Regulations 1993, SI 1993/152; the Genetically Modified Organisms (Contained Use) Regulations 1993, SI 1993/15; the Genetically Modified Organisms (Deliberate Release) Regulations 1992, SI 1992/3280; and the Genetically Modified Organisms (Deliberate Release) Regulations 1995, SI 1995/304. The Genetically Modified Organisms (Contained Use) (Amendment) Regulations 1996, SI 1996/967 and the Genetically Modified Organisms (Risk Assessment) (Records and Exemptions) Regulations 1996, SI 1996/1106 revoke and replace the earlier Regulations to take account of Council Regulation No. 2309/93 (OJ L241 24.8.93). The Genetically Modified Organisms (Deliberate Release and Risk Assessment – Amendment) Regulations 1997, SI 1997/1900 amend SI 1992/3280 and SI 1996/1106 to implement Directive 97/35/EC (OJ L169 27.6.97 p. 72) which adapted Directive 90/220/EEC to reflect technical progress. The Genetically Modified Organisms (Contained Use) (Amendment) Regulations 1998, SI 1998/1548 exempt novel food and novel food ingredients which are now covered by the Novel Food Regulations.

Latest position

In December 1996 the Commission issued a report on the review of Directive 90/220 and possible amendment to streamline applications to release genetically modified organisms and to tighten risk assessment (COM (96)630). The Commission has drafted an amending Directive (COM (98)85 OJC 139 4.5.98 p. 1) which would streamline authorisation procedures but would introduce new monitoring requirements. It was generally supported by the Council of Ministers in Luxembourg on 16–17 June 1998. Ministers held an orientation debate on the proposed Directive on 21 December 1998 and declared that Members States would take into account the principles for risk assessment and monitoring when applying the existing Directive. The draft amending Directive has been revised (COM (99)139 OJC 139 19.5.99 p. 7). Ministers reached a political agreement on 24–25 June 1999 and a Common Position on 9 December 1999 (Common Position No. 12/2000 OJC 64 6.3.2000 p. 1). The Commission has produced an opinion on amendments to the Common Position from the Parliament (COM (2000)293).

In June 1997 the Commission adopted adaptations to Directive 90/220 to extend existing information requirements to include the labelling of new products containing genetically modified organisms. The Regulation also requires those notifying GMOs under Directive 90/220 to include molecular data for inclusion on a register. Member States had until 31 July 1997 to implement the measure that will be integrated into amendments to Directive 90/220. It has been implemented in the UK by the Genetically Modified Organisms (Contaminated Use) (Amendment) Regulations 1998, SI 1998/1548.

8.2.5 Access to Environmental Information Directive

90/313/EEC: Council Directive of 7 June 1990 (OJ L158 23.06.90 p. 56).

The Directive seeks to improve environmental protection by giving access to environmental information held by public authorities.

Implemented by the Environmental Information Regulations 1992, SI 1992/3240 which came into force on 31 December 1992 and the Environmental Information (Amendment) Regulations 1998, SI 1998/1447. Information held in certain public registers is available under the Environmental Protection Act 1990 and the Water Resources Act 1991.

Latest position

The Commission is to carrying out a review of the Directive and is expected to propose amendments in May 2000 to implement the Aarhus Convention on Access to Information, Public Participation and Justice in Environmental Matters adopted in June 1998.

The Freedom of Information Bill will revoke the Regulations and will enable the Secretary of State to make Regulations to implement the Aarhus Convention.

8.2.6 Ozone depletion

Council Regulations on substances that deplete the ozone layer (EEC) No. 594/91 OJ L67 14.03.91 p. 1, and EC Reg. No. 3093/94 OJ L333 22.12.94 p. 1.

Amended by 92/3952 (OJ L405 31.12.92 p. 41) and 93/2047 (OJ L185 28.07.93 p. 20).

Implemented the Montreal Protocol to the Vienna Convention for the Protection of the Ozone Layer. The Regulation specified maximum levels of production, use and supply of chlorofluorocarbons (CFCs), hydro-chlorofluorocarbons (HCFCs), trichoroethane and carbon tetrachlorine. See the Environmental Protection (Controls on Substances that Deplete the Ozone Layer) Regulations 1996, SI 1996/506.

Latest position

The Commission has proposed a further Regulation to reflect amendments to the Montreal Protocol which would lead to the elimination of all ozone-depleting substances (COM (98)398 OJC 286 15.9.98 p. 6). The December 1998 Council of Ministers reached political agreement on the new Regulation and a Common Position in February 1999 (Common Position No. 19/1999 OJC 123 4.5.99 p. 28) in the light of which the Regulation has been amended (COM (99) 67 OJC 83 25.3.99 p. 4; COM (99) 392). The Commission has provided an opinion on the Parliament's amendments to the Common Position (COM (2000) 96). See the Commission proposal for a Council Decision on the amendment of the Montreal Protocol COM (99) 392.

8.2.7   Nitrates Directive

91/676/EEC: Council Directive of 12 December 1991 concerning the protection of waters against pollution caused by nitrates from agricultural sources (OJ L375 31.12.91 p. 1).

The Directive imposes a requirement on Member States to designate all zones vulnerable to pollution from nitrate compounds and to take action against further contamination.

The Directive goes beyond the existing limited powers under the Water Resources Act 1991 and the Nitrate Sensitive Areas (Designation) Order 1990, SI 1990/1013. Implemented by the Protection of Water Against Agriculture Nitrate Pollution (England and Wales) Regulations 1996, SI 1996/888.

Latest position

In 1997 the Commission produced a report on the implementation of the Directive (COM (97) 473 and COM (98) 16) on which the Parliament has commented (OJC 341 9.11.98 p. 35) calling for speedier action to implement and enforce the Directive. The Commission is taking legal action against Germany, Luxembourg, France, Belgium and The Netherlands for failure to abide by the Directive.

8.2.8   Hazardous Waste Directive

91/689/EEC: Council Directive of 12 December 1991 on hazardous waste (OJ L377 31.12.91 p. 20).

Amended by 94/31 (OJ L168 02.07.94 p. 28)

See also 94/67/EC: Council Directive of 16 December 1994 on the incineration of hazardous waste (OJ L365 31.12.94 p. 34).

Will eventually replace 78/319/EEC: Council Directive of 20 March 1978 on toxic and dangerous waste.

The Directive seeks to harmonise definitions of hazardous waste across the Community. Annexes specify categories of waste, constituents of waste and the properties of such waste. The Directive also prescribed requirements for a hazardous waste permitting system, for the production of waste management plans by competent authorities, and for the packaging and labelling of hazardous waste. A Council Decision of 22.12.94 made under Directive 91/689 established a list of 200 types of hazardous waste (OJ L356; 31.12.94 p. 14).

Implemented in part by Part II of the Environmental Protection Act 1990 and the Environmental Protection (Duty of Care) Regulations 1991, SI 1991/2839. The Special Waste Regulations 1996, SI 1996/972 as amended by the Special Waste (Amendment) Regulations 1996, SI 1996/2019 and the Special Waste (Amendment) Regulations 1997, SI 1997/251 implement the Directive and the list of hazardous wastes adopted by the Council. See also Department of the Environment Circular 14/96.

Directive 94/67 has been implemented by the Environmental Protection Act (Prescribed Processes and Substances) (Amendment) (Hazardous Waste Incineration) Regulations 1998, SI 1998/767 which came into force on 13 April 1998.

Latest position

In December 1996 Environment Ministers asked the Commission to produce proposals to update the control of waste incineration. The Commission circulated a discussion paper on proposals for an amending Directive requiring separate collection of hazardous wastes from households and municipal sources. In October 1998 the Commission proposed a Directive to extend controls to most forms of waste not covered by the 1994 Directive to reduce further emissions from waste incinerators, particularly dioxins and furans, mercury, cadmium and acid gases (COM (98)558OJC 372 2.12.98 p. 11). In December 1997 the Commission proposed an amending Directive to extend the control of toxic emissions to discharges to water (COM (97)604 OJC13 17.1.98 p. 6). The Council of Environment Ministers in June 1999 reached a political agreement on an amended proposal for a Directive on the incineration of waste which now incorporates a former proposal for a Directive amending Directive 94/67 (COM (99)330) and a Common Position in November 1999 (Common Position No. 6/2000 OJC 25 28.1.2000 p. 17).

8.2.9 Implementation of Environmental Directives

91/692/EEC: Council Directive of 23 December 1991 standardising and rationalising reports on the implementation of certain Directives relating to the environment (OJ L337 31.12.91 p. 48).

Amended, for example, Directive 82/884/EEC.

Implemented by Part II of the Environmental Protection Act 1990, the Waste Management Licensing Regulations 1994, SI 1994/1056 and the Waste Management Regulations 1996, SI 1996/634.

8.2.10 Habitats Directive

Council Directive 92/43/EEC of 21 May 1992 on the conservation of natural habitats and of wild fauna and flora (OJ L206 22.07.92 p. 7) and amending Directive 97/62/EC of 27 October 1997 taking account of technical and scientific progress (OJ L305 8.11.97 p. 42).

The Directive seeks to achieve bio-diversity through conservation. Under the Directive a network of special areas of conservation are to be established across Europe. The UK has submitted a list of 340 sites as candidate SACs to the European Commission.

Implemented by the Conservation (Natural Habitats, etc.) Regulations 1994, SI 1994/2716 governing the designation of special areas of conservation (SACs) and special protection areas for birds (SPAs) and their protection from any development which adversely affects their integrity. The 1988 General Development Order has been replaced by the Town and Country Planning (General Permitted Development Order) 1995, SI 1995/418, with effect from 3 June 1995, to make all permitted development subject to the Conservation (Natural Habitats, etc.) Regulations.

8.2.11 Wild Birds Directive

79/409/EEC: Council Directive of 2 April 1979 on the conservation of wild birds (OJ L103 25.04.79 p. 1).

Amended by 81/854 (OJ L319 07.11.81 p. 3), 85/411 (OJ L233 30.08.85 p. 33), 86/122 (OJ L100 16.04.86 p. 22), 91/244 (OJ L115 08.05.91 p. 41), 94/24 (OJ L164 30.06.94 p. 9) and 97/49 (OJ L223 13.8.97 p. 9).

The Directive prescribed detailed requirements on the system of species protection to be adopted by each Member State.

Implemented by the Wildlife and Countryside Act 1981, which created a number of criminal offences and legal protection for sites of special scientific interest, the Conservation (National Habitats, etc.) Regulations 1994, SI 1994/2716 and the Wildlife and Countryside Act 1981 (Amendment) Regulations 1995, SI 1995/2825.

8.2.12 Air Quality Limits Directive

80/779/EEC: Council Directive of 15 July 1980 on air quality limit values and guide values for sulphur dioxide and suspended particulates (OJ L229 30.08.80 p. 30).

Amended by 81/857 (OJ L319 07.11.81 p. 18), 89/427 (OJ L201 14.07.89 p. 53) 90/656 (OJ L353 17.12.90 p. 59), and 91/692 (OJ L377 31.12.91 p. 48).

The Directive specified maximum concentration values for sulphur dioxide emissions at ground level and in smoke as suspended particulates.

Implemented by the Air Quality Standards Regulations 1989, SI 1989/317, Part I Environmental Protection Act 1990, the Clean Air Act 1993 and the Air Quality Standards (Amendment) Regulations 1995, SI 1995/3146.

Note the UK's National Air Quality Strategy of March 1997 and the Air Quality Regulations 1997, SI 1997/3043 which introduced the system of local air quality management under Part IV of the Environment Act 1995. The Labour Government undertook a review of the National Air Quality Strategy prior to the publication of its Air Quality Strategy in January 2000.

96/62/EC: Council Directive of 27 September 1996 on ambient air quality assessment and management (OJ L296 21.11.96 p. 55). A framework Directive setting out measures to harmonise air quality management, monitoring and provision of information on air quality. A series of Directives will set standards for individual pollutants.

99/30/EC: Council Directive of 22 April 1999 relating to limit values for sulphur dioxide, nitrogen dioxide and oxides of nitrogen, particulate matter and lead in ambient air (OJ L163 29.6.99 p. 41).

Latest position

Council Decision of 27 January 1997 establishing a reciprocal exchange of information and data on ambient air quality in Member States (OJ L35

5.2.97 p. 14). The Commission has proposed an EU strategy to reduce acidification by setting national emission ceilings for pollutants (COM (97)88 OJC 190 21.6.97 p. 9). The Commission has also proposed a Directive imposing limits for benzene and carbon monoxide which represent reductions of 70 per cent and up to a third respectively (COM (98)591 OJC 53 24.2.99 p. 8). The Parliament provided its comments in December 1999 (OJC 194 11.7.2000 p. 56). The Council of Ministers adopted a Common Position (No. 29/2000 OJC 195 11.7.2000 p. 1), as a result of which the proposed Directive has been amended (COM (2000)223). The Commission has adopted a further proposal for a Directive under the 96/62 framework Directive prescribing national ceilings for ambient levels of ozone in the air (COM (99)125). The Portuguese Presidency hopes to be able to reach a compromise before the June Council meeting. On 22 June 2000 Ministers agreed a proposed Directive imposing ceilings on emissions of sulphur dioxide, nitrogen dioxide, volatile organic compounds and ammonia from existing plants.

8.2.13 Diesel Emissions Directive

88/77/EEC: Council Directive of 3 December 1987 on the approximation of the laws of the Member States relating to the measures to be taken against the emission of gaseous pollutants from diesel engines for use in vehicles (OJ L036 09.02.88 p. 33). The Directive applies to vehicles over 3.5 tonnes with diesel engines.

Amended by 91/542/EEC (OJ L295 25.10.91 p. 1) and by 96/1/EC of 22 January 1996 (OJ L040 17.02.96 p.l).

Implemented by the Motor Vehicles (Type Approval) (Amendment) Regulations 1997, SI 1997/191.

97/68/EC (OJ L59 27.2.98 p. 1) Directive on the approximation of the laws of Member States relating to measures against the emission of gaseous and particulate pollutants from internal combustion engines to be installed in non-road mobile machinery.

Implemented by the Non-Road Mobile Machinery (Emission of Gaseous and Particulate Pollutants) Regulations 1999, SI 1999/1053.

99/96/EC: Parliament and Council Directive of 13 December 1999 on the approximation of the laws of the Member States on measures to be taken against the emission of gaseous and particulate pollutants from compression ignition engines and from positive ignition engines fuelled with natural gas or liquified petroleum for use in vehicles and amending Directive 88/77/EC (OJ L44 16.2.2000 p. 1).

2000/25/EC: Parliament and Council Directive on action to be taken against the emission of gaseous and particulate pollutants by engines intended to power agricultural or forestry tractors (OJ L173 12.7.2000).

Latest position

Ministers reached political agreement on a proposed Directive on emission standards for heavy vehicles at the Brussels Environment Council on 21 December 1998.

8.2.14 Vehicular Pollution Directive

94/12/EC: Council and Parliament Directive of 23 March 1994 (OJ L100 19.04.94 p. 42) relating to measures to be taken against air pollution from emissions from motor vehicles.

96/44/EC: Commission Directive of 1 July 1996 (OJ L210 20.8.96 p. 25) on the approximation of the laws of Member States relating to measures to be taken against air pollution from motor vehicle emissions.

98/69/EC: Council and Parliament Directive of 13 October 1998 (OJ L350 28.12.98 p. 1) relating to measures to be taken against air pollution by emissions from motor vehicles.

99/94/EC: Parliament and Council Directive of 13 December 1999 on the availability of consumer information on fuel economy and the emission of carbon dioxide in the marketing of new passenger cards (OJ L12 18.1.2000 p. 16).

Latest position

The Commission has reached a voluntary agreement with the European Automobile Manufacturers' Association to reduce carbon dioxide emissions from new cars which was endorsed by Ministers at the Luxembourg Council meeting on 6 October 1998 (see COM (98)495) and has issued a Recommendation on the reduction of CO_2 emissions from passenger cares (OJ L40 13.2.99 p. 49). Similar agreements have been reached with the Korean Automobile Manufacturers' Association (OJ L100 20.4.2000 p. 55) and the Japanese Automobile Manufacturers' Association (OJ L100 20.4.2000 p. 57). The Commission has a proposal for a scheme to monitor emissions of CO_2 from new passenger cars (COM (98)348 OJC 231 23.7.98 p. 6) which has been amended (COM (99)58 OJC 83 25.3.99 p. 9) in the light of the Common Position adopted by Ministers in February 1999 (Common Position No.18/1999 OJC 123 4.5.99 p. 13). The

Parliament offered amendments in December 1999 (OJC 194 11.7.2000 p. 46). The Commission has provided an opinion on the Parliament's amendments to the Common Position (COM (2000)44) and has proposed a Directive on measures to be taken against air pollution by emissions from motor vehicles (COM (2000)42).

8.2.15 Environmental Impact Assessment Directive

Council Directive 85/337/EEC of 27 June 1985 on the assessment of the effects of certain public and private projects on the environment (OJ L175 05.07.85 p. 40).

Implemented by the Town and Country Planning (Environmental Impact Assessment) (England and Wales) Regulations 1999, SI 1999/293 and the Transport and Works (Assessment of Environmental Effects) Regulations 1995, SI 1995/1541. The Offshore Petroleum Production and Pipe-lines (Assessment of Environmental Effects) 1998, SI 1998/968 came into force on 30 April 1998. The Environmental Assessment (Forestry) (England and Wales) Regulations 1999, SI 1999/2228 came into force on 6 September 1999. The Public Gas Transporter Pipeline Works (Environmental Impact Assessment) Regulations 1999, SI 1999/1672 came into force on 15 July 1999.

Amending Directive 97/11/EC of 3 March 1997 (OJ L73 14.3.97 p. 5) amends the 1985 Directive by extending the categories of developments requiring an environmental impact assessment and introducing new rules for determining when environmental assessments are required and their content.

Implemented by the Transport and Works (Assessment of Environmental Effects) Regulations 1998, SI 1998/2226; the Offshore Petroleum Production and Pipelines (Assessment of Environmental Effects) Regulations 1999, SI 1999/360; the Environmental Impact Assessment (Fish Farming in Marine Waters) Regulations 1999, SI 1999/367; the Highways (Assessment of Environmental Effects) Regulations 1999, SI 1999/369; the Environmental Impact Assessment (Land Drainage Improvement Works) Regulations 1999, SI 1999/1783; the Harbour Works (Environmental Impact Assessment) Regulations 1999, SI 1999/3445; and the Environmental Impact Assessment (Forestry) (England and Wales) Regulations 1999, SI 1999/2228. See also DETR Circular 2/99 on environmental impact assessment. The DETR has consulted on draft Transport and Works Act (Applications and Objections Procedure) Rules, proposed Water Resources (Environmental Impact) Regulations and the DTI has consulted on Electricity Works (Assessment of Environmental Effects) Regulations.

Latest position

The Commission has presented a re-examined proposal for a further amending Directive (COM (96)723 OJC 95 24.3.97 p. 31) and a proposal for a Directive on the assessment of the effects of certain plans and programmes on the environment (COM (96)511 OJC 129 25.4.97 p. 14) – see the amendments suggested by the Parliament OJC 341 9.11.98 p. 18 and the Commission's amended proposal (COM (99)73 OJC 83 25.3.99 p. 13). The latter would apply to structure, unitary development and local plans and to programmes in sectors such as transport, energy, waste and water management, industry, tourism. A policy debate was held at the Luxembourg Council on 24–25 June. On the basis of a compromise produced by Finnish Presidency the Environment Council on 13–14 December 1999 reached political agreement on the proposed Directive and adopted a Common Position on 30 March 2000 (Common Position No. 25/2000 OJC 137 16.5.2000 p. 11).

8.2.16 New Municipal Waste Incinerator Directive

89/369/EEC: Council Directive of 8 June 1989 on the prevention of air pollution from new municipal waste incineration plants (OJ L163 14.06.89 p. 32).

The Directive introduces tougher emission standards for incinerators authorised after 1 December 1990. A Directive is expected to extend the emissions standards prescribed by the Hazardous Waste Incineration Directive to new incinerators.

Implemented by Part I of the Environmental Protection Act 1990.

Latest position

The Commission has produced a draft Directive on the incineration of all non-hazardous waste which will replace the 1989 Directive COM (98)558 OJC 372 2.12.98 p. 11. A political agreement was reached at the Council of Ministers in June and a Common Position in November 1999. The Parliament has suggested amendments on which the Commission has provided an opinion (COM (2000)280).

8.2.17 Ozone Pollution Directive

Council Directive 92/72/EEC of 21 September 1992 on air pollution by ozone (OJ L297 13.10.92 p. 1). Implemented by the Ozone Monitoring and Information Regulations 1994, SI 1994/440. 1994 EC Regulations on ozone-depleting substances have been implemented by the Environmental Protection (Controls on Substances that Deplete the Ozone Layer) Regulations 1996, S1 1996/506.

8.2.18 Agriculture and the environment

Council Regulation (EEC) No 2078/92 of 30 June 1992 on agricultural production methods compatible with the requirements of the protection of the environment and the maintenance of the countryside (OJ L215 30.07.92 p. 85).

8.2.19 Risks of existing substances

Council Regulation (EEC) No 793/93 of 23 March 1993 on the evaluation and control of the risks of existing substances (OJ L084 05.04.93 p. 1).

8.2.20 Packaging and Packaging Waste Directive

Council Directive 94/62/EC of 20 December 1994 (OJ L365 31.12.94 p. 10).

The Directive encourages recycling and prescribes minimum common standards to be achieved throughout the Union. It must be implemented by Member States by 1 July 1996. By July 2001 Member States must recover 50–65 per cent and recycle 25–45 per cent by weight of all packaging waste. The targets will be tightened thereafter. To meet the targets each Member State is required to establish systems for the return or collection of used packaging from consumers and the reuse or recovery of packaging waste. After 1997, only packaging complying with the requirements of the Directive will be allowed on the European market. Commission Decision of 28 January 1997 establishes the identification system for packaging materials pursuant to the Directive (OJ L50 20.2.97 p. 28). The Commission has also published a draft Directive to introduce standard symbols for use on 'recyclable' and 'reusable' packaging.

Implemented by the Producer Responsibility Obligations (Packaging Waste) Regulations 1997, SI 1997/648, under the Environment Act 1995 which came into effect on 6.3.97 as amended by the Producer Responsibility (Packaging Waste) (Amendment) Regulations 1999, SI 1999/1361 and the Producer Responsibility (Packaging Waste) (Amendment) (No 2) Regulations 1999, SI 1999/3447.

Latest position

The Commission has produced a discussion paper proposing increases in the minimum recycling and recovery rates for packaging waste as the basis for a draft Directive by the end of 1999.

8.2.21 Landfill of Waste Directive

Council Directive 99/457/EC of 22 April 1999 (OJ L182 16.7.99 p. 1).

Latest position

The DETR is consulting on the implementation of the Directive at present.

8.2.22 Integrated Pollution Prevention and Control Directive

Council Directive 96/61/EC(OJ L257 10.10.96 p. 26) provides a general framework for integrated pollution prevention and control and promotes the principle of sustainable development. It will apply to new installations from October 1999 and to existing installations from October 2007. The Commission has begun the preparation of technical guidance on the industrial processes covered by the Directive.

Implemented by the Pollution Prevention and Control (England and Wales) Regulations 2000, SI 2000/1973.

Latest position

The Commission has circulated a consultation paper on the extension of IPPC to smaller industrial operations which are largely excluded from the Directive and has included the proposal in the legislative programme for 1997. However, the informal meeting of Environment Ministers on 18–20 April 1997 requested the Commission to prepare a wider strategy on environmental controls for small- and medium-sized enterprises. The Commission has begun to draft guidance on the 'best available techniques' for specific industrial sectors. See the Commission Decision of 31 May 1999 on a questionnaire relating to the 1996 Directive (OJ L148 15.6.99 p. 39)

8.2.23 Civil Liability for Environmental Damage

A draft Directive in 1989 proposed a strict liability regime for damage to the environment by waste (COM (89)282; OJC 251 4.10.89). The draft was revised in 1991 (COM (91)219; OJC 192 23.7.91 p. 6) but was not proceeded. In 1993 the Commission issued for consultation the Green Paper on 'Civil Liability for Environmental Damage' (COM (93)47). (UK Government Response 8 October 1993 and Law Society response).

The key objective of a community wide system of environmental liability would be to remove differences in civil liability regimes in Member States which might distort competition. The Green paper proposed the application of strict liability for damage; the imposition of obligations on persons responsible to pay for the restoration of damage to the environment; and where a number of separate polluters are responsible for damage or where a particular polluter cannot pay because he is uninsured or insolvent, the clean-up and compensation obligations should be funded by joint compensation fund arrangements involving compulsory levies on various industry sectors.

The Commission's 1995 Work Programme suggested that the focus is now on the production of a communication on the introduction of a framework system of civil liability for environmental damage. In 1994 the Commission launched two studies which would serve as the basis for decision on the guiding principles for legislation: a comparative analysis of the rules governing liability for environmental damage in individual Member States (undertaken by McKenna & Co.); and analysis of the economic impact of introducing liability for environmental damage. The studies were released in April 1996 and are available from Unit B3, DGX1, European Commission, Rue de la Loi B1049 Brussels.

Latest position

The former Environment Commissioner Ritt Bjerregaard led a debate within the Commission focusing on three possible options as a way forward: a European Directive establishing a liability regime to cover personal injury, damage to property and environmental damage; a general Directive covering environmental damage alone; or accession to the Lugano Convention on civil liability for environmental damage. The latter would impose strict liability and would allow citizens' action. All three options are opposed currently by France, Germany and the UK. On 9 February 2000 the Commission adopted a White Paper on environmental liability COM (2000)66 on which comments are requested by 1 July.

8.2.24 Noise

Directive 2000/14/EC: Council and Parliament Directive of 8 May 2000 on the approximation of the laws of Member States relating to the noise emission in the environment by equipment for use outdoors (OJ L162 3.7.2000 p. 1). The first product of the 1996 Green Paper on Future Noise Policy (COM (96)540) and the Commission's proposal for a framework Directive (COM (98)46 OJC 124 22.4.98 p. 1).

8.2.25 Emissions Trading

In March 2000 the Commission issued a Green Paper (COM (2000)87) for comment on the institution of a system for emissions trading within the EU for the energy sector and big industrial installations. The scheme is intended to provide a means of enabling the EU to reduce the emission of greenhouse gases to which it is committed under the 1997 Kyoto Protocol.

APPENDIX 1

List of potentially contaminative land uses[1]

1. Agriculture: burial of diseased livestock.

2. Extractive industry: coal mines, coal preparation plants, oil refineries and petrochemicals; mineral workings, mineral processing works. (NB: includes loading, transport, sorting, forming and packaging and similar operations.)

3. Energy industry: gas works; coal carbonisation plants; oil refineries; power stations.

4. Production of metals: metal processing; heavy engineering; electroplating and metal finishing. (NB: includes scrap metal treatments.)

5. Production of non-metals and their products: mineral processing; asbestos works; cement, lime and gypsum manufacture, brickworks and associated processes.

6. Glass-making and ceramics – including glazes and vitreous enamel.

7. Production and use of chemicals.

8. Engineering and manufacturing processes: manufacture of metal goods (including mechanical engineering industrial plant or steel work, motor vehicles, ships, railway or tramway vehicles, etc.); storage, manufacture or testing of explosives, propellants, small arms, etc.; electrical and electronic equipment manufacture and repair.

9. Food processing industry: pet foods or animal feedstuffs; processing of animal by-products (including rendering or maggot farming but excluding slaughterhouses and butchering).

10. Paper, pulp and printing industry.

---

[1]   Listed in First DoE Consultation Paper: 3 May 1991.

11. Timber and timber products industry: chemical treatment and coating of timber and timber products.

12. Textile industry: tanning, dressing, fellmongering or other process for preparing, treating or working leather; fulling, bleaching, dyeing or finishing fabrics or fibres; manufacture of carpets or other textile floor-coverings (including linoleum works).

13. Rubber industry: processing natural or synthetic rubber (including tyre manufacture or retreading).

14. Infrastructure: marshalling, dismantling, repairing or maintenance of railway rolling-stock; dismantling, repairing or maintenance of marine vessels (including hovercraft); dismantling, repairing or maintenance of road transport or road haulage vehicles; dismantling, repairing or maintenance of air and space transport systems.

15. Waste disposal: treating sewage or other effluent or storage, treatment or disposal of sludge (including sludge from water treatment works); treating, keeping, depositing or disposing of waste including scrap (to include infilled canal basins, docks or river courses); storage or disposal of radioactive materials.

16. Miscellaneous: dry-cleaning operations; laboratories for educational or research purposes; demolition of buildings, plant or equipment for any of the activities mentioned above.

Suggested wording for sample preliminary enquiries

[*Enquiries 1–6 are a set of enquiries which could be used in any transaction. Some of the sub-parts could be omitted if it was clear that they were irrelevant, e.g. cooling towers (legionella), PCBs and electrical transformers, etc. as these may be more appropriate for commercial properties. Their significance in domestic cases should not be ignored, however.*

Enquiries for use in commercial transactions – or residential transactions which may be thought of as 'high risk' – follow.

The replies to the enquiries may raise issues beyond the competence of the solicitor, and in appropriate circumstances it may be necessary to refer the answers to an independent consultant for interpretation. At the very least, the replies should put a solicitor on notice of potential problems which may require further specialist advice or investigation.

In any event, the answers should not be relied on as conclusive proof of the state of the land to be bought; further on-site investigations may have to be recommended to the client.]

1. Uses of the property

(a) Please give details of the current use of and the activities carried on at the property.

(b) Has there been a change in the nature of the use of or activities carried on at the property during the seller's ownership or occupation? If so, please give details.

(c) Please give details of the use of, and activities carried on at, the property prior to the seller's period of ownership or occupation, and, in particular, whether the property has ever been used for any one or more of the following:

[delete as required]

Agriculture: burial of diseased livestock.

Extractive industry: coal mines, coal preparation plants, oil refineries and petrochemicals; mineral workings, mineral processing works. (NB: includes loading, transport, sorting, forming and packaging and similar operations.)

Energy industry: gas works; coal carbonisation plants; oil refineries; power stations.

Production of metals: metal processing; heavy engineering; electroplating and metal finishing. (NB: includes scrap metal treatments.)

Production of non-metals and their products: mineral processing; asbestos works; cement, lime and gypsum manufacture, brickworks and associated processes.

Glass-making and ceramics – including glazes and vitreous enamel.

Production and use of chemicals.

Engineering and manufacturing processes: manufacture of metal goods (including mechanical engineering industrial plant or steel work, motor vehicles, ships, railway or tramway vehicles, etc.); storage, manufacture or testing of explosives, propellants, small arms, etc.; electrical and electronic equipment manufacture and repair.

Food processing industry: pet foods or animal feedstuffs; processing of animal by-products (including rendering or maggot farming but excluding slaughterhouses and butchering).

Paper, pulp and printing industry.

Timber and timber products industry: chemical treatment and coating of timber and timber products.

Textile industry: tanning, dressing, fellmongering or other process for preparing, treating or working leather; fulling, bleaching, dyeing or finishing fabrics or fibres; manufacture of carpets or other textile floor-coverings (including linoleum works).

178

Rubber industry: processing natural or synthetic rubber (including tyre manufacture or retreading).

Infrastructure: marshalling, dismantling, repairing or maintenance of railway rolling-stock; dismantling, repairing or maintenance of marine vessels (including hovercraft); dismantling, repairing or maintenance of road transport or road haulage vehicles; dismantling, repairing or maintenance of air and space transport systems.

Waste disposal: treating sewage or other effluent or storage, treatment or disposal of sludge (including sludge from water treatment works); treating, keeping, depositing or disposing of waste including scrap (to include infilled canal basins, docks or river courses); storage or disposal of radioactive materials.

Miscellaneous: dry-cleaning operations; laboratories for educational or research purposes; demolition of buildings, plant or equipment for any of the activities mentioned above.

(d) Is any neighbouring property used for:

any industrial purposes which, in the event of a major accident, may require immediate evacuation of the property?

any prescribed process within the meaning of Part I of the Environmental Protection Act 1990?

any purposes involving handling hazardous substances?

[*Practitioners may feel that they need to define phrases such as 'hazardous substances' along the following lines:*

any substance or substances referred to in EC Directive 76/464/EEC List I and List II of families and groups of substances as follows:

List I
organohalogen compounds and substances which may form such compounds in the aquatic environment;
organophosphorus compounds;
organotin compounds;
substances in respect of which it has been proved that they possess carcinogenic properties in or via the aquatic environment;
mercury and its compounds;
cadmium and its compounds;
persistent mineral oils and hydrocarbons of petroleum origin; and

persistent synthetic substances which may float, remain in suspension or sink and which may interfere with any use of water.

List II

The following metalloids and metals and their compounds:

zinc	*copper*	*nickel*	*chromium*
lead	*selenium*	*arsenic*	*antimony*
molybdenum	*titanium*	*tin*	*barium*
beryllium	*boron*	*uranium*	*vanadium*
cobalt	*thallium*	*tellurium*	*silver*

Biocides and their derivatives not appearing in List I.

Substances which have a deleterious effect on the taste and/or smell of the products for human consumption derived from the aquatic environment, and compounds liable to give rise to such substances in water.

Toxic or persistent organic compounds of silicon, and substances which may give rise to such compounds in water, excluding those which are biologically harmless or are rapidly converted in water into harmless substances.
Inorganic compounds of phosphorus and elemental phosphorus.

Non-persistent mineral oils and hydrocarbons of petroleum origin.

Cyanides, fluorides.

Substances which have an adverse effect on the oxygen balance, particularly: ammonia, nitrates; and/or

substances controlled by Directives created pursuant to the said Directive 76/464/EEC together with asbestos and any other substance compound or element generally regarded as being toxic and/or harmful and/or hazardous to health; and/or

noxious gases – those gases which by virtue of their physical or chemical properties are considered to be toxic, carcinogenic, irritant, asphyxiant, flammable or explosive and may pose a risk to human health or the built environment, including inter alia: methane (and landfill gas), carbon monoxide, carbon dioxide, hydrogen cyanide,

*hydrogen sulphide, phosphine, sulphur dioxide, formalde-
hyde and radon*

though this may be considered as going too far.]

(e) Are there any storage tanks over or underground on the property or on any adjoining or neighbouring property? If so please provide details of:

- their location;

- their age and condition;

- any substances stored in them, including details of nature and volume;

- any spillages or leakages from them;

- facilities for inspection;

- results of any inspections carried out.

(f) Are there, or has there ever been, any electricity sub-station trans-formers, capacitors or other oil-filled electrical switchgear containing PCBs located on the property or any neighbouring property? If so, please give details of their location and condition and any steps proposed or taken to remove them from the property.

(g) Are any neighbouring properties used, or have they ever been used, for any of the uses mentioned above or for any other purpose which does or may lead to interference of an environmental nature on the property?

(h) Is the seller aware of any proposal to use the property or any neighbouring property for any of the uses mentioned above or for any other purpose which does or may lead to interference of an environmental nature on the property?

2. Condition of the property

(a) Is there any contamination or pollution on the property, or in or on any adjoining or neighbouring property? If so, please give details.

(b) Is there any stained soil or significant evidence of damage to vegetation on the property?

(c) Are there currently, or have there been previously, any flooring, drains, or walls located within the property that are stained by substances other than water or are emanating noxious odours?

(d) Please confirm that no hazardous substances have been used in the structure or fabric of any building on the property. If such confirmation cannot be given please give full details of the materials used and of any action taken to identify and remove any such materials from the property.

(e) Has the seller any reason for believing or suspecting that some potential liability or detriment arising from pollution or related environmental matters, whether of the property or neighbouring property, may attach to the owners or occupiers of the property at any foreseeable future date?

(f) Please confirm that no polluting incident has taken place, or is taking place on the property. If such an incident is taking, or has taken, place please provide the following particulars:

- full details of the accident or incident;

- copies of any reports, correspondence, court orders, notices or recommendations relating to the accident or incident;

- details of any remedial work carried out, including certificates of satisfactory completion.

3. Waste

(a) Is there any waste on the property? If so, please indicate the quantity, and whether it is industrial, commercial, domestic or special waste.

(b) Is the property being or has it ever been used as, or does it or has it ever comprised in whole or in part a waste landfill site? If so, please provide copies of any Waste Disposal or Waste Management Licences granted in respect of the property and any reports or material correspondence relating thereto. In particular, please specify what measures have been taken to close the landfill, and what steps are being or have been taken to limit, control, contain and/or monitor any emissions of any substance likely to emanate from the property.

[*methane emissions, particularly*]

(c) Has any adjoining or neighbouring land been used in any way (including, but not limited to, use for the deposit, disposal or treatment of waste) which might impact on the state and condition of the property by pollution or contamination, either directly or indirectly (e.g. by watercourses or otherwise)? If so, please provide details.

(d) Is the seller aware of any proposal to deposit waste on the property or any adjoining land?

4. Inspections, complaints, notices and proceedings

(a) Have there been any complaints from or disputes with the Environment Agency, the local authority, any other statutory authority or any other person regarding the state and condition of the property or the use of the property, or any neighbouring property? If so, please supply full details.

(b) Has the Environment Agency or the local authority inspected the property or given notice of its intended inspection of the property or any neighbouring property? Please supply copies of any survey or test results carried out in relation to the property pursuant to such inspection.

(c) Has any notice been served in respect of the property or any neighbouring property by the Environment Agency, the local authority or any other statutory authority which is of current effect? If so, please give details of such notices and any appeals.

(d) Is there any reason why any statutory body might enter the property or any neighbouring property and/or take any steps to avoid pollution to the environment or harm to health, or any indication that the authority might do any of those things? If so, please supply full details.

(e) Are there any proceedings in progress or in prospect, or any circumstances which may result in such proceedings, which have led or may lead to the owner of the property being liable to fines, penalties and/or costs of remedial measures? If so, please supply full details.

[*criminal and clean-up liability*]

(f) Are there any proceedings in progress or in prospect, or any circumstances which may result in such proceedings, which have led or may lead to the owner of the property being liable to pay damages in respect of any environmental incident, accident, escape or emission? If so, please supply full details.

[*civil liability*]

(g) Has the seller ever had cause to make a complaint about any neighbouring property or institute, or bring any claim, action or proceedings against the owners of any neighbouring property in respect of any environmental matter?

5. Reports and investigations

(a) Have there been any soil or site investigations, environmental surveys or samplings of the soil/water or atmosphere carried out on the property or any neighbouring property, whether by the local authority or any other person? If so, please provide details, and provide a copy of any relevant report.

(b) Has any environmental audit, investigation or environmental assessment been carried out in relation to the property or any proposed use of or development of the property? If so, please supply a copy of the same.

6. Miscellaneous

(a) Have any buildings on the property ever been associated with sick building illnesses or other related problems?

(b) Have any construction debris, hazardous substances, unidentified waste materials, tyres, automotive or industrial batteries or any other waste materials, rubbish, debris or refuse been dumped above ground, buried and/or burned on the property?

(c) Have any current or past buildings on the property included material containing asbestos (*inter alia* as roofing, cladding or insulation)? If so, please give full details of its age, condition, quantity and location.

(d) Has any urea formaldehyde foam insulation been used within the fabric of any building on the property? If so, please give full details of its age, condition, quantity and location.

(e) (i) Is the property located in an area which is known or thought to be at risk from radon gas?
   (ii) Have any investigations been carried out on the property in relation to the possible presence of radon gas? If so, when and what were the results?
   (iii) Has any action been taken as a result of any radon investigation results? If so, what were they and were they successful?

(f) Are there any cooling towers or evaporative condensers on the property which may give rise to any risk of legionella? If so, please give details of any steps taken to maintain them.

(g) Does the property lie within 150 metres of any overhead or underground electricity cables transmitting electrical power in excess of 132,000 volts?

(h)   Have any complaints about noise been made or received in relation to the property or any neighbouring property? If so, please give full details.

(j)   Please confirm that no lead, PCBs or any other deleterious or potentially deleterious materials have been used on, or in the structure or fabric of any building on, the property. If such confirmation cannot be given please give full details of the materials used and of any action taken to remove these materials from the property.

[*Some of these enquiries may overlap with earlier ones, or those that follow. Unnecessary duplications should be avoided.*]

[*The following enquiries relate to commercial transactions or residential transactions of high risk.*]

7.   Emissions and deposits

(a)   Are any emissions or deposits made to air, water, land or sewer from any activity carried out on the property, whether in liquid, solid or vapour form? If so, please provide details of nature, type, rate, frequency, quantity and location of any such emission or deposit.

[*This may seem repetitive of other enquiries, but is intended to focus both seller's and buyer's attention on the possible need for authorisation for any such emission, and lead into Enquiry 8.*]

Not all emissions need a formal licence, but they may be problematic if they occur, e.g. smoke may not require an LAAPC licence, but may be a statutory nuisance. It is vital to know what emissions are occurring and where in case the buyer is taken to inherit any nuisances or problems by failing to take steps to stop them.]

8.   Licences, permits and authorisations

(a)   Are any activities carried on at the property for which is required any licence, permit, authorisation or consent issued under any environmental legislation? If so, please confirm that all such licences, etc. have been obtained, are currently in force and supply copies.

(b)   Please confirm that all conditions or obligations attached to any licences, permissions, authorisations and consents have been and are being complied with, that the seller is not aware of any proposals to vary or revoke any such consent or any circumstances likely to lead to the variation or revocation of any such consent.

(c) Please give details of any appeals or other proceedings, correspondence, notices, discussions or negotiations with any relevant body with respect to the grant, revocation, renewal or variation of any contract, agreement, consent, permit, licence, authorisation or arrangement relating to any environmental matter on the property or any neighbouring property.

[*This enquiry is intended to focus on those emissions and other activities for which formal authorisation is required – IPC/IPPC/ LAAPC processes, waste deposit and treatment, water abstraction, water discharges, discharges of trade effluent to sewer, authorisations for radioactive material and waste and hazardous substances. Are the licences in existence, in force and complied with?*

Some may be transferred to the buyer, others may have to be the subject of an application by the buyer.]

9. Hazardous substances

Are there, or have there ever been, any radioactive substances or wastes, any explosives or other hazardous materials present, used, kept or disposed of on the property or any neighbouring property? If so, please give details of the substances, their quantities, dates of storage, use, etc. and any steps taken or proposed to remove them from the property.

10. Environmental insurance

(a) Does the property have the benefit of any environmental insurance? If so, please supply a copy thereof.

(b) Has an application ever been made for such insurance cover, whether or not it was successful? If so, please provide a copy of the proposal.

APPENDIX 3

Suggested lease clauses

[*A variant of this clause was used in leases granted by the Welsh Development Agency to tenants on an industrial estate. When the Welsh Development Agency was prosecuted for water pollution offences, it successfully defended itself on other grounds. In the course of the judgment, however, reference was made to the lease clause and the comment was made that the clause had the effect of passing the obligation of compliance with water pollution legislation on to the tenant, thus exonerating the landlord.*

See: *National Rivers Authority* v. *Welsh Development Agency* [1993] EGCS 160.

The clause could be readily adapted to meet other forms of potential environmental liability besides water pollution, to which this clause is exclusively directed.

It should be borne in mind, though, that it is against public policy to contract out of, or indemnify oneself against, a criminal liability, so it remains to be seen what effect this sort of lease clause may have.]

'Not to discharge or permit or suffer to be discharged any solid matter or any fluid of a poisonous or noxious nature (with the exception of human sewage) from the demised premises into any drains or sewers as aforesaid that does in fact destroy, sicken or injure the fish in or contaminate or pollute the water of any stream or river and further not to do or omit or permit or suffer to be done any act or thing whereby the waters of any stream or river may be polluted or the composition thereof so changed as to render the landlord liable to any action or proceedings by any person whatsoever ... '

APPENDIX 4

Suggested agreement on liabilities for contaminated land

SCHEDULE

Agreement on liability for remediation under Part IIA EPA 1990

Part I

1   BACKGROUND

The Parties acknowledge that they are or may be held to be responsible for all or part of the costs of a Remediation Action in respect of the Property and have agreed the basis on which they wish to divide that responsibility

2   DEFINITIONS AND INTERPRETATION

In this schedule:

2.1   'Body of Competent Authority' means the body specified as being the regulator of contaminated land in accordance with Part IIA of the Environmental Protection Act 1990, the Contaminated Land (England) Regulations 2000 and all and any guidance notes circulars and other documentation issued thereunder or any statutory modification or re-enactment thereof

2.2   'Buyer' means

2.3   'Exclusion' 'Apportionment' and 'Attribution' have the meanings attributed to them in the Contaminated Land (England) Regulations 2000

2.4   'Legislation Relating to Contaminated Land' means Part IIA of the

Environmental Protection Act 1990 the Contaminated Land (England) Regulations 2000 and all and any guidance notes circulars and other documentation issued thereunder or any statutory modification or re-enactment thereof

2.5 'Limitation On The Recovery Of Remediation Costs' has the meaning attributed to it by Part IIA of the Environmental Protection Act 1990, the Contaminated Land (England) Regulations 2000 and all and any guidance notes circulars and other documentation issued thereunder or any statutory modification or re-enactment thereof

2.6 'the Parties' means [the Seller and the Buyer or *(as the case may be)*]

[2.7 'the Property' means [all of the Properties *or* Property No.(s.) *(numbers)*]

2.8 'Remediation Action; means any action specified as being required to cause land to cease to be contaminated within the meaning of Part IIA of the Environmental Protection Act 1990, the Contaminated Land (England) Regulations 2000 and all and any guidance notes circulars and other documentation issued thereunder or any statutory modification or re-enactment thereof

2.9 'Remediation Notice' means the document served by the Body of Competent Authority which specifies any Remediation Action

2.10 'Seller' means

3 APPORTIONMENT OF LIABILITIES

3.1 If a Body of Competent Authority serves a Remediation Notice in respect of the Property on persons which include the Parties the provisions of this paragraph of this schedule shall come into effect

3.2 The Parties shall pay the costs of any Remediation Action or part thereof in accordance with the provisions set out in Part II of this schedule

3.3 The Parties confirm that they are content for the provisions of Part II of this schedule to be applied to the costs of the Remediation Action and that a copy of this agreement may be provided to the Body of Competent Authority concerned

3.4 The Parties confirm and accept that the provisions of Part II of this schedule shall be applied and that the Body of Competent Authority shall as between the Parties make such determinations on the questions of Exclusion Apportionment and Attribution as shall give effect to the terms of Part II of this schedule and that the Body of Competent Authority shall not as between the Parties apply the tests set out in any Legislation Relating to Contaminated Land for the time being in force

3.5 The Parties confirm that the transaction the subject of this agreement and the terms of Part II of this schedule are not intended nor are they part of any larger series of transactions which are intended to have the effect of increasing the share of costs theoretically to be borne by any person who would benefit from a Limitation on The Recovery of Remediation Costs and that the Body of Competent Authority should not therefore seek to disregard this agreement

3.6 If the Body of Competent Authority should notwithstanding paragraph 3.5 disregard this agreement and apply the normal tests set out in any Legislation Relating to Contaminated Land for the time being in force and this has the effect that the Parties share the costs of the Remediation Action in a way other than that set out in Part II of this schedule Part II of this schedule shall nevertheless apply as between the Parties and they shall be entitled to insist on reciprocal indemnities the one against the other such that the costs of the Remediation Action shall be adjusted as between them in order to restore the financial position to that which would have prevailed had the Body of Competent Authority applied Part II of this schedule and not disregarded this agreement

4   INDEMNITY

4.1 Full details have been disclosed to the Buyer of all and any matters which may have the result that the Property be designated as contaminated land within the meaning of Part IIA of the Environmental Protection Act 1990 and the Buyer accepts and acknowledges that the Seller is therefore entitled to be excluded from the categories of person liable to contribute to the cost of any remediation works at on or under the Property and that the Buyer will bear any such liability as would otherwise have attached to the Seller

4.2 The Buyer shall indemnify and keep indemnified the Seller against any liability which may be incurred by the Seller for the costs of remediation works at on or under the Property occasioned by the failure of any body of competent authority to exclude the Seller from such liability under the terms of the said Part IIA

Part II

[*Insert substantive details of apportionment and payment of the costs of the Remediation Action agreed by the parties.*]

APPENDIX 5

Share purchase agreement

[For a commentary on these clauses, the reader is referred to the text of Chapter 4.]

THIS AGREEMENT is made the day of **[year]**

BETWEEN

1.   The Vendor

2.   The Purchaser

THE PARTIES HEREBY AGREE as follows:

1.   Interpretation

1.1   In this Agreement:

'Assets' means the assets owned by the Company and listed at Schedule [ ];

'Business' means the business owned by the Company;

'Company' means [ ] Limited registered number [ ];

'Completion' means the completion of the sale and purchase on the Completion Date;

'Disclosure Letter' means the disclosure letter written by the Vendor to the Purchaser on the date of this Agreement (including the documents annexed to it);

'Environmental Contamination' means any release, leakage, discharge, deposit, emission, spillage or other escape of Hazardous Substances into the atmosphere, water or on to land occurring or having occurred (in any case) on or from the Property and any buildings, Plant and Equipment situated therein or thereon;

'Environmental Indemnity' means the indemnity given by the Vendor to the Purchaser;

'Environmental Law' means all laws (whether statutory or common law and whether civil or criminal), insofar as they relate to the control and prevention of pollution of land, water or the atmosphere due to the release, discharge, spillage, entry, deposit, emission or other escape of Hazardous Substances or to noise, odour or other nuisances and the production, transportation, storage, treatment, recycling or disposal of waste and the protection of human health and life;

'Environmental Liabilities' means:

(i)   any fines or penalties (whenever imposed) in respect of any breaches prior to Completion by the Vendor or the Company or its predecessors in title or their officers, agents or employees of any Environmental Law and all costs and expenses reasonably incurred in connection with such proceedings;

(ii)   any liability to third parties (whenever arising) resulting wholly or partly from:

    (a)   the state or condition of the Property prior to or at Completion;

    (b)   activities or operations of the Vendor or the Company or its predecessors in title or those deriving title therefrom at the Property;

(iii)   all costs of remedial or clean-up action incurred or suffered by the Purchaser in order to meet the requirements of any competent authority or a Court of competent jurisdiction and arising in consequence of (a) or (b) above and whether carried out by the Purchaser, the competent authority or another;

(iv)   all costs of remedial or clean-up action arising in consequence of (a) or (b) above which the Independent Environmental Consultant, appointed pursuant to Clause [ ] hereof, has reported as being, in his opinion, necessary to meet the reasonable requirements of any competent authority or Court of competent jurisdiction had such authority or Court been made fully aware of the condition of the Property;

(v)   the cost of reasonable measures taken in respect of the Property to prevent or mitigate any risks presented by the Property to human health or safety, property, air quality, surface or underground water or soil by reasons of Environmental Contamination arising prior to Completion;

(vi)   for the purposes of clause (iv) above and Clause 6 and the Warranties it is agreed that the expression 'remedial and clean-up action' shall include proper investigation of the Environmental

Contamination giving rise to any Environmental Liability, removal of defective plant or structures contributing to Environmental Contamination and appropriate treatment of contaminated material, whether by destruction, removal, containment or otherwise;

'Environmental Licences' means the permits, licences, authorisations, consents or other approvals required by any Environmental Law;

'Hazardous Substances' means any organism, products, wastes, pollutants, contaminants or other substances (whether in solid or liquid form or in the form of a gas or vapour and whether alone or in combination with any other substance) which may, either alone or in combination, be harmful to man or to the life or health of any other living organisms or deleterious to the environment;

'Independent Environmental Consultant' means the independent environmental consultant appointed pursuant to Clause [ ];

'Licences' means all licences, authorisations and approvals (including but not limited to the Environmental Licences and the other permits) that are required for the exploitation of the Business;

'Property' means the real property of the Business;

'Prudent Operating Practice' means the standard of practice attained by exercising that degree of skill, diligence, prudence and foresight which could reasonably be expected from a skilled and experienced operator engaged in the same or a similar type of undertaking as or to that of the Vendor in operating the Business under the same or similar circumstances;

'Shares' means all the issued shares in the capital of the Company;

'Warranties' means the warranties, representations and undertakings on the part of the Vendor contained in Schedule I;

'Waste' means any packaged or stored substance which constitutes material or effluent or other unwanted surplus substance arising from the application of any process (whether toxic, dangerous or otherwise) which requires to be disposed of.

2.   Sale and Purchase

2.1   The Vendor as beneficial owner will sell, and the Purchaser will buy, the Shares.

2.2   Each of the Shares will be sold and bought free from any claim, charge, lien, encumbrance, equity or third-party right, and with all rights attached to it including the right for the Purchaser to receive and retain any dividends or other distributions declared, made or paid after the execution of this Agreement.

2.3   The Vendor waives all rights of pre-emption over any of the Shares conferred by the Articles of Association of the Company or otherwise.

2.4   The Purchaser shall not be obliged to complete the purchase of any of the Shares unless the purchase of all the Shares is completed simultaneously.

3.   Consideration

3.1   The Consideration for the sale of the Shares will be the sum of £[amount] ([amount] Pounds) (being £[amount] per Share); accordingly the Vendor will be entitled to receive the sum specified.

3.2   The Consideration will be paid in cash on Completion by way of a single banker's draft drawn on a Clearing Bank in favour of the Vendor's Solicitors or by such other method as may be agreed between the parties. The Vendor's Solicitors are authorised to receive the Consideration on behalf of the Vendors and payment to them will be a good and sufficient discharge to the Purchaser and the Purchaser will not be further concerned as to the application of the moneys so paid.

4.   Conduct of Business prior to Completion

4.1   The Vendor covenants and agrees that, prior to the Completion Date, it shall in respect of the Business comply with each of the following:

4.1.1   it shall conduct the Business only in the ordinary and usual course, it shall use its best endeavours to keep intact the Property, the Plant and Equipment, the Intellectual Property, the business organisation and Goodwill, and (save as otherwise agreed between the Vendor and the Purchaser) maintain good relationships with suppliers, creditors, distributors, employees, customers and others having business with them, and it shall immediately notify the Purchaser of any event or occurrence or emergency material to the Business;

4.1.2   it shall comply with the provisions of any Laws applicable to operation of the Business, and in particular any Environmental Laws, and shall make sure that none of the warranties granted hereunder are breached or otherwise materially affected;

4.1.3   it shall comply with the provisions of all Licences, the terms and conditions of all contracts to which the Vendor is a party and any requirements, obligations, covenants or like matters associated with title in the Property;

4.1.4   it shall maintain in full force and effect insurance coverage of a and amount customary in its business.

5.   Warranties by the Vendor

5.1   The Vendor:

5.1.1   hereby agrees with the Purchaser that all of the Warranties shall be repeated and shall have effect as if made and given at the Completion Date;

5.1.2   warrants, represents and undertakes to the Purchaser in the terms of the Warranties, provided however that the Purchaser shall not be entitled to claim that any fact or combination of facts constitutes a breach of any of the Warranties if and to the extent that such fact or combination of facts has been fairly and reasonably disclosed (and nothing has knowingly been withheld by the Vendor which would render them untrue, inaccurate or misleading) in the Disclosure Letter;

5.1.3   agrees that the Purchaser is entering into this Agreement in reliance on each of the Warranties and the Disclosure Letter;

5.1.4   shall indemnify the Purchaser against any reasonable costs (including legal costs on a full indemnity basis), expenses or other liabilities which it may incur, either before or after the commencement of any action, as a result of any breach of any of the Warranties;

5.1.5   undertakes that, in the event of any claim being made against it the Purchaser under the Warranties or by a third party under any clause whatsoever, it will not make any claim against any of the Employees on whom it may have relied before agreeing to any term of this Agreement or authorising any statement in the Disclosure Letter.

6.   Indemnity and Environmental Indemnity

6.1.1   The Vendor undertakes to the Purchaser that in the event of a breach of any of the Warranties, the Vendor shall pay to the Purchaser, or in the case of liability to any other person which has not been discharged, the person to whom the liability has been incurred, an amount equal to such liability or to the damages resulting to the Purchaser from such breach, whichever is the higher.

6.1.2   The Vendor hereby indemnifies the Purchaser against all Environmental Liabilities.

6.2   Each of the Warranties, Indemnities and Environmental Indemnity shall be construed as a separate warranty or indemnity, as the case may be, and shall not be limited or restricted by reference to, or inference from, the terms of any other warranty or indemnity or any other term of this Agreement.

6.3   The Environmental Indemnity shall be limited to 75 per cent of all Environmental Liabilities arising in connection with the Business provided that any such Environmental Liability occurred on or before the Completion Date. Where any incident of Environmental Contamination is or shall be discovered at the Property at any time after the Completion Date, the Purchaser shall, where there is any dispute as to the existence or scope of the Vendor's liability as a result of such incident under any Environmental Liability:

6.3.1   instruct the Independent Environmental Consultant to make such enquiries and investigations as he shall consider appropriate and to determine as soon as practicable to what extent the instant of Environmental Contamination was reasonably likely to have occurred in whole or in part on or prior to the Completion Date; and

6.3.2   instruct the Independent Environmental Consultant to determine whether the remedial and clean-up action proposed to be undertaken by the Purchaser is the minimum reasonably required in order to bring the [premises] into compliance with Environmental Law.

6.4   The Independent Environmental Consultant shall be appointed by mutual agreement of the Vendor and the Purchaser upon notification by the Purchaser to the Vendor that it wishes an Independent Environmental Consultant to be appointed to resolve any dispute as described in Clause [ ]. If the Vendor and the Purchaser shall fail to agree upon an appointee within 14 days of the Purchaser notifying the Vendor of its wish to make an appointment, either the Vendor or the Purchaser may apply to the President for the time being of the British Chambers of Commerce to appoint an Independent Expert.

6.5   The Vendor and the Purchaser shall jointly instruct the Independent Environmental Consultant to report in accordance with Clause [ ] above. The professional fees of the Independent Environmental Consultant shall be borne by the Vendor and the Purchaser proportionally in 75:25 shares respectively. The Vendor and the Purchaser shall provide such information and all necessary access to their respective properties, plant, equipment, records and personnel as the Independent Environmental Consultant shall reasonably require. The opinion of the Independent Environmental Consultant pursuant to this clause shall be conclusive and binding on the parties, but without prejudice to the right of the Purchaser to commence and serve legal proceedings to the extent that any damage to Purchaser or liability to third parties would not be eliminated by the remedial and clean-up action as determined under Clause [ ].

6.6   The Vendor hereby unconditionally and irrevocably undertakes to the Purchaser that it shall, prior to Completion or as soon as reasonably practicable thereafter (and in any event within one month of the day of Completion), remove or have removed, and dispose or have disposed from the Property in accordance with all Environmental Laws any Waste. The Vendor shall indemnify and keep indemnified the Purchaser against any and all costs, damages, fines, judgments and expenses (including legal fees) and liabilities whatsoever incurred in connection with the removal of such Waste.

6.7   Any sum due from the Vendor to the Purchaser under the Environmental Indemnity shall be paid within [ ] days of:

6.7.1   completion of any remedial and clean-up action undertaken by the Purchaser;

6.7.2   the Purchaser incurring the cost of the remedial and clean-up action carried out by any person other than the Purchaser; or

6.7.3   the date of payment of any liabilities to third parties, fines or awards (and all expenses incurred in connection therewith); provided that the Purchaser shall at the same time pay 25 per cent of any such sum due under the Environmental Indemnity.

7.   Limitations on Warranties, Indemnity and Environmental Indemnity

7.1   The Purchaser acknowledges that in entering into this Agreement it has not relied on any warranties or representations whatsoever other than the Warranties, indemnities or the Environmental Indemnity contained in this Agreement and that it has relied on the Disclosure Letter and no other warranties or representations whatsoever have been made by or on behalf of the Vendor.

7.2   The Purchaser shall not be entitled to make any claim under this Agreement (whether in contract or tort) if or to the extent that:

7.2.1　the facts, matters or circumstances in respect of which the claim arises are fairly and reasonably disclosed (and nothing has been knowingly withheld by the Vendor which would render them untrue, inaccurate or misleading) in the Disclosure Letter (or in any documents annexed to the Disclosure Letter); or

7.2.2　in respect of any claim made under the Environmental Indemnity, the claim arises or is increased as a result of the passing, or any change in, any Environmental Law made after the Completion Date; or

7.2.3　the facts, matters or circumstances in respect of which the claim arises occurred with the prior written consent of the Purchaser after the date hereof but on or before Completion.

7.3　The Purchaser shall not be entitled to make any claim under this Agreement (whether in contract or tort) unless the Purchaser gives to the Vendor written notice of the claim (giving details of the breach or nature of the claim and the Purchaser's best estimate of the amount of the claim) as soon as reasonably practicable after the Purchaser has become aware of the facts giving rise to the claim and in any event within, in the case of any claim under the Environmental Indemnity, [ ] years of the Completion Date and, in any other case, within [ ] years of the Completion Date, and commences and serves legal proceedings in respect of any such claim within [ ] months of the date any such notice is given.

7.4　If the Purchaser becomes aware of any claim or threatened claim against the Purchaser which may constitute or give rise to a claim under the Warranties or becomes aware of any Environmental Liability, the Purchaser shall as soon as practicable thereafter notify the Vendor giving full details thereof. The Purchaser shall not compromise, settle or discharge any such claim or make any admission of liability without first consulting with the Vendor and the Purchaser shall consider any reasonable request of the Vendor in connection with any negotiations or proceedings concerning any claim or potential claim under the Warranties or any Environmental Liability.

7.5　The following limitations shall apply:

7.5.1　the Vendor shall have no liability in respect of any single claim under this Agreement (whether in contract or tort) if the amount for which the Vendor would (in the absence of this Clause [ ]) be liable to the Purchaser in respect of that claim is equal to or less than £[amount];

7.5.2　the Vendor shall have no liability in respect of any claims under this Agreement (whether in contract or tort) if the aggregate amount for which the Vendor would (in the absence of this

Clause [ ] be liable to the Purchaser in respect of that claim is equal to or less than £[amount].

7.6 The Purchaser shall take all reasonable steps to avoid or mitigate any loss, damage or liability which might give rise to a claim against the Vendor under this Agreement (whether in contract or tort).

7.7 Any amount payable or paid by the Vendor to the Purchaser under the Warranties shall be treated as a reimbursement of the Purchase Price payable hereunder.

7.8 In the event of any circumstances arising which do or may give rise to an Environmental Liability and which fall within the terms of the Environmental Indemnity, the Purchaser shall not (where practicable) make any public statement regarding such circumstances without prior consultation with the Vendor on the text of any such public statement before it is made.

7.9 Subject to Clause [ ], no breach of the Warranties or of any other provisions of this Agreement nor any misrepresentation or statement of fact whatsoever shall give rise to any right of the Purchaser to rescind or terminate this Agreement following its signing by the parties hereto.

7.10 The aggregate liability of the Vendor in respect of (a) all claims including, where relevant, the fees of the Independent Environmental Consultant, made under the Environmental Indemnity shall be 75 per cent. of £[amount] and (b) all other claims under this Agreement (whether in contract or tort) shall not in any event exceed the further amount of £[amount].

7.11 The Purchaser shall not be entitled to recover under the Warranties if and to the extent that the Purchaser has recovered any indemnity under any applicable insurance.

8. Termination by the Purchaser

8.1 This Agreement may be terminated by the Purchaser from the date hereof prior to the Completion Date if:

8.1.1 physical damage has occurred or hazard has arisen at the Property after the date hereof or any proceedings have been issued by a third party against the Vendor which (whether (in any case) alone or where the effect of which when combined with the effect of other such events) would render the Vendor unable to carry on the Business (or a material part thereof) from the Properties on or after the Date of Completion; or

8.1.2   any incident of material Contamination shall have occurred after the date hereof which would give rise to Environmental Liability.

SIGNED BY THE PARTIES NAMED ABOVE

SCHEDULE I

WARRANTIES

1.   Environmental Matters

1.1   The Company has obtained all Environmental Licences necessary to own and operate the Assets and to carry on the Business at the Property and has at all times complied with all applicable Environmental Law and the terms and conditions of the Environmental Licences (whether express or implied) and, without undue expenditure and effort on the part of the Company, can continue to so comply.

1.2   The Company has not received any notice or other communication (including without limitation any abatement, enforcement, prohibition, revocation, remediation, works, charging, or other notice of a relevant nature, judgment, demand letter or communication relating to clean-up action in relation to pollution or protection of the environment or nuisance or any communication) from which it appears that it may be or is alleged to be in violation of any Environmental Law or Environmental Licence or that any Environmental Licence may be subject to modification, suspension or revocation and there are no circumstances likely to give rise to such violation or modification, suspension or revocation.

1.3   The Company is not engaged in and the Vendors are not aware of any facts which make it likely or desirable that it should be engaged in any appeal in respect of any Environmental Licence or any conditions contained therein or any review thereof or any refusal of any Environmental Licence and the Vendors have no reason to believe that those Environmental Licences which have been applied for but which have not yet been granted or are pending will not be granted within a reasonable period of time and on acceptable terms.

1.4   Full details of any remedial work carried out at the Property and affecting Environmental Contamination and of any environmental assessment, audit, review or investigation conducted by or on behalf of the Company are contained in or annexed to the Disclosure Letter.

1.5   There are no facts or circumstances which interfere or prevent compliance with any Environmental Law or which may give rise to any common law or legal liability or otherwise form any claim or action related to the pollution or protection of the environment.

1.6   The Company has not refused to comply with or prevented or sought to prevent any other person from complying with the requirements of any inspector or other officer appointed under the Environmental Laws.

1.7   During the [ ] years prior to the date hereof, the Company has not used, disposed of, generated, stored, transported, dumped, released, deposited, buried or emitted any Hazardous Substance at, on, from or under any of the Property or at, on, from or under any other premises.

1.8   No other person has used, disposed of, generated, stored, transported, dumped, released, deposited, buried or emitted any Hazardous Substance at, on, from or under any of the Property.

1.9   During the [ ] years prior to the date hereof, the Company has not disposed of any Hazardous Substance in the past in connection with the business in such a way that its disposal would now constitute a breach of any Environmental Law.

1.10   To the best of the Vendors' knowledge and belief warranties [ ] to [ ] (inclusive) would be true if given in respect of any other person who owns or occupies or carries on business on property which adjoins either the Property or any property occupied by the Company insofar as relates to his adjoining property or to activities carried on there or in respect of whose activities or business wherever carried on the Company or its activities is or is likely to be affected.

1.11   Full details have been disclosed to the Purchaser of all expenditure which has been incurred or which the Vendor is aware will be required to be incurred by the Purchaser to comply with any applicable Environmental Law or any condition attaching to any Environmental Licence.

APPENDIX 6

Illustrative terms for inclusion in a facility agreement

[*For a commentary on these clauses, the reader is referred to the text of Chapter 5.*]

A.   Definitions

'Environmental Claim' means, with respect to any person, any notice, claim, demand or similar communication (written or not) by any other person alleging potential liability for investigatory costs, clean-up costs, governmental response costs, natural resources damages, property damages, personal injuries, fines or penalties arising out of, based on or resulting from:

(a)   the presence, or release into the environment, of any Material of Environmental Concern at any location, whether in surface or ground water or on or under land and whether or not owned by such person; or

(b)   circumstances forming the basis of any violation, or alleged violation, of any Environmental Law or Environmental Consent;

'Environmental Consent' means any consent, permit, licence, approval, ruling, exemption or other authorisation required under applicable Environmental Laws;

'Environmental Laws' means any law (which includes an order or decree, any form of delegated legislation, a treaty and a directive or regulation made by virtue of powers conferred by a treaty) of a Governmental Authority regulating, relating to or imposing liability or standards of conduct concerning, environmental protection matters, including without limitation, in relation to the manufacture, processing, distribution, use, treatment, storage, disposal, transfer or handling of Materials of Environmental Concern, as now or may at any time hereafter be in effect;

['Environmental Report' means the environmental report dated [ ], 200[ ] prepared by the Borrower with respect to the Borrower [and its Subsidiaries];]

'Governmental Authority' means any nation or government, any state or political sub-division thereof and any entity exercising executive, legislative, judicial, regulatory or administrative functions of any of the foregoing;

'Material of Environmental Concern' means chemicals, pollutants, contaminants, wastes, toxic substances, petroleum and petroleum products and distillates, and all hazardous substances defined or regulated as such in or under any Environmental Law.

B. Conditions precedent

( ) A copy of the Environmental Report accompanied by a certificate from an officer of the Borrower confirming that, after having made all appropriate inspections and investigations, the Borrower [and its Subsidiaries] [is/are] in compliance in all material respects with the Environmental Laws in the jurisdictions in which [it/they] carr[ies/y] on business.

( ) Evidence satisfactory to the Bank that effective insurance cover is in place for risks in relation to Environmental Claims to such extent as is in accordance with industry practice.

C. Representations and warranties

[( ) The Environmental Report is true, complete and accurate in all material respects, does not omit any material fact in relation to the compliance by the Borrower [and its Subsidiaries] with Environmental Laws and the Borrower is not aware of any material fact or circumstance which has not been disclosed to [the Managers,] the Agent or the Banks which, if disclosed, would be likely at the date of this Agreement to be relevant in relation to any material liability of the Borrower [or any of its Subsidiaries], or any liability of the [Managers,] the Agent or the Banks in their respective capacities as such under this Agreement, under or in respect of Environmental Laws;]

( ) [each of] the Borrower [and its Subsidiaries] is in full compliance with all Environmental Laws which are currently applicable to its business and all Environmental Consents required in respect thereof have been obtained from the appropriate authorities and are in full force and effect [except where the failure to comply with any such Environmental Laws or to obtain any such Environmental Consents would not reasonably be expected (i) materially and adversely to affect the ability of the Borrower to fulfil its obligations under this Agreement or (ii) to result in any liability to [the Managers,] the Agent or the Banks in their respective capacities as such during the normal course of this Agreement];

( )   no litigation, arbitration or administrative proceeding is current, pending or, to the knowledge of the Borrower, threatened under any Environmental Laws to which the Borrower [or any of its Subsidiaries] is or will be named as a party;

( )   there are no material compliance or enforcement orders currently outstanding against the Borrower [or any of its Subsidiaries] arising under any Environmental Laws; and

( )   there is no Environmental Claim pending or, to the knowledge of the Borrower, threatened against the Borrower [or any of its Subsidiaries] and, so far as the Borrower is aware after due enquiry, there are no past or present actions, activities, circumstances, conditions, events or incidents including without limitation the release, emission, discharge or disposal of any Material of Environmental Concern, which could reasonably be expected to form the basis of any Environmental Claim against the Borrower [or any of its Subsidiaries].

D.   Covenants

( )   Comply with [, and ensure compliance by its Subsidiaries with,] all Environmental Laws applicable to the operations of the Borrower [and its Subsidiaries] and obtain from the appropriate authorities all Environmental Consents required in respect thereto [, except where the failure to comply with any such Environmental Laws or to obtain such Environmental Consents would not reasonably be expected (i) materially and adversely to affect the ability of the Borrower to fulfil its obligations under this Agreement or (ii) to result in any liability to [the Managers,] the Agent and the Banks in respect thereof in their respective capacities as such during the normal course of this Agreement];

( )   maintain [, and ensure that each of its Subsidiaries maintains,] insurance on and in relation to [its/their respective] business[es] and assets with reputable underwriters or insurance companies against such risks, including, without limitation, risks in relation to Environmental Claims, and to such extent as in accordance with good industry practice; [( ) as soon as practicable, and in any event within [ ] days, after the end of each of its financial years, deliver to the Agent in sufficient copies for the Banks a certificate of an officer of the Borrower stating that there has been no change to any of the matters set out in the Environmental Report or, if there has been any change, setting out of the details thereof, its effect on the Borrower's obligations regarding Environmental Laws as set out in this Agreement and the steps the Borrower is taking in respect thereof;

[( ) if the Borrower fails to provide a certificate in respect of the

Environmental Report as required by Clause [ ]) (and without prejudice to the rights of the Banks under Clause ( ) ([Events of Default]), permit [, and cause its Subsidiaries to permit,] any representative of the Agent and/or the Banks at any reasonable time (i) to visit and inspect any of the places at which the Borrower [or any of its Subsidiaries] carries on its business and (ii) to examine any of the books and records of the Borrower [and any of its Subsidiaries], for the purpose of conducting an environmental audit of the business of the Borrower, the cost of such audit to be reimbursed by the Borrower on demand if such audit establishes that the Borrower is in breach of this Agreement in relation to Environmental Laws;]

( )   if:

    (i)   the Borrower [or any of its Subsidiaries] receives any notice alleging that it is not in compliance with any applicable Environmental Law; or

    (ii)   the Borrower [or any of its Subsidiaries] becomes aware that there any Environmental Claim pending or threatened against it; or

    (iii)   there occurs any (or any threatened) release, emission, discharge or disposal of any substance which could reasonably be expected to form the basis of any Environmental Claim against the Borrower (or any of its Subsidiaries);

and, in the case of any of the foregoing, there is a reasonable likelihood that the same could materially and adversely affect the ability of the Borrower to perform its obligations under this Agreement or result in liability to [the Managers,] the Agent and/or the Banks in their respective capacities as such during the normal course of this Agreement then:

( )   the Borrower shall promptly upon the occurrence of any of the foregoing provide to the Agent a certificate of an officer of the Borrower specifying in detail the nature of such event and the actions which the Borrower [or, as the case may be, such Subsidiary] intends to take in response thereto; and

( )   upon the written request of the Agent, submit to the Agent at reasonable intervals a report providing any update of the situation resulting from such event; and it will not make or permit any material change in the nature of its business or commence any new type of business materially different from its business at the date of this Agreement [or commence any business which would have been defined as a contaminative use under s.143 of the Environmental Protection Act 1990 or which may have the result of causing any land of the Borrower to be designated as contaminated or a special site within the meaning of Part IIA of the Environmental Protection Act 1990.]

E.   Indemnity

The Borrower shall indemnify [the Managers,] the Agent and the Banks [and any receiver appointed under any of the Security Documents] and their respective employees, agents, directors and officers (the 'Indemnified Parties') against all claims, costs, expenses or liabilities (a 'Liability') of whatever kind or nature suffered or incurred by any Indemnified Party arising out of or in connection with any order, requirement or demand made against any Indemnified Party by any Governmental Authority in respect of a breach or alleged breach by the Borrower [or any of its Subsidiaries] of any Environmental Law or arising out of or in connection with any action taken by the Indemnified Parties to clean up, improve, remove any substance (hazardous or otherwise) or take any other action of whatever kind taken with a view to disposing of the assets subject to the Security Documents.

F.   Clauses to be inserted in the Certificate of Title or in the Facility Agreement as Representations and Warranties

( )   [So far as the Borrower is aware [during the Borrower's occupation]] there has been no storage disposal generation or treatment of any hazardous substances at the Property in contravention of any statute or regulation relating thereto.

( )   [During the Borrower's period of ownership] there has been no spill, discharge, leak, emission, injection, escape, dumping or release of any kind onto the Property with respect to any business carried on at the Property or into the environment surrounding the Property other than releases as permissible or allowable under applicable consents or licences.

APPENDIX 7

Suggested terms and conditions of appointment of environmental consultants

[The clauses contained in this suggested agreement have been drafted on the basis of other, well-established precedents for similar consultancy agreements, adapted for use in the environmental field.

Most firms of consultants have standard terms and conditions which are substantially briefer, and usually much more restrictive of the client's rights, than this model, and those standard terms may well be adequate, once the main restrictions have been dealt with (for commentary, please see text).

As a clean-sheet approach, the aim of which is to protect the client first and foremost, the following model is suggested as the basis for initial bargaining. Many consultants will relent and accept conditions other than their own if the client is assertive enough on the important points.]

Date: 20

Parties:

1. 'The Client': _____ [Limited] [PLC] (registered no. _____)

   whose registered office is at _____

2. 'The Consultant': _____[Limited] [PLC] (registered no. _____)

   whose registered office is at _____.

Recitals:

(A) The Consultant is engaged in business offering consultancy services in relation to environmental matters and has considerable skill, knowledge and experience in that field.

(B) In reliance upon that skill, knowledge and experience the Client wishes to engage the Consultant to provide services in relation to environmental matters and the Consultant agrees to accept the engagement on the following terms.

1. Interpretation

1.1   In this Agreement:

'Affiliate' means any company, partnership or other entity which directly or indirectly controls, is controlled by or is under common control of either the Client or the Consultant;

'Control' means the legal power to direct or cause the direction of the general management and policies of the party in question;

'Agreement' means this instrument and any and all Schedules to this Agreement as the same may be amended, modified or supplemented from time to time in accordance with these provisions;

'The Board' means the Board of Directors from time to time of the Client;

[*Clearly, if the client is not a company but, say, a firm of solicitors, this will need redefining.*]

'The Commencement Date' means ;

'Confidential Information' means all unpatented designs, drawings, data, specifications, manufacturing processes, testing procedures and all other technical business and similar information relating to the Project or relating to the business of the Consultant or its operation including all readable or computer or other machine readable data, logic, logic diagrams, flow charts, orthographic representations, coding sheets, coding, source or object codes, listings, test data, test routines, diagnostic programs or other material relating to or comprising software which is part of the Project;

'Documents' means all records, reports, documents, papers and other materials whatsoever originated by or on behalf of the Consultant pursuant to this Agreement;

'The Project' means the job specification set out in Schedule 1;

'Services' means the services more particularly set out in Schedule 2; and

'The Site (s)' means the property and places more particularly set out in Schedule 3.

[*Relevant definitions have been relegated to Schedules in view of the potentially complex definition of the type of works required which may be necessary.*]

1.2 The headings in this Agreement are inserted only for convenience and shall not affect its construction.

1.3 Where appropriate words denoting a singular number only shall include the plural and vice versa.

1.4 Reference to any statute or statutory provision includes a reference to the statute or statutory provisions as from time to time amended, extended or re-enacted.

2. Duration

2.1 The Consultant shall commence the provision of the Services on the Commencement Date and shall continue to provide the Services until termination of this Agreement as provided in Clause 6.

3. Positive obligations of the Consultant

3.1 The Consultant shall provide the Services at the Site provided that it may provide the Services at such other place or places as may be necessary for the due performance of them.

3.2 The Consultant shall keep detailed records of all acts and things done by it in relation to the provision of the Services and at the Client's request shall make them available for inspection and/or provide copies to the Client.

3.3 The Consultant shall at all times during the period of this Agreement:

    3.3.1 faithfully and diligently perform those duties and exercise such powers consistent with them which are from time to time necessary in connection with the provision of the Services;

    3.3.2 obey all lawful and reasonable directions of the Board;

[Clearly, if the client is not a company but, say, a firm of solicitors, use of the term 'Board' is inappropriate.]

    3.3.3 use its best endeavours to promote the interest of the Client and its Affiliates.

3.4 *Confidentiality*

    3.4.1 The Consultant agrees to treat as secret and confidential and make no disclosure of and to ensure that its personnel shall treat as secret and confidential and make no disclosure of the Confidential Information, the Documents and all other matters arising or coming to its or their attention in connection with the provision of the Services and not at any time for any reason whatsoever to disclose them or permit them to be disclosed to any third party except as permitted hereunder to enable the Consultant to carry out its duties and obligations. The Consultant shall procure that its personnel and all others of its employees having access to any of the Confidential Information, the Documents or such matters shall be subject to the same obligations as the Consultant and shall enter into a suitable secrecy agreement in a form approved by the Client or, insofar as this is not reasonably practicable, the Consultant shall take all reasonable steps to ensure that its employees are made aware of and perform such obligations.

3.4.2   The Consultant agrees to treat as secret and confidential and not at any time for any reason to disclose or permit to be disclosed to any person or persons or otherwise make use of or permit to be made use of any information relating to the Client's technology, technical processes, business affairs or finances or any such information relating to any Affiliate, suppliers, or customers of the Client where knowledge or details of the information was received during the period of this Agreement.

3.4.3   The obligations of the parties under this Clause 3.4 shall survive the expiry or the termination of this Agreement for whatever reason.

3.5   *Liability*

3.5.1   The Client will be relying upon the Consultant's skill, expertise and experience and also upon the accuracy of all representations or statements made and the advice given by the Consultant in connection with the provision of the Services and the accuracy of any Confidential Information or Documents conceived, originated, made or developed by the Consultant in connection with the provision of the Services and the Consultant hereby agrees to indemnify the Client against all loss, damage, costs, legal costs and professional and other expenses of any nature whatsoever incurred or suffered by the Client or by a third party whether direct or consequential including but without limitation any economic loss or other loss of turnover, profits, business or goodwill as a result of such reliance.

3.5.2   The Consultant accepts:

3.5.2.1   liability for death or personal injury howsoever resulting from the Consultant's negligence or that of its employees or sub-contractors; and

3.5.2.2 liability for damage to property howsoever resulting from the Consultant's negligence or that of its employees or sub-contractors where such negligence has arisen or arises in connection with the provision of the Services or in connection with any other activities undertaken by the Consultant pursuant to or for any purpose related to this Agreement. The Consultant hereby agrees to indemnify the Client against all and any liability, loss, damage, costs and expense of whatsoever nature incurred or suffered by the Client or by any third party whether arising from any disputes, contractual, tortious or other claims or proceedings which seek to recover loss and/or damage incurred by reason of any such death, personal injury or damage to property. The Consultant's personnel shall at all times be deemed to be the Consultant's employees whether such personnel are at the Site or anywhere else.

3.5.3 The Consultant's liability under Clauses 3.5.1 and 3.5.2 above shall be limited to the sum of £[ ].

[*One could seek to omit any clause voluntarily limiting the liability of the Consultant, but this is unlikely to escape scrutiny. One will inevitably have to concede some limitation – the question is how much.*

Suitable limits would be a sum equivalent to the Consultant's insurance cover – typically £2m–£5m. It should nevertheless be borne in mind that insurance can be difficult to obtain, and in any event, if a claim has already been brought against a consultant, the limit of £5m may already have been exhausted.]

3.5.4 The Consultant expressly acknowledges that the provisions of this Clause 3.5 satisfy the requirements of reasonableness specified in the Unfair Contract Terms Act 1977 and that it shall be estopped from claiming the contrary at any future date in the event of any dispute with the Client concerning the Consultant's liability hereunder.

3.5.5 The Consultant undertakes and agrees to take out and maintain for the whole period of the Project adequate insurance cover with an insurance office of repute to cover the liability accepted by it in this Clause 3.5 and agrees to produce at the Client's request a copy of the insurance policy or policies and relevant renewal receipts for inspection by the Client.

[Insurance is available for consultants on the specialist market, so one should resist inclusions which seek to limit this requirement in some way, e.g. by adding words such as 'insofar as such cover is commercially available at suitable premiums'.]

3.5.6   The provisions of this Clause 3.5 shall survive the termination of this Agreement for any reason.

3.6   If the Consultant shall consider it necessary to use the services of a third party whether for information or for the supply of goods or services including without limitation manufacture of models, prototypes, mock-ups, artwork, drawings, printing, photography, testing and the like, the Consultant shall except in matters of a minor and obvious nature obtain the prior consent of the Client before using such services.

3.7   The Consultant shall indemnify the Client against all and any liability, loss, damage, cost and expense of whatsoever nature incurred or suffered by the Client or any third party as a result of the activities of the Consultant in undertaking the Project.

4.   Payment

4.1   In consideration of the provision of the Services, the Client shall pay to the Consultant the fees as set out in Schedule 4.

4.2   All payments to the Consultant shall be made against the Consultant's invoices which shall be presented at the end of each calendar month during the term of this Agreement in respect of the provision of the Services provided in each such month. All payments shall be made by the Client within [30] days following receipt by the Client of the Consultant's invoice. All payments shall be made by the Client by a cheque or bank transfer to the account of the Consultant at a bank to be nominated in writing by the Consultant.

4.3   Payment by the Client shall be without prejudice to any claims or rights which the Client may have made against the Consultant and shall not constitute any admission by the Client as to the performance by the Consultant of its obligations hereunder. Prior to making any such payment, the Client shall be entitled to make deductions or deferments in respect of any disputes or claims whatsoever with or against the Consultant.

5.   Obligations of the Client

5.1   Throughout the period of this Agreement the Client shall [if applicable] insofar as possible afford the Consultant such access to the Site and the

Client's information records and other material relevant to the Project as the Consultant may require to provide the Services provided always that the Client shall [if applicable] be obliged to afford such access only during its normal business hours. Further the Client shall [if applicable]:

5.1.1 advise the Consultant of the rules and regulations which are then in force for the conduct of personnel at the Site. The Consultant shall ensure that its personnel comply with any such rules and regulations;

5.1.2 make available such working space and facilities at the Site as the Consultant may reasonably require. Such working space and facilities shall be comparable to but not better than those given by the Client to its own personnel of similar status;

5.1.3 make available appropriate personnel to liaise with the Consultant;

5.1.4 secure and otherwise keep safe all and any property of the Consultant.

[Clearly, this clause has no function if the Client is not the owner of the Site, but the investigation is being carried out in anticipation of an acquisition.]

6. Termination

6.1 This Agreement shall terminate automatically on completion of the Project by the Consultant to the satisfaction of the Client by the service of a written notice to that effect from the Client, but such termination shall be without prejudice to any provision intended to operate thereafter.

6.2 Upon any breach by the Consultant of any of its duties and obligations under this Agreement in relation to the provision of the Services, the Client shall have the rights specified in Clauses 6.2.1 and 6.2.2.

6.2.1 The Client shall have the right to seek an order for specific performance together with a mandatory injunction against the Consultant in addition to bringing a claim in damages. The Consultant expressly acknowledges that the Client is relying upon the Consultant to perform all the Consultant's duties and obligations in connection with the provision of the Services and that, upon any breach by the Consultant of any such duties and obligations, the Client may not wish to exercise its right to terminate this Agreement pursuant to Clause 6.2.2 and thereafter to engage the services of another consultant to complete the provision of the Services seeking to recover the cost thereof as damages from the Consultant since any such other consultant will not have the familiarity with the Client's business affairs necessary to enable such other consultant to provide the Services pursuant to the terms of this Agreement. By reason of the foregoing the Consultant hereby agrees that, in circumstances where it is in breach of its duties and obligations in connection with the provision of the Services and the Client elects to affirm this Agreement and claim for damages, the claim for damages will be an inadequate remedy for the Client and, subject always to the discretion of the Court, the Client shall be entitled to an interlocutory order for specific performance together with a mandatory injunction (if the circumstances are appropriate to the grant of such an injunction) either or both in terms compelling the Consultant and its personnel thereafter to provide the Services pursuant to this Agreement. The Consultant further hereby agrees that such relief shall not affect the Client's right to seek to recover any loss and damage suffered by it in respect of the Consultant's prior breach of its duties and obligations in connection with the provision of the Services.

6.2.2   The Client shall have the right to terminate this Agreement forthwith by notice in writing to the Consultant and to engage another consultant to complete the provision of the Services. Following any such termination of this Agreement the Consultant shall indemnify the Client against all loss, damage, cost including management and similar costs, expenses including professional fees and expenses and all other expenditure or loss of opportunity or revenue whatsoever incurred or suffered by the Client as a result of the Consultant's breach. This indemnity shall survive the termination of this Agreement.

6.3   In addition to and notwithstanding the Client's rights of termination pursuant to Clause 6.2 either party may terminate this Agreement forthwith by notice in writing to the other if the other:

6.3.1   commits a breach of this Agreement which in the case of a breach capable of remedy shall not have been remedied within 30 days of the receipt by the other of a notice from the innocent party identifying the breach and requiring its remedy;

6.3.2   is unable to pay its debts or enters into compulsory or voluntary liquidation (other than for the purpose of effecting a reconstruction or amalgamation in such manner that the company resulting from such reconstruction or amalgamation if a different legal entity shall agree to be bound by and assume the obligations of the relevant party under this Agreement) or compounds with or convenes a meeting of its creditors or proposes a voluntary arrangement with its creditors or has a receiver or manager or administrative receiver, or administrator appointed or ceases for any reason to carry on business or takes or suffers any similar action which in the opinion of the party giving notice means that the other may be unable to pay its debts.

6.4   The Client shall have the right to terminate this Agreement forthwith by written notice to the Consultant if the Consultant shall have been prevented by any cause from providing the services for an aggregate period of [20] working days in any period of [12] calendar months.

6.5   Upon termination of this Agreement:

6.5.1   for whatever reason, the Consultant shall deliver up to the Client all of the Confidential Information, Documents and copies thereof in the possession, power, custody or control of either of them at the time and shall execute all such deeds and documents as the Client's legal advisers may require to transfer and assign to the Client the property and intellectual property in such Confidential Information and Documents and the Consultant shall not thereafter utilise or exploit the Confidential Information or Documents in any way whatsoever;

6.5.2   for whatever reason, the Client shall have the right to utilise and exploit the Confidential Information and the Documents in any way whatsoever without restriction;

6.5.3   by the Consultant pursuant to Clause 6.3 the Client shall remain liable to pay to the Consultant all sums which have accrued due and owing to the Consultant hereunder.

6.6   Termination of this Agreement for whatever reason shall not affect the accrued rights of the parties arising in any way out of this Agreement as at the date of termination and, in particular but without limitation, the right to recover damages against the other and all provisions which are expressed to survive this Agreement shall remain in force and effect.

7.   Assignment

7.1   Subject to the provisions of Clause 7.2 below neither party shall assign, transfer, sub-contract or in any other manner make over to any third party the benefit and/or burden of this Agreement without the prior written consent of the other.

[The question of the assignability of rights under the Agreement is a vexed one. It is common practice for persons other than the Client – a purchaser of assets from the Client, for example – to want the right to

sue the Consultant if they have in some way relied on the report in their assessment of risk. They will usually demand the assignment of rights under the contract, and the Client could be advised to include a term allowing the unilateral assignment of rights by the Client alone.

The Consultant will be very reluctant to allow this, however, as the range of potential claimants may become enormous, and jeopardise the Consultant's insurance position.

In addition, Consultants will resist any attempt to force them to act as the Client's 'insurer' against environmental risk – the right to sue being traded off against a contract price in a transaction. Their view is that the Client should be more concerned to get the right information for their own purposes, and to look no further.

Including this clause will, however, give the Client freedom to negotiate assignment on an ad hoc basis when and if required.

One freedom which the Client may need to reserve is the freedom to disclose the report to a funder.]

7.2   The Client shall be entitled without the prior written consent of the Consultant to assign, transfer or in any manner make over the benefit and/or burden of this Agreement to an Affiliate or to any 50/50 joint venture company where it is the beneficial owner of 50 per cent of the issued share capital thereof or to any company or partnership with which it may merge or to any company or partnership to which it may transfer its assets and undertaking provided that such Affiliate or other company or partnership undertakes and agrees in writing to assume, observe and perform the rights and powers and/or duties and obligations of the Client under the provisions of this Agreement being assigned, transferred or otherwise made over.

7.3   This Agreement shall be binding upon the successors and assigns of the parties hereto and the name of a party appearing herein shall be deemed to include the names of its successors and assigns provided always that nothing shall permit any assignment by either party except as expressly provided.

8.   Governing law jurisdiction

8.1   The validity, construction and performance of this Agreement shall be governed by English law.

8.2   All disputes, claims or proceedings between the parties relating to the validity, construction or performance of this Agreement shall be subject to the non-exclusive jurisdiction of the High Court of Justice in England to which the parties hereto irrevocably submit. Each of the parties irrevocably consents to the award or grant of any relief in any such proceedings before the High Court of Justice in England. Either party shall have the right to take proceedings in any other jurisdiction for the purposes of enforcing a judgment or order obtained from the High Court of Justice in England.

9.   Force majeure

9.1   Neither party shall be in breach of this Agreement if there is any total or partial failure of performance by it of its duties and obligations under this Agreement occasioned by any act of God, fire, act of government or state, war, civil commotion, insurrection, embargo, prevention from or hindrance in obtaining any raw materials, energy or other supplies and any other reason beyond the control of either party. If either party is unable to perform its duties and obligations under this Agreement as a direct result of the effect of one of those reasons, that party shall give written notice to the other of the inability which sets out full details of the reason in question. The operation of this Agreement shall be suspended during the period (and only during the period) in which the reason continues. Forthwith upon the reason ceasing to exist the party relying upon it shall give written notice to the other of this fact. If the reason continues for a period of more than [90] days and substantially affects the commercial intention of this Agreement, the party not claiming relief under this Clause 9 shall have the right to terminate this Agreement upon giving 30 days written notice of such termination to the other party.

10.   Illegality

10.1   If any provision or term of this Agreement or any part thereof shall become or be declared illegal, invalid or unenforceable for any reason whatsoever including but without limitation by reason of the provisions of any legislation or other provisions having the force of law or by reason of any decision of any Court or other body or authority having jurisdiction over the parties or this Agreement including the EU Commission and the European Court of Justice, such terms or provisions shall be divisible from this Agreement and shall deemed to be deleted from this Agreement in the jurisdiction in question provided always that, if any such deletion substantially affects or alters the commercial basis of this Agreement, the parties shall negotiate in good faith to amend and modify the provisions and terms of this Agreement as may be necessary or desirable in the circumstances.

11.   Amendment, etc.

11.1   This Agreement shall not be amended, modified, varied or supple-
        mented except in writing signed by a duly authorised representative of
        each of the parties.

11.2   No failure or delay on the part of either party hereto to exercise any right
        or remedy under this Agreement shall be construed or operated as a
        waiver thereof nor shall any single or partial exercise of any right or
        remedy as the case may be. The rights and remedies provided in this
        Agreement are cumulative and are not exclusive of any rights or reme-
        dies provided by law.

11.3   The text of any press release or other communication to be published by
        or in the media concerning the subject matter of this Agreement shall
        require the approval of each party.

11.4   Each of the parties hereto shall be responsible for its respective legal
        and other costs incurred in relation to the preparation of this Agreement.

12.   Notice

12.1   Any notice or other document to be given under this Agreement shall be
        in writing and shall be deemed to have been duly given if left or sent by:

    12.1.1   first class post or express or air mail or other fast postal
             service; or

    12.1.2   registered post; or

    12.1.3   telex, facsimile or other electronic media to a party at the
             address or relevant telecommunications number for such party
             or such other address as the party may from time to time desig-
             nate by written notice to the other[s].

12.2   All such notices and documents shall be in the English language. Any
        notice or other document shall be deemed to have been received by the
        addressee two working days following the date of dispatch of the notice
        or other document by post or, where the notice or other document is
        sent by hand or is given by telex, facsimile or other electronic media,
        simultaneously with the delivery or transmission. To prove the giving of a
        notice or other document it shall be sufficient to show that it was
        dispatched.

Contacts

BIO-WISE

Dept of Trade and Industry
PO Box 83
Didcot
Oxfordshire OX11 0BR

Tel: 0800 432 100
Fax: 01235 432 997
Web: www.biowise.org.uk

British Gas

Head Office

100 Thames Valley Park Drive
Reading
Berkshire RG6 1PT

Tel: 020 7935 3222
Fax: 0118 935 3484

British Geological Survey

Kingsley Dunham Centre
Nottingham NG12 5GG

Tel: 0115 936 3100
Fax: 0115 936 3593

British Railways Board

Euston House
24 Eversholt Street
London NW1 1DZ

Tel: 020 7928 5151
Fax: 020 7557 9027

British Waterways Board (BWB)

Headquarters

Willow Grange
Church Road

Watford
Herts WD1 3QA

Tel: 01923 226 422
Fax: 01923 226 081

Regional Offices

Midlands and South West
Peels Wharf
Lichfield Street
Fazeley
Tamworth B78 3QX

Tel: 01827 252 000
Fax: 01827 288 071

North East
1 Dock Street
Leeds LS1 1HH

Tel: 0113 281 6800
Fax: 0113 281 6886

North West
Navigation Road
Northwich CW8 1BH

Tel: 01606 723 800
Fax: 01606 871 471

Southern
Brindley Suite
Willow Grange
Church Road
Watford WD17 4QA

Tel: 01923 208 700
Fax: 01923 208 787

Certa

America House
2 America Square
London EC3N 2LU

Tel: 020 7903 6500
Fax: 020 7903 6588

Church Commissioners for England

1 Millbank
Westminster
London SW1P 3JZ

Tel: 020 7898 1000
Fax: 020 7898 1001

Coal Authority

Mining Reports Dept
200 Litchfield Lane
Berry Hill
Mansfield
Nottingham NG18 4RG

Tel: 01623 427 162
Fax: 01623 622 072
DX: 716176 Mansfield-5

Commission of the European Communities

Jean Monnet House
8 Storey's Gate
London SW1P 3AT

Tel: 020 7973 1992
Fax: 020 7973 1900
Web: www.cec.org.uk

Companies House

Companies House
Crown Way
Cardiff CF4 3UZ

Tel: 029 2038 8588
Fax: 029 2038 0900
DX: 33050 Cardiff-1

Council for Licensed Conveyancers

16 Glebe Road
Chelmsford

Essex CM1 1QG

Tel: 01245 349 599
Fax: 01245 341 300
DX: 121925 Chelmsford-6

Council of Mortgage Lenders

3 Savile Row
London W1X 1AF

Tel: 020 7437 0655
Fax: 020 7734 6416
DX: 81550 Savile Row W1

Council for the Protection of Rural England

25 Buckingham Palace Road
London SW1W 0PP

Tel: 020 7976 6433
Fax: 020 7976 6373
Web: www.greenchannel.com/cpre

Country Landowner's Association

16 Belgrave Square
London SW1X 9PQ

Tel: 020 7235 0511
Fax: 020 7235 4696
Web: www.cla.org.uk

Countryside Agency

John Dower House
Crescent Place
Cheltenham GL50 3RA

Tel: 01242 521 381
Fax: 01242 584 270
Web: www.countryside.gov.uk

Countryside Council for Wales

Plas Penrhos
Ffordd Penrhos
Bangor
Gwynedd LL57 2LQ

Tel: 01248 385 500
Fax: 01248 355 782
Web: www.cw.gov.uk

Department of the Environment, Transport and the Regions

Eland House
Bressenden Place
London SW1E 5DU

Web: www.detr.gov.uk

Environment and energy helpline:
0800 585 794
General enquiries:
020 7890 3000
Countryside planning policy (PD1):
020 7890 3978
Minerals and waste (PD2):
020 7890 3871
Development control (householder):
020 7890 3943
Development control (telecoms):
020 7890 3942
Environmental impact assessment
(PD5): 020 7890 3894
International planning (PD5B):
020 7890 3908
Planning research (PD5C):
020 7890 3906
Development plans:
020 7890 3925
Crown development (PCD):
020 7890 3913
Statistics (PLUS3):
020 7890 5502

Directorate General XI

(Environment, Nuclear Safety and Civil
Protection)
European Commission
200 Rue de la Loi
B1049 Brussels
Belgium
Tel: 00 322 299 1111

Drinking Water Inspectorate

Floor 2/A2
Ashdown House
123 Victoria Street
London SW1E 6DE

Tel: 020 7944 5956
Fax: 020 7944 5969

Energy and Environmental Programme

Royal Institute of International Affairs
Chatham House
10 St James's Square
London SW1Y 4LE

Tel: 020 7957 5711
Fax: 020 7957 5710

English Heritage

23 Savile Row
London W1X 1AB

Tel: 020 7973 3000
Fax: 020 7973 3001
Web: www.english-heritage.org.uk

English Nature

Northminster House
Northminster Road
Peterborough PE1 1UA

Tel: 01733 455 000
Fax: 01733 568 834

The Environment Agency

Enquiry line: 0645 333 111
Pollution reporting line: 0800 807 060
Email: enquiries@environment-
agency.gov.uk
Web: www.environment-agency.gov.uk

Head Office

Rio House
Waterside Drive
Aztec West
Almondsbury
Bristol BS32 4UD

Tel: 01454 624400
Fax: 01454 624409
DX: 121225 Almondsbury-2

Regional Offices

Anglian Region
Kingfisher House
Goldhay Way
Orton Goldhay
Peterborough PE2 5ZR

Tel: 01733 371 811
Fax: 01733 231 840

Midlands Region
Sapphire East
550 Streetsbrook Road
Solihull B91 1QT

Tel: 0121 711 2324
Fax: 0121 711 5824

North-East Region
Rivers House
21 Park Square South
Leeds LS1 2QG

Tel: 0113 2440191
Fax: 0113 2461889

North-West Region
Richard Fairclough House
Knutsford Road
Warrington WA4 1HG

Tel: 01925 653 999
Fax: 01925 415 961

South-West Region
Manley House
Kestrel Way
Exeter EX2 7LQ

Tel: 01392 444 000
Fax: 01392 444 238

Southern Region
Guildbourne House
Chatsworth Road
Worthing
West Sussex BN11 1LD

Tel: 01903 820 692
Fax: 01903 821 832

Thames Region
Kings Meadow House
Kings Meadow Road
Reading RG1 8DQ

Tel: 0118 953 5000
Fax: 0118 950 0388

Welsh Region
Rivers House/Plas-yr-Avon
St Mellons Business Park
St Mellons
Cardiff CF3 0LT

Tel: 029 2077 0088
Fax: 029 2079 8555

West Region
SEPA West
5 Redwood Crescent
Peel Park
East Kilbride G74 5PP

Tel: 01355 574 200
Fax: 01355 574 688

Environmental Auditors Ltd

Environmental Auditors House
Redhouse Farm
Newtimber
West Sussex BN6 9BS

Tel: 01273 857500
Fax: 01273 857550

Environmental Data Association

Environmental Auditors House
Redhouse Farm
Newtimber
West Sussex BN6 9BS

Tel: 01273 857500
Fax: 01273 857550

Environmental Law Foundation

Unit 309
16/16a Baldwins Gardens
London EC1N 7RJ

Tel: 020 7404 1030
Fax: 020 7404 1032

Environmental Risk Insurance Services Ltd

Environmental Auditors House
Redhouse Farm
Newtimber
West Sussex BN6 9BS

Tel: 01273 857500
Fax: 01273 857550

European Environment Agency

Kongens Nytoru 6
1050 Copenhagen K
Denmark

Tel: 00 45 3336 7100
Fax: 00 45 3336 7199
Email: eea@eea.eu.int
Web: www.eea.eu.int

Forestry Commission

231 Corstorphine Road
Edinburgh EH12 7AT

Tel: 0131 334 0303
Fax: 0131 334 3047
Web: www.forestry.gov.uk

Health and Safety Executive

Rose Court
2 Southwark Bridge
London SE1 9HS

Tel: 020 7717 6000
Fax: 020 7717 6717
Web: www.hse.gov.uk

HMSO

See The Stationery Office

Incorporated Society of Valuers and Auctioneers (ISVA)

3 Cadogan Gate
London SW1X 0AS

Tel: 020 7235 2282
Fax: 020 7235 4390
Web: www.isva.co.uk

Institute of Historic Building Conservation

C/o Richard Morrice
Old Laundry Cottage
Mote Road
Ivy Hatch
Sevenoaks TN15 0NT

Tel: 020 7973 3132

International Network for Environmental Management

Osterstrasse 58
20259 Hamburg
Germany

Tel: 00 49 40 4907 1600
Fax: 00 49 40 4907 1601
Web: www.inem.org

Joint Committee of National Amenity Societies

St Ann's Vestry Hall
2 Church Entry
London EC4V 5HB

Tel: 020 7236 3934
Fax: 020 7329 3677

Landmark Information Group Ltd

7 Abbey Court
Eagle Way
Exeter EX2 7HY

Tel: 01392 441 700
Fax: 01392 441 709

Lands Tribunal

48/49 Chancery Lane
London WC2A 1JR

Tel: 020 7936 7200
Fax: 020 7936 7215
DX: 44452 Strand

Landscape Institute

6–8 Barnard Mews
London SW11 1QU

Tel: 020 7738 9166
Fax: 020 7738 9134
Web: www.l-i.org.uk

Law Society of England and Wales

The Law Society's Hall
113 Chancery Lane
London WC2A 1PL

Tel: 020 7242 1222
Fax: 020 7831 0344
Web: www.lawsociety.org.uk
DX: 56 Lond/Chancery Ln WC2

Ipsley Court
Berrington Close
Redditch
Worcs B98 0TD

Tel: 020 7242 1222
(local) 01527 517 141
Fax: 01527 510 213
DX: 19114 Redditch

Local Government Association

26 Chapter Street
London SW1P 4ND

Tel: 020 7834 2222
Fax: 020 7664 3030
Web: www.lga.gov.uk

Millennium Estates

30 Station Road
Cuffley
Herts
EN6 4HE

Tel: 01707 873 126

Ministry of Agriculture, Fisheries and Food

Whitehall Place
London SW2A 2HH

Tel: 0645 335 577
Fax: 020 72708419
Web: www.maff.gov.uk/maffhome.htm

National Radiological Protection Board

Radon Survey
Chilton
Didcot
Oxon OX11 0RQ

Tel: 01235 831 600
Fax: 01235 833 891
NRPB Radon Freephone:
  0800 614 529

OECD Paris Centre

2 rue André Pascal
75775 Paris Cedex 16
France

Tel: 00 33 145 248 200
Web: www.oecd.org

Office for the Supervision of Solicitors

Victoria Court
8 Dormer Place
Leamington Spa
Warwickshire CV32 5AE

Tel: 01926 820 082
Fax: 01926 431 435
DX: 292320 Leamington Spa 4

The Planning Inspectorate

Tollgate House
Houlton Street
Bristol BS2 9DJ

Switchboard:
  0117 987 8000
Planning appeals:
  0117 987 8752/8754
Enforcement appeals:
  0117 987 8075
Lawful use appeals:
  0117 987 8546
Advertisement appeals:
  0117 987 8612
Appeals costs:
  0117 987 8824
Local plan inquiries:
  0117 987 8540

Planning Inspectorate for Wales

Cathays Park
Cardiff CF1 3NQ

Tel: 029 2082 3892
Fax: 029 2082 5622

Pollution Legal Liability

Environment Impairment Liability Dept
AIG Europe (UK) Ltd
The AIG Building
120 Fenchurch Street
London EC3M 5BP

Tel: 020 7626 7866
Fax: 020 7623 3762

Railtrack Board

Railtrack House
Euston Square
London NW1 2EE

Tel: 020 7344 7100
Fax: 020 7577 9000

Ramblers Association

1–5 Wandsworth Road
London SW8 2XX

Tel: 020 7339 8500
Fax: 020 7339 8501
Web: www.charitynet.org/-ramblers

Royal Commission on the Ancient and Historical Monuments of Wales

Crown Buildings
Plas Crug
Aberystwyth
Ceredigion SY23 1NJ

Tel: 01970 621 233
Fax: 01970 627 701

Royal Commission on the Historical Monuments of England

National Monuments Centre
Kemble Drive
Swindon SN2 2GZ

Tel: 01793 414 700
Fax: 01793 414 707

Royal Courts of Justice

Strand
London WC2A 2LL

Tel: 020 7936 6000
DX: 44450 Strand

Royal Institute of British Architects

66 Portland Place
London W1N 4AD

Tel: 020 7580 5533
Fax: 020 7255 1541
Web: www.riba.org

Royal Institution of Chartered Surveyors

12 Great George Street
Parliament Square
London SW1P 3AD

Tel: 020 7222 7000
Fax: 020 7222 9430
Web: www.rics.org.uk
DX: 2348 Victoria SW1

Royal Town Planning Institute

26 Portland Place
London W1N 4BE

Tel: 020 7636 9107
Fax: 020 7323 1582

The Stationery Office

PO Box 29
St Crispins House
Duke Street
Norwich NR3 1GN

Tel: 0870 600 5522
Fax: 0870 600 5533

Web: www.the-stationery-office.co.uk

Town and Country Planning Association

17 Carlton House Terrace
London SW1Y 5AS

Tel: 020 7930 8903
Fax: 020 7930 3280

United Kingdom Environmental Law Association Ltd

C/o Dr Christina Hill (General
Secretary)
Honeycroft House
Pangbourne Road
Upper Basildon
Berkshire RG8 8LP

Tel: 01491 671 631
Fax: 01491 671 631
Web: www.greenchannel.com/ukela

Water Service Companies

Anglian Water Services Ltd
Anglian House
Ambury Road
Huntington PE29 3NZ

Tel: 01480 323 000
Fax: 01480 323 115

North-West Water
Dawson House
Liverpool Road
Great Sankey
Warrington WA5 3LW

Tel: 01925 234 000
Fax: 01925 233 360

Northumbrian Water
Abbey Road
Pity Me
Durham DH1 5FJ

Tel: 0191 383 2222
Fax: 0191 384 1920
DX: 60863 Durham-6

Severn Trent Water
2297 Coventry Road
Birmingham B26 3PU

Tel: 0121 722 4000
Fax: 0121 722 4800

South-West Water
Peninsular House
Rydon Lane
Exeter EX2 7HR

Tel: 01392 446 688
Fax: 01392 434 966
DX: 119850 Exeter-10

Southern Water
Southern House
Yeoman Road
Worthing
West Sussex BN13 3NX

Tel: 01903 264 444
Fax: 01903 691 435
DX: 400500 Goring-by-Sea-3

Thames Water Utilities Ltd
Rose Kiln Court
Rose Kiln Lane
Reading
Berks RG2 0HP

Tel: 0118 925 1515
Fax: 0118 925 1516

Welsh Water
Cambrian Way
Brecon
Powys LD3 7HP

Tel: 01874 623 181
Fax: 01874 624 167

Wessex Water PLC
Wessex House
Passage Street
Bristol BS2 0JQ

Tel: 0117 929 0611
Fax: 0117 929 3137

Yorkshire Water
Western House
Western Way
Halifax Road
Bradford BD6 2LZ

Tel: 01274 306 063
Fax: 01274 804 022

Water Supply Companies

Bournemouth and West Hampshire
Water PLC
George Jessel House
Francis Avenue
Bournemouth BH11 8NB

Tel: 01202 590 059
Fax: 01202 597 022

Bristol Water PLC
PO Box 218
Bridgwater Road
Bristol BS99 7AU

Tel: 0117 966 5881
Fax: 0117 963 4576

Cambridge Water Company
41 Rustat Road
Cambridge CB1 3QS

Tel: 01223 247 351
Fax: 01223 214 052

Cholderton and District Water Company
Estate Office
Cholderton
Salisbury
Wiltshire SP4 0DR

Tel: 01980 629 203
Fax: 01980 629 307

Essex and Suffolk Water Company
Hall Street
Chelmsford
Essex CM2 0HH

Tel: 01245 491 234
Fax: 01245 212 345

Folkestone and Dover Water Services Ltd
The Cherry Garden
Cherry Garden Lane
Folkestone
Kent CT19 4QB

Tel: 01303 298 800
Fax: 01303 276 712

Hartlepool Water PLC
3 Lancaster Road
Hartlepool TS24 8LW

Tel: 01429 868 555
Fax: 01429 858 000

Mid Kent Water PLC
Rockfort Road
Snodland
Kent ME6 5AH

Tel: 01634 240 313
Fax: 01634 242 764

North Surrey Water Ltd
Millis House
The Causeway
Staines
Middlesex TW18 3BX

Tel: 01784 455 464
Fax: 01784 426 333

Portsmouth Water PLC
PO Box 8
West Street
Havant
Hants PO9 1LG

Tel: 023 9249 9888
Fax: 023 9245 3632
DX: 50008 Havant

Severn Trent Water PLC
Bromwich Rd
Lower Wick
Worcester WR2 4BN

Tel: 01905 424 300
Fax: 01905 427 326

South-East Water PLC
3 Church Road
Haywards Heath
West Sussex RH16 3NY

Tel: 01444 448 200
Fax: 01444 413 200

South Staffordshire Group PLC
Green Lane
Walsall
W Midlands WS2 7PD

Tel: 01922 638 282
Fax: 01922 631 779

Sutton and East Surrey Water PLC
London Road
Redhill
Surrey RH1 1LJ

Tel: 01737 772 000
Fax: 01737 766 807

Tendring Hundred Water
Services Ltd
Mill Hill
Manningtree
Essex CO11 2AZ

Tel: 01206 399 200
Fax: 01206 399 210

Three Valleys Water PLC
PO Box 48
Bishops Rise
Hatfield
Herts AL10 9HL

Tel: 01707 268 111
Fax: 01707 277 333

Wrexham Water PLC
Packsattle
Wrexham Road
Rhostyllen
Wrexham
Clwyd LL14 4EH

Tel: 01978 846 946
Fax: 01978 846 888

Yorkshire Water
Museum Street
York YO1 2DL

Tel: 08451 242 424
Fax: 01274 731 830

Welsh Local Government Association

10/11 Raleigh Walk
Atlantic Wharf
Cardiff CF1 5LN

Tel: 029 2046 8600
Fax: 029 2046 8601
DX: 81550 Savile Row W1

Welsh Office

Cathays Park
Cardiff CF1 3NQ

Tel: 029 2082 5111
Web: www.wales.gov.uk

Planning Division
  Tel: 029 2082 3585
  Fax: 029 2082 5622
Environment Division
  Tel: 029 2082 3174
  Fax: 029 2082 5008
Local Government Division
  Tel: 029 2082 3060
  Fax: 029 2082 5096
Planning Inspectorate
  Tel: 029 2082 3866
  Fax: 029 2082 5150

Index